MW01673327

Money + Love Manifestation Blueprint- The Law Of Attraction (2 in 1): 50+ Manifesting Techniques, Meditations, Hypnosis& Affirmations For Abundance, Wealth+ Twin Flames/ Soul Mate

Manifesting Money & Abundance Blueprint- The Law Of Attraction: 25+ Advanced Manifestation Techniques, Meditation & Hypnosis For Conscious Wealth Attraction Raising Your Vibration

By Spiritual Awakening Academy

Table of Contents

Chapter 1
What is Manifestation?

Have you ever wondered what it would be like to project your hopes and dreams into the environment and hope for a good outcome? If that is you, then consider Manifestation, or manifesting your dreams for a successful future.

Here you will be learning what Manifestation is on both a spiritual and a psychological level according to what many professionals and practicing individuals have to say. This is where Manifestation came from and how it works with both a spiritual and a psychological component in order to be most effective.

Spiritual Manifestation is the theory that by using meditation and positivity, paired with good and constructive thinking, it is possible to make your dreams and aspirations manifest into reality. This theory would include the thinking, that if you really want something, and hold that thought at the forefront of your thinking, it will form in your reality to become a tangible thing.

On the spiritual spectrum, to meditate should most likely, or could in theory include your higher power, this would amplify and increase the chances of Manifestation working for you. Meditate with full balance in which way you feel is right for you. Once you have reached your higher power in a state of euphoria and heightened oneness, think or project the thing which is desired most, and it will happen.

Accessing what is known as the highest state of meditation or near highness is difficult. In many spiritual aspects, it is only possible once you complete a cleansing of your body and soul. Knowing what your beliefs are and who or what your higher power might be will amplify the way Manifestation works for you.

Experts say that Manifestation works best when in the most comfortable of atmosphere and with as little stress as possible.

For example, one might be seeking a Tesla… in most cases that would make for a calm atmosphere, but when one is seeking salvation or healing in one way or another for themselves or a needy loved one, depending on the beliefs across the board, stress and high anxiety might be hard to rid yourself of.

It's important in order to meditate and achieve your goal, no matter the desire, you attempt to open communication with your deity or open your third eye, also depending on your beliefs. With each system of belief, one thing holds consistent, and that is that spirituality is a common key-term used.

That spirituality might be different belief to belief, but if you can achieve the level of highness through your specific spirituality, then you can get that Tesla, or healing, home, money, whatever the desire may be.

Gandhi once said that "the spirit, as manifest in truth and love possessed him utterly. My creed is service of god, and therefore humanity, and service means pure love." Gandhi meant that in so many ways, but the most littoral way to assume it, is if you can achieve those things physically and spiritually, then Manifestation and other achievements, are only a thought away.

On the other hand, to think of Manifestation psychologically, one must consider their mental status. Can you believe in something so grand that you can have faith in a thing before it can be ever seen? Is it possible, for you to wrap your mind around the process before it's practice and brought to fruition?

The concept of Manifestation on a psychological level means that on some level, people can become aware of how their thought, goals, beliefs, wishes, and general mindset can influence current and future experiences. Essentially with the idea of Manifestation, what one desires and is attracted to, can come to light through what you think, say, do, and in the way you act.

Similar, to what Gandhi said about humanity and love, if you have a dark soul/personality, it is less likely you can achieve even the lowest level of headspace in order to manifest even the slightest desire. Think about it like the quote, "what you put out in the world will always come back to you. But never how you predict."

If you put garbage into the universe, you will reap garbage, or negative karma… the utter reverse of blessings and Manifestations. If you sow goodness and kindness… "love" as Gandhi suggested, then your body has most likely been cleansed, as has you mind, enough to achieve something higher and thus Manifestation can work.

Can, however is the word to look at. Depending on your mindset and thought process, your psychological analysis of Manifestation must be on a level consistent with belief. In that sense, spiritual and psychological are nearly one in the same, but not… at the same time.

Ask for what you want and be prepared to get it.

Ralph Waldo Emerson said, "once you make a decision, the universe conspires to make it happen." The universe conspiring in your favor is perhaps one of the greatest gifts one can be given.

Stop waiting for someone to elevate your game, if you wait around for others, you might just miss what is out there for you. You are already equipped with everything you need to manifest your own greatness. You are all given the measurement of faith within yourselves to project and receive.

Considering belief when referring to mind and spirit, you need to remember that in order to manifest your desires, you must believe first in what is inevitable.

Cause and effect can be like Manifestation. Because you can think it, the cause being putting it out in the universe, believing in the outcome and the effect is like achieving your Manifestation and gaining from it, be it for your gain or someone else's.

In all honesty, it's already yours, you only need to claim that it is, and receive what has always been waiting for you.

Rhonda Byrne said, "every single second is an opportunity to change your life because in any moment you can change the way you feel." Albert Einstein said "imagination is everything. It is the preview of life's coming attractions."

Both of those support a healthy mindset. Seeing is believing and likewise. If you can't imagine your life the way you want, then how are you going to project your Manifestation and receive the outcome? Thinking and seeing your thoughts visualized into your future is not as hard as one might think.

Projecting is pushing an idea into the atmosphere and hoping it comes back for the good. Manifestation is projection while pushing an idea into the atmosphere and KNOWING it will come back for the good.

"Destiny is not a matter of chance, it is a matter of choice," William Jennings Bryan.

Choose to have the right mindset.

Do you suffer from depression? Anxiety? Stress induced issues? Well, to learn that destiny is not a matter of chance, not the game of Life hoping to not lose it all, it is your choice what happens. Manifest your depression away, gain a mindset that through affirmation and Manifestation that you will no longer be depressed.

It can happen… take it from Rumi, "the universe is not outside of you. Look inside yourself, everything that you want, you already are."

Believe your psychological self can accept something not so tangible and make it as such.

Jim Carrey is a funny man, not a philosopher, scientist, or the like. We watch him in the movies and see his characters, and think that's brilliant, or we don't like this one, we love the other. Let's cry with Mr. Popper and laugh with The Mask but not many of you think of him for quotes on intentions and accomplishing what is impossible.

"Our intention is everything. Nothing happens on this planet without it. Not one single thing has ever been accomplished without intention," Jim Carry.

Think on that. How is it possible, without the right mindset to create intention and project it… Manifest it?

Think I am, not I want to be. Know you are, not you hope to someday be. Intentions are the root and Manifestation is the bud to an even bigger plant that comes in many names. Success, achievement, accomplishment, happiness, having what you need, some of what you want… that is only one thought away.

There are so many other quotes by famous people, some you know, and others you don't. Knowing the quotes are by someone famous isn't what's important, it's the power behind the words, and the reality there. Remembering that power and accessibility are only things if you make them things.

A car has the ability to run. It can start and zoom down the road at the speed you desire, but that car is going nowhere if you don't start it. It can't start itself it isn't going anywhere without you first projecting the end goal of the journey, or at very least the start of it. Think of your dreams like a car, happiness and a life well deserved… it's there, hanging out somewhere in the universe, but it will NEVER be used if you don't spark it first.

You have to make the first move… spiritually, mentally, emotionally, it doesn't matter if it's there, it always has been and will always be, but without you taking the first step, it will stay there, unused and wasted.

In the following chapters, you will learn the various ways of accessing your proper mindset and learning to manifest in your own unique way. You will learn how to visualize and focus on the goal, much like ball players, you have to see the end result you want before it's even there.

You will be given a figurative toolbox of everything needed to achieve Manifestation.

You will know exactly what an affirmation is, and how it can help you do anything from cure your depression, to gain your dream job. Along with that, you will know the seven main laws to attract and manifest in the way that is right for you.

We will discuss with you the difference between choices and decisions and how you need to consider both in making your life available for Manifestation. Ultimately, one will discover how to speak to yourself.

Humans are their own worst enemy. People say such mean things, but the way we speak to ourselves and about ourselves is perhaps the grossest thing we could do. Putting oneself down just because that's what everyone else does, will never allow Manifestation to work due to psychological blockage. You do you, be nice to you, love you… you are all you have sometimes… why would you want to run yourself away.

Love who you are and do it on purpose.

Your thoughts and words can affect your body and mind, the way you project and the doubts that set in on top of your hopes and dreams. You will learn how to think positively and speak affirmations of faith for your daily life.

While considering the above motivations, the topic of conscious living will be touched on, as well as elevations of vibrational response… this is the way you should respond to the vibrational frequencies of everyone and everything around you, and in turn, the universe is responding to your vibrations. This is a huge power to your advantage when Manifestation comes to play.

After leaning that, you will find a chapter on intentions and how to set them. There are many ways to make an intention and many ways to use your spiritual self to set them into place. Intentions are important while manifesting, and perhaps one of the most beneficial aspects. Intentions can be as small as sending good vibes into the world, and as big as intentions to become somebody that everybody will admire.

Creative methods and timelines for seeing projections come to fruition are often two of the biggest questions asked during Manifestation. Humans want it to happen here and now, and in some cases it does, but the term "be patient" may be more prevalent here than anywhere.

Lastly, becoming a master of Manifestation is the ultimate goal, but one can't achieve this unless their spiritual and psychological selves are ready. Continuing without first getting those two aspects, if only those two in check is of the utmost importance.

Finding who you are, seeing what can be done, having faith in yourself and others, knowing where you belong, and loving yourself and others… those are all good steps to take in making sure you are ready to continue. Also, knowing what you believe and do it with great passion.

Here are a few tips for the above things in making sure your mind, and spiritual self are ready.

- Finding who you are.
  - By this time, you should have some idea as to who you are. This doesn't mean who others think you are, sometimes others don't know you as well as you know yourselves.
  - Find who you are as a person, what you love to wear, what your favorite things to do are.
  - And do this without taking anyone else into consideration.
  - If you must consider someone, only consider your close loved ones, parents, husband/wife/partner, children, and the like, but express first that this is who you have always been, and you would like them to accept you the way you are.
  - This step will also work when thinking of sexuality and coming to others with the results of your revelation, or perhaps you have known and it's time to tell others.
- Seeing what can be done.
  - In seeing what can be done through Manifestation, you might consider reading materials on the subject… likely why you are here.
  - You could also speak to others who practice and achieve good results through Manifestation.
  - Talking to the leader of your belief system about manifesting through meditation, affirmation, and self-assurance is a good start.
  - Study, and know the facts, and if after all that, you still don't know, ask again.

- In the end, it's best to always try it yourself, you are the best judge of your own end results.
- Having faith in yourself.
    - Believing in you is key. If you don't have faith in your capabilities, even in simple tasks, then Manifestation can not be possible.
    - Learning your own abilities even with the help of others first helps your self-worth, and faith in oneself, but you might have to be good with the next step to do this one.
    - Practice makes perfect.
- Having faith in others.
    - If you can't trust yourself, you are likely not trusting others.
    - Trusting others comes with practice, and it doesn't mean you are trusting everyone.
    - Find the few and follow them… be their friend, let them be yours.
    - Always trust your deity, higher power, parishioners of your belief system… unless they have given you a good reason not to.
    - If that's the case, reevaluate who you have chosen and see what went wrong.
    - Have good judgement of character.
- Knowing where you belong.
    - Knowing where you belong and with whom you belong is important.
    - Trying to make yourself fit like a round peg into a square hole will only hinder you.
    - Knowing your friends and true loved ones is what's most important when considering where you belong.
    - Considering the right organizations, clubs, sports, events, and spiritual affiliations that fit your needs is also important for a healthy development towards mindfulness and spirituality towards achieving Manifestation.
- Love yourself.
    - Just like having faith in yourself, you need to love who you are.
    - Self-worth and self-esteem can be largely affected by what people say and do to you, but loving yourself no matter what will cause your mind and soul to heal.
    - Loving yourself also makes you a prime candidate to love others openly and to be a good example for those struggling in that department.
- Love others.
    - Sometimes this can be the hardest mindset to get behind.
    - Psychologically, you know… KNOW, that it's hard to love someone that doesn't love you back.
    - This doesn't mean a romantic love, but a kindness type of love.
    - In loving others, you can truly find the good wherever you look… even in the darkest places.
- Know what you believe.

- This one is a hard one. Belief is a difficult subject, especially while trying to find who you are, but once you have done that, finding who and/or what you believe in is important.
- Some say they don't believe in anything, but that isn't entirely true. The wind blows, but we don't see it, but we believe it's there… even if you have to focus on the wind, be a good person, and love yourself and others, you can believe Manifestation will work.

To conclude this chapter, you should focus on these thoughts… you are loved, you are worth it, you are good enough to achieve what you believe, you can project and manifest the desires of your heart… you can be the best version of you.

You can believe.

Chapter 2
How Do I Begin?

Here, it will be discussed as to what methods are best to first get started and some of the ways that a person will need to clear their mind and find out what exactly they are seeking before they can begin a Manifestation practices.

When doing most anything, you can't start in the middle or at the end of the process and get the same finishing results… you must always start at the beginning. The same holds true with Manifestation. End results can only be achieved if and only if you do the work from start to finish.

Here, you will learn the exact steps you will need to take in order to achieve your end goal and how to get there with little to no problems.

First, it is important to do the steps in chapter one in order to be in the highest state of consciousness and spirituality to make the connection.

Once you are ready spiritually and mentally, then it is time to move on to these steps.

- Realization.
    - Realizing the need for Manifestation is the first step to achieving your manifested wishes.
    - Realizing that Manifestation is even a thing and can be achieved no matter your belief system.
    - Realizing that what you want has always been there for you and will always be there.
    - Realizing that if you do nothing about that, it will never come true.
    - Its time for you to take the first step… realize that.

Through realization, you will learn how to study, research, and ask what is needed to continue heading towards your goals and learning how to manifest your hopes and wishes.

Think of it like a test at school, if you try to take the test without studying first, you will likely fail. The same can be said with Manifestation. If you try it without at least the basic knowledge and tools needed, then you will most likely fail.

It doesn't matter if you feel you are a busy person, you will need to find the time for reading and surrendering yourself to self-chosen ignorance. Admitting that we don't automatically know it all out of the gate sometimes can be the hardest thing to do.

Think of finding out that Manifestation is a thing like hearing about a life hack that could have saved you so much trouble through the years, but you didn't know about it… well, now you do. It could have been helping you all along, but since you didn't know it existed, then you can't fault yourself.

Now that you know that you can achieve your goals through Manifestation, and once you learn how, it will become the most life changing thing you have discovered.

Learning is important when making the decision to implement anything into your life, Manifestation and the like is the same… be educated before you act.

- Understanding.
    - Understand that learning how to achieve Manifestation is not for everyone.

- Understand that only by having a clean mind, body, and soul can you even attain said goal.
- Understand that only you, with great training, and understanding, can even contemplate Manifestation.

Understanding and education often go hand in hand. If you can't understand what you are learning, then in the end, you may never achieve the highest achievements… be it educationally or in reference to Manifestation.

In referencing understanding, one must know themselves… in that knowledge of self and the way your mind and body works brings you to another level.

For example, you wouldn't go sky diving if your body and mind weren't physically and mentally ready. Physically so, due to the weight one has to be to partake and the condition your body would need to be inside and out to participate. Mentally due to the fact that you will be plummeting towards the ground at a break-neck speed with only a rip-cord to save you.

You might be wondering what skydiving has to do with understanding what it takes to practice Manifestation. Well, more than you might know. Like driving a car or taking a test without being ready, the right steps need to be taken for both.

For the act of lunacy or adrenaline, depending on the spectrum you fall on regarding jumping out of a plane, you can't second guess YOUR ability to act in the way that will result in saving your life. Like Manifestation, while it's not got a life-threatening aspect, it CAN cause you mental and even spiritual anguish if not ready.

Like said many times over to this point… understanding who you are, what you can handle, your mental health, and your spiritual health is TOP priority.

So, like the situation of jumping out of a plane, you won't be doing it without a full understanding, practice, training, and then ultimately confidence in YOURSELF.

- Preparedness.
  - Being prepared to begin your journey is important.
  - Knowing the tools needed is also important.
  - Knowing yourself and the stages from chapter one, have each been addressed.
  - Knowing that your mind is ready and, also that you have the faith to believe in Manifestation.

Preparedness means to make certain that you are ready for whatever it is that you are going to embark on. To say that you believe in Manifestation is one thing, but again, if you do not have the knowledge, understanding, and the tools to start, then your simply not ready.

Being ready to begin your journey through Manifestation doesn't need to be taken lightly. One would assume that since you have gotten this far, you have at very least a minimal desire to learn what Manifestation is, or how to achieve it at its highest.

Benjamin Franklin said that "by failing to prepare, you are preparing to fail."

Abraham Lincoln said it this way, "give me six hours to chop down a tree and I will spend the first four sharpening the axe."

Both men have been revered through history as being influential and knowledgeable, also for being prepared for the challenges that were ahead of them. Franklin didn't always jump headfirst into an idea, it started as a thought, a spark, then with preparedness and research it grew… sure, trial and error was largely a thing during his life and many others, but never without basic understanding.

Lincoln didn't mean that he literally needed four hours to sharpen a blade. He meant that no matter how much time you feel you have, there is never a reason not to stop and prepare. To chop down a tree with a dull blade would have taken far more than six hours, likely, but if the blade was sharp, then two would be enough.

Take the time to sharpen your mind, spirit, body, and be prepared.

- Gathering the tools.
  - Gather all the things needed to begin, this does not mean real tools or even tangible items.
  - Simply prepare a clean and relaxed environment, free of as much stress and negativity as possible.
  - Dress comfortably and prepare your intention, projection, or affirmation in the way your belief system allows, or that you have been taught… this will differ person to person.

Just like any carpenter, or laborer of any kind, tools are needed to do the job they have chosen or been given for their life. Like Manifestation, you have been given the chance to achieve higher understanding and in the end the gifts that are hanging in the divide for you.

What is yours is yours, but only if you know how to get it. You can't build a house with only your hands, or have it built for that fact. The person doing the work, be it you or someone you trust, the TOOLS needed to do that specific job are essential to the end goal being what you want.

The proper tools for manifesting towards you end goal are going to be discussed in depth further on in the reading. Be sure you understand these are not hammers, and nails… these are the mental, physical, and spiritual things you will need to achieve you desires.

Sure, tangible things might be needed depending on your practice, candles, sage, spices, pillows, blankest, cloth, and such, those would also be part of your tool arsenal, but in no way should you consider gathering the tangible tools until you know you are ready with the mental, physical, and spiritual ones.

- Believing.
  - Knowing beyond a shadow of a doubt that Manifestation is real, is key.
  - Believe in yourself and others you trust.
  - Believe in your higher power, deity, or the process of Manifestation.
  - Seeing is believing and believing is seeing… but remember that sometimes you need to believe in things you can't see too.

Believing in something is what it takes to act towards or for the thing you hope to achieve as your goals and aspirations for yourself and your life. Humans tend to not dedicate their time towards things and people they don't believe in and trust.

Unless you are forced into it, one doesn't often do a job they don't believe in, practice something they don't believe one hundred-precent. We don't put time and energy into people we feel aren't worth it and we can't believe will amount to good one way or another.

On the other hand, even if you have gotten this far… believing is only half the battle. As discussed in chapter one briefly, if you are not prepared in the ways needed, it's likely you are not purely cleansed and true, it won't matter how much you believe Manifestation will works… it won't for you.

Believing in yourself would be the first real step towards cleansing oneself.

Facing the fact that the monsters in this world are usually human hurts. Sometimes it doesn't matter how much said monster wants to change, it isn't over night. On the other hand, most humans aren't purely darkness… it's hard to live your life that dark.

Even if you feel you are the worst person on earth, it's not too late to believe in yourself. By believing and seeking the help you need mentally, spiritually, and physically, Manifestation can only be a few steps away. By manifesting your dreams, also making sure they are pure and good, you may even get closer to becoming the kind of person you have always wanted to be.

It is NEVER too late to become that person. No matter how old or young you are, you are worth it, you are beautiful, and you have a soul worth the light.

- Seeing.
    - Know that seeing in this sense means something figurative.
    - You must see the end result, picture it and think it into fruition through Manifestation.

Seeing your aspirations and goals is not something everyone can do. Some people have trouble seeing the future like that, others often fear thinking about what they want or never even try due to fearing failure. Through Manifestation, affirmation, and believing in the possibility of the future desired, it can become easy for you to do something great through meditation and Manifestation.

Studies show that there are three main kinds of people when dealing with seeing your dreams and aspirations for your life, even as simple as believing in the fact that the universe is waiting for you to ask and receive. Knowing which category, you fall under will help you continue this list of steps towards achieving your Manifestation goals.

-Seers-By being a literal seer, you can picture things in your minds eye. Think of the juicy apple and actually… visualize the sweet, crispness, the dew dripping off the waxy coating. For seers, it's hard to believe that NOT ALL PEOPLE see the way you do.

Those that can are lucky, to physically see the thing you desire in your minds eye makes it that much easier to project the thing you want or need towards achieving Manifestation.

Just because you don't fall in this category, does not mean how you project isn't considered seeing the end goal, it's just seeing through your other senses.

-Hearers-Being a hearer means that you can hear that still small voice in the back of your mind. (No this is not referencing schizophrenia or a mental break) it simply means that you are more in tune with your conscious, verbal self, or what you may call it.

You're welcome… for some of you that just cleared up so much for you. Thinking you have been going crazy your whole life by hearing it, has just been cleared up in a simple paragraph… don't worry, you are among a grand percentage of people who can do the same… and no, they aren't crazy either.

Know that some hearers can also be seers, and vice versa, but it doesn't not mean that is the only truth… you can only be one or the other or have a combination of hearing and the next one.

Being a hearer sometimes makes the thought process better, but hearers often have trouble shutting off their brain… downfalls and perks of being able to do this.

Another benefit is that IF you can't see the dream or desire, you can project mentally through the use, of your still-small-voice. Let it see for you and manifest your desires.

-Hands on-if you are a person who practices better with hands on experience… seeing and hearing isn't there for you, or might be but not as prevalent, you CAN achieve Manifestation, but with a few more steps.

If you practice hands on learning, then likely you have hopes and dreams, but they are thoughts for you. Those that are fortunate enough can project thoughts without first seeing or hearing it, but some can't.

For those that can't and you have gotten to the end, ready to achieve that which you have manifested, if you are struggling, then do something hands on… draw what you want so you can visualize… write a short story about you with the outcome you wish… those are both hands on things that can help you visualize, project, and achieve Manifestation in ways you might not have been able to before.

- Meditation/Relaxation.
    - Gain a heightened sense of relaxation through meditation or relaxing in the way you see fit.
    - Concentrate on what the end result you want is and know it's only moments away.

As spoke about in chapter one and will be expounded beyond further into the chapters, finding the optimal form of mediation for you is going to help in the long run. If you're a seer, hearer, or hands on learner, you will need to first be comfortable in order to reach your highest thinking to attain the result you are going for.

- Achieving I.
    - Achieving I is the portion of meditation in which you have finally gotten to that state of happy and highness.
    - Be it meditation or relaxation, you have finally achieved it, live there in that headspace for as long as possible.
    - Once you have learned how to achieve that state, perfect it by learning how to make it better… you can only get better from here.

Achieving I is the first level of achievement in the steps towards manifesting your aspirations. There are two in the steps process, but this one simply means that one, you have learned the way you learn the best, two, you have learned that it's possible, three, you have found the category you are able to see best in, and four, you have been able to achieve the vision/projection/intention you want.

That means you are ready to continue. Achieving this is usually the half-way point, and is only done during the high point of meditation/prayer and the like.

- Concentration.
    - Once you are achieving the highness of euphoria in which way you have chosen, concentrate on your higher power, deity, or the thing you wish to guide you.
    - If you have none of those, then make sure to think about the steps of Manifestation and/or the person who guided you towards said steps.

This is self-explanatory, meaning you must concentrate to hold that imagine (in whichever way you must see it.) Hold it, concentrate on it and send it out into the universe.

- Prayer/Projection/Intention/Manifestation.
    - This section loosely depends on the individual. Choosing the way you will achieve your end goal, or Achieving II heavily depends on your method.
    - If you choose prayer, then pray to the powers that be for the end result that YOU want.

    - Through projection, project your thoughts, hopes, dreams, and goals towards the end result that YOU want.
    - The same goes for Intention. If this requires more materials, as some belief systems would, gather those and have them on hand.
    - Manifestation is truly the end result for all of them, projection, intention, and prayer will all get you to the same conclusion if done the right way.

Again, this one is self-explanatory in the fact that this is literally the act of sending the thought into the world and believing it will come back to you in the way and time the universe sees fit.

- End Goal.
    - Know what you want.
    - Push it out into the universe.
    - Don't give it a timeline, good things are worth waiting for.
    - Don't begin to doubt it will come true if it doesn't happen when and how you want.
    - Look for the small stuff, sometimes Manifestations don't end in a face slap, but rather a sweat and almost soft end result that could easily be passed up if you don't sit back and look and listen.
- Achieving II.
    - Achieving II is as simple as that… it is the receiving of the gift.

The end goal is the action of receiving the gift that you put out into the world. This is after you have come down from the high of Manifestation. Sometimes seconds after, other times weeks, months, or years later… not often that long you will find yourself with the ending that you had manifested.

For example if you manifested becoming a famous actress/actor it is out there for you and will happen, but not until you go out and get it for yourself. It's the gentile push you need to go to acting school, try out for the role… you will never know until you try.

The universe expects you to claim the gifts it has for you… get it and use it. Again, like a car doesn't run by itself… a gift doesn't open itself.

Chapter 3
What's the Best Way to Manifest?

In this chapter the discussion of some of the best ways to manifest will be covered. Topics such as the tools needed for manifesting (visualization) and how to use them in order to get the best results will be featured. This may also include various activities that one can do to help with their meditation while manifesting such as seeing, hearing, and hands on scripting as discussed in chapter two.

The following are the tools you will need to attain purity of mind, body, and soul, in order to begin the process of Manifestation.

Two types of tools will be talked about…

-Figurative-the tools you will need to make your inner self at the level needed to practice Manifestation.

-Physical-the tools you might need to meditate, based on beliefs and practices. (This will most likely be an example-based portion of the lesson.) It is impossible to name all beliefs and the physical tools they use to achieve mediation and Manifestation.

First the figurative tools needed to purify yourself to continue your manifesting journey.

- Compassion and giving.

Compassion is concern for others who are misfortunate or downtrodden. Those that have not been given the things you have, have not been offered the goodness of life, or have suffered loss of any form. This is in reference to people, animals, any living thing. Compassion is given freely and without needing, wanting, or requiring ANYTHING in return.

Giving is providing caring and emotional support for others. Loving others. Seeking health and wellness for others over yourself. Parents, teachers, pastors, humanity in general… these are those that should naturally have this, but unfortunately that isn't always the case.

You MUST give to others in order to purely achieve the right spiritual and mental balance. You MUST have each of these tools to be worthy of Manifestation. You can be worthy… each person is given the capability to do so, but it can not be done with the subtraction of any of these.

Bring caring and compassion to the table when beginning the process of Manifestation… your mind and soul will thank you… as will all those you have helped in the process, (although you should NEVER practice either of these, just for the thanks… it negates the reasoning and actions behind it.)

- Understanding.

Understanding is the ability to understand and comprehend something. This is also being sympathetically aware of other people… their feelings. By understanding you must also learn to be tolerant and to be forgiving.

Learning to tolerate people and things that could sometimes bother you is important. Being tolerant of someone slower than you in the line at the store, a child that learns differently, a person whose thoughts don't form the way yours do. You should learn to tolerate the differences and in turn learn to love.

On the other hand, pick your battles. This means that if something is bothering you, making you mad, or setting you on edge… be calm, and only delve into the battle if there is an important reason to have one. Only if it will benefit the other person by being persistent about something being the way it should.

The best example of this is parents and children, or bosses and employees. As humans, we WANT things the way we want them. If someone doesn't do it the exact way you want, then sometimes you need to tolerate the fact that not all kids, people in general do things the same… it's not always going to be your way.

Lastly in this category… if you have been wronged or hurt by anyone for any reason… forgiving them is the ONLY way you can set your mind at ease. You will never be psychologically ready to practice Manifestation, or anything for that fact, without practicing forgiveness first.

In turn, that does not mean you will forget but learn from the experience. To forgive doesn't mean you have to allow that person back into your life.

- Proper knowledge of mediation.

As said before and will be expounded on later, the proper knowledge of meditation is important. How it needs to be done to suit your individual and spiritual needs will make the whole process that much easier.

When coming to a state of mediation… the knowledge of how, when, and why will help you… again, you don't take a test without first having the understanding and fundamental knowledge of the process and how it should work for you.

- Good habits.

Good habits are the behaviors that are beneficial to ones physical, mental, and general health. This is often tied to high levels of discipline and control.

Some examples of good habits are…

-Exercise.

-Minimal to no consumption of harmful things for your body.

-A balance diet.

-Monogamy or fully agreed upon habits of relationships.

The list can go on and on. Again, what is good for one person may not be what is good for the next, however by listening to your inner voice or others around you that love you if you can't hear said voice, you will quickly learn if what habits you practice are good or bad.

Know that not all input from others is criticism, it is often loved ones merely opening up to you about the things they see as harmful or concerning behavior.

- Charity.

Charity is giving to others and the process of selfless actions towards bettering those that can't or have limitations towards bettering themselves. In order to utilize this tool, that doesn't mean you have to give of all your free time, volunteer for everything… it means if you have abundance give, if you have extra time give, if you have something you hold dear to you, volunteer when you can.

When your done with your glasses, give them to clubs and organizations that can fix them for kids and the elderly that can't afford them. When your kids have outgrown their coats, give them to other children, put them in a park on a tree, over a fence, on a bench, if you feel it will embarrass someone by you going up to them.

Start a lending library… conduct a free movie night for your neighbors outside with a projector, parents, listen to your children's friends… sometimes they need you more than you might realize. Start a coat tree where people can come and put their used or new coats on the branches so others can come in anonymity and get what they need.

Do good.

- Affirmations of faith.

Affirmations will be talked about later as to what they are and what you need to do, but affirmations of faith simply are spiritual claiming of the good things surrounding your belief system. For example, in Manifestation, this could be *I will get the healing desired, my higher power is going to move in this need, I will get the new car I need to get back and forth to work, church, place of practice,* excreta.

- Affirmations of self.

This is literally the same as affirming through faith, only there is no religious aspect to this. This is helping yourself out of your mental health issues, learning to love yourself, doing better through daily saying of affirmations. First thing in the morning and several times through the day is best.

You can start by writing the affirmations down, then eventually, you will memorize them.

Examples of affirmations of self are…

-Today is going to be a good day.

-I am beautiful no matter what anyone says.

-I don't have to be thin to be beautiful.

-My skin color does not make me who I am, I make me who I am.

-Bullies are just people that have hidden scars that are coming out in the way of hurt.

-I can be anything I want to be.

-I will graduate, achieve, succeed.

-I will not cut or harm myself today, I will talk to others that I love about my wants to and the thoughts I have that I can't at this time control.

-I can control my thoughts, it's just going to take time.

-I love you, (meaning yourself)

There are so many things that you can use to make it specific for you.

- Gratitude.

Gratitude is the thankfulness for things you have and have been given. It is thanking those around you for the time they give, the money they attribute, and the charity they do for you.

You might have at one point been the child in need of a coat… adopted by a lovely family, taken seriously when being hurt. Being grateful for those who are in your life for the good is the only way to live.

How can you EXPECT people to be thankful for your time, money, and contributions, if you aren't in return for those things that others have done for you?

- Visualization

Visualization is seeing what you want, need, dream of, desire. By identifying if you are a seer, hearer, or hands on person, you can learn in which way visualization will work for you.

- Knowledge of projection.

Projection means more than one thing… it could mean an estimate of future situations based on present situations or seeing blips of future events. Or simply meaning you can see the things you want for your future.

This is simply the step after visualization. You need to see, then you must project the positivity out into the world. However, this can also be done to the negative, it is important that you know the difference.

If you think hate, you project it. It you think harm on others and project it, if you mean it or not, harm can cone to them. If you project hate of self, others will see that, and they too will contribute to your negative self-worth/self-esteem.

Knowing projection and how it works before Manifestation is perhaps the most important.

- Love.

This one should be the simplest tool to bring to the table. It isn't though.

Love doesn't always come naturally to some people. Others think that as long as you love your four and no more then that is love. This simply isn't the case.

You must love yourself, humanity, your higher power if you have one. You must love those that don't love you. Sometimes this can only come after forgiveness, but again loving someone does not mean you love the things they do or even ever have them in your life again but love regardless.

Next, you will learn the tangible tools you might need in order to set an intention towards Manifestation. Again, this does not have to be done to attain, however it is needed to know how to do it through intentions in various religions.

Sometimes intentions can be set through mediation and prayer, while other times intentions are set through action using tools. Here, you will learn the difference.

The best example of intentions with the use of tools would come from paganism.

Intentions are set by practicing Pagans regardless of the deities that are served. These are physical intentions that require tangible tools. Those tools can include, but are not limited to…

1. Candles.

Be sure when creating an intention with a candle that you coordinate the color of the candle with the intention that you wish to make.

-Green for money.

-Red for love.

-White for spirit.

And so on, but make sure you research first to use what's best for you.

Never blow a candle out after the intention, use water, a snuff, or damp fingers.

2. Lighting source

Decide if matches, a lighter, or secondary candle are best for you. Keep in mind that while you are meditating, the candle or candles will be lit. Creating the best meditation and intention making environment is key.

3. Paper.

If burning an intention, you will need a fire source and paper to write the intention on. Small scroll like papers of light parchment works best.

4. Cauldron.

Keep a cauldron or dish of water near for putting out the paper as it burns or for sitting the flaming script to finish burning. The last is the best of both decision… a good cauldron is made of cast iron.

5. Writing utensil.

This is self-explanatory. You will require a way to write, pen, pencil, wax, whichever the need to create the papered intention to burn.

Remember that this might differ from belief system to belief system, but the core to it all will be common. If you can set an intention then you are closer to Manifestation than you first thought you were.

By being ready in your body, mind, and soul, you are now ready to move forward through the steps. It's only after you have reached this level of wholeness that you can even think about setting an intention and manifesting it.

Think of it like a child that wants something badly. If they are good and kind and ask for it, then likely the thing will be gotten for them. On the other hand, if the child is bad, throws tantrums, demands the item, they should not or will likely not get it.

The same can be said for Manifestation. Here are the tools, go forth and be the builders of your own destiny.

Through intention, visualization, and meditation you can assure you are nearly ready to practice Manifestation. Not completely so, but with a little more research and proactive and positive thinking, if you think it you can have it.

Remember this out of all that has been talked about, it's all in good timing and will happen how it's meant and for the betterment of your future. Don't rush things, take it slow, feel out the desires of your heart, and go for what feels right. Be you, do you, and know that as long as you are following the steps and in the right headspace, it's not as hard as you once thought.

Later, when you achieve and receive, think back to this passage and evaluate what it is like to be on both ends of the process. Think about now when you are only learning, and reference the journey as you take it from start to finish.

Chapter 4
What are Affirmations?

Here, we will be discussing what affirmations are in depth and what they can do to help a person with their individual journey toward the life of their dreams and achieving their goals. This will be the chapter where specific types of wording will be discussed and how you can set your mindset for the day with an intent that can attract the results you desire most.

As talked about in chapters past, affirmations can make or break the way you act, and the mindset you are in. as said before, it is possible to take yourself from chronic and debilitating states of mind and leave that headspace and enter a whole new reality for your life.

Famous plus-size model Ashley Graham said, "you are bold, you are brilliant, and you are beautiful."

"Will Smith offered… "our thoughts, our feelings, our dreams, our ideas are physical in the universe. That if we dream something, if we picture something, it adds a physical thrust towards realization that we can put into the universe."

Claude M. Briston said, "it's the repetition of affirmations that leads to belief, and once that belief becomes deep convictions, things begin to happen."

Each of these prove that affirmations are a powerful thing. They are the tools to feeling like you are worthwhile and that things can happen for you when others and even yourself, say it can't. Contrary to the fact that you may be one of the main reasons you doubt yourself and others, that can change. As talked about briefly before, affirmations are either of faith or to use in making one's self worth and esteem better.

You quickly become what you believe or what others say are true about you even if they aren't true in reality. Some examples of what others might say about you that could easily be misconstrued and bounce back to yourself and the way you treat yourself and what you feel is true are.

-Your ugly.

-Your body type doesn't not appeal to me.

-You are to tall, to short, to skinny, to fat.

-What you like doesn't matter.

-Who you are doesn't matter.

-You will never amount to anything.

-Give up.

Out of each of these, they all hurt the same, but after a while, we tend to begin to believe what people have said to us. If we start to believe it, then that is the time we need to consider altering our way of thinking by using affirmations of self.

A great reference for this is Adolf Hitler. He was a man of great influence that did many horrible things to people that didn't deserve it. For those that survived the horrors that was the holocaust, they had to live on with the thought that some group of persons thought they weren't good enough because their hair wasn't blonde and eyes weren't blue.

Could you imagine being thrown out of somewhere because they only cater to hazel eyed people? Or cared about the color of skin you have?

Imagine trying to gain good self-esteem after surviving such things. After people had told you that you weren't worth loving because of a trait that didn't match what fit their perfect image.

It's possible however to get past that. Not easy, but possible. Through affirming yourself and changing your mindset, it can often change the mindset of others or at very least, cause them to leave you alone.

If you get to the point through affirmation where things don't bother you any longer, then in turn don't react to what they have to say, often they quit saying it because they aren't getting the thing they want the most… a reaction.

Daily affirmations or affirmations of self are merely true and positive statements or declarations of aspirations and goals you wish to achieve for yourself through affirming truth and light in your life. Lear to love yourself again this way.

These affirmations will then become empowering mantras that can and often will have a profound effects on the conscious and unconscious mind, body, and your soul.

This comes back to the thought of being ready both mentally and spiritually. It is impossible to do either unless you can believe the truths about yourself and learn to love who you are or at very least who you can be. Affirmations also are the key to creating the life of your dreams! If you can dream it (not meaning while you are asleep per se, but rather think it) it can become the new reality for your life.

Perfect examples of successful people that have used affirmation to gain the success they desired in their life are…

-Top salespeople in their chosen profession.

These are the people who have worked hard for what they want, but through affirmation, they knew they were going to achieve the end goal. Setting affirmations and practicing Manifestation go hand in hand towards said end goal.

-Entrepreneurs.

Again thinking that you can have what you want and knowing it can come true through affirming ones self that becoming an entrepreneur is what you have always wanted.

Or perhaps you were one before, but with a small and unknown business… this thought process would then bring you into the light and out of the darkness of unknowing.

-Presidents.

It is possible that even a president or elected royalty might need to affirm their self-worth to know they are good enough for the job. Something with such a high stress level and demanding performances involving millions of people would need to be addressed. It's not a job for the faint of heart.

And more so, not a job for someone that didn't feel worthwhile.

-Bestselling authors.

-Award winning actors

The two above are great examples of self-affirmation or daily affirmations. There are thousands upon thousands of authors and actors/actresses out there, but it takes something special to gain the top rating bill of being award winning or bestselling.

Great faith and affirmation can be one of the tools those people could have used to get to the level desired.

-Olympic athletes, and so on…

They have all figured out that using willpower to fuel their success isn't enough. You need to let go of any, and all negative thoughts and fill your mind with new thoughts and images that are positive and stated in the present tense.

How do you do this you might ask?

The process you use to do this begins with daily affirmations, which are simply statements that describe a goal in its already completed state. Basically, telling yourself you can and will do something, believing it can and will come true, and knowing that soon, the old way of doing it will be but a distant memory.

A few examples of affirmations are…

-I am gracefully walking across the stage as I receive my degree at my dream university.

-I am receiving my first paycheck at my new high paying job doing what I love to do.

-I am celebrating as I cross the finish line of the marathon I have been training for.

There is some research that now proves that in times in high-stress level environments, those who use daily affirmations have lower stress levels and more success than those who don't.

The perfect example as to what a daily Affirmations is, is that affirmations are to the mind the same as what exercise is to the body. They are both needed to keep ones-self healthy and happy, but they are equal in importance. Repeating affirmations helps to reprogram the unconscious mind for success. It can help to eliminate negative and limiting beliefs and energy in order to put you back where you need to be in order to be happy and keeping from the one that was keeping you trapped.

It helps to replace the words I can't with I can, I won't be able to with I will be able to. Make sure to replace your fears and doubts with confidence and charisma.

Keep in mind that affirmations are reminders to your unconscious mind to stay focused on your goals and to come up with solutions as to how to get away from past and negative though processes.

They can also create higher vibrations… vibrations will be talked about in depth later on in the chapters, but they can be used for achieving happiness, joy, appreciation, and gratitude that then, through affirmations and Manifestation can draw people, resources, and opportunities to you so that you are able to achieve your goals.

It's also good to know that affirmations can go the other way too. Telling yourself mean and negative things will also affirm to you that is the truth and therefore that is who you are and what you deserve. Putting negative into the atmosphere will only reap negativity.

Some examples of these types of affirmations will shock you. You may think that you have never sent out a negative affirmation about yourself, but chances are some of these have come from your own mouth… and many times perhaps.

-This outfit makes me look fat.

-Everything I eat goes to my hips.

-I might as well give up.

-I am never going to meet someone that will love me the way I love them.

-I can never catch a break

-I can never have anything nice.

-There is no point to this.

-Everyone hates me.

-I hate everyone.

-I might as well die.

-I'm ugly.

-I eat too much/I eat too little.

-I'm too short/I'm too tall/I'm too fat/I'm too skinny.

-I will never love who I am because of what people say about me.

The only way to counteract these thoughts are by putting forth positive affirmations of faith, self, or through daily affirmations.

A few ways to create positive affirmations and what can be said day to day to make both you feel better and cause others to leave you alone.

The daily use of positive affirmations interrupts and eventually replaces all the negative thoughts and beliefs you have been thinking and believing about yourself for so long. To achieve this, you must continually fill your thought process with thoughts and images of the new reality you wish to create.

Here are a few guidelines for creating powerful daily affirmations that work, there are so many ways to turn the negative away, but the only way it can even begin is by you making the first step.

Waking up on day one and saying and thinking, projecting, visualizing, and eventually affirming that you are worth life, and everything in between is the key to opening the new connection with yourself.

The guidelines for creating effective affirming statements. Writing them down and saying them helps. You may want to write these down so that you can use them day to day.

- Start with the words *I am!*
  - These are the two most powerful words you can say.
  - Affirming that you are talking about your "self" is important.
- Use the present tense.
  - I am.
- Be positive.
  - This will happen.
  - Things are going to get better.
  - Again… I will, it will, they will!
- Affirm what you want, not what you don't want.
  - Only say things that you want to come to light.
  - Never use what you feel others want for you as a way to affirm who you are.
- Keep it brief.
  - Short and sweet affirmations are easy to hold onto.
  - I am going to be brave.
  - I am not ugly.
  - I am going to pass the test.
  - I am worth it.
- Make it suited to your individual needs.
  - Make sure that what you need is stated.
  - If you are needing a job because you lost your last one and can hardly pay the bills. *I am going to get the promotion.*
- Make sure there is nothing negative in the verse.
  - Nothing such as *I guess I am pretty, I think I may be worth it, I might pass the test.*
- Make it specific.
  - Again, tailoring the affirmation to fit your needs and making it as specific to yourself as others works best.
- Include at least one dynamic emotion or feeling word.

- Happy. *I am going to be happy at my new job.*
- Excellent. *I am going to have an excellent day.*
- Am going. *I am going to get my driver's license today.*
- Splendid. *I am going to be happy today, it will be a splendid day.*

- Make affirmations for yourself, not others.
    - Making sure you use "I" not they, we, your, it.

Now that the basic fundamentals have been laid out for you… some examples of affirmations of self, or daily affirmations are…

-I am joyfully driving my new red Porsche Carrera convertible down the Pacific Coast Highway in Malibu.

-I am sipping mimosas on a beach far away from all the drama.

-I am gleefully walking into the school happy for being me.

-I am so happy to be the new kindergarten teacher.

-I am grateful that I am now in love with who I am.

-I am so happy and grateful that I am now earning $150,000 a year.

-I am so happy and grateful that I am now celebrating having achieved my ideal weight of 140 pounds.

Make sure to take at least five minutes every day to repeat your affirmations – preferably out loud with high energy and enthusiasm. Sometimes that's hard to do first thing in the morning, but early morning and right before you go to bed are the best for making it a good day, or planning on towmorrow being that day.

Once you have learned how to do this, it will become evident quickly that you are seeing results that you want.

You can also write down three to five affirmations for yourself that affirm you having already achieved a few of your goals. Then you can write down the time of day that you will commit to practicing your affirmations.

You can also do a few affirmations during these times.

-Mid-day when you need a pick-me-up?

-After meditation.

-During high stress times.

-When starting to doubt yourself.

-When others are continuing to bully you into thinking what they say is true.

Hold yourself accountable for continuing to balance your life with affirmations. Remember that the art of affirmation is profound, but can be soft and subtle at the same time.

Despite the popularity of this technique, some people just don't know how to use affirmation properly, especially towards Manifestation. When creating affirmations of self and faith on a daily level, it is best to think about that even the smallest collection of words can make a massive difference towards achieving your end results. Since words literally have the power to change the future, it is best to take a few minutes even now to take your affirmation skills to a higher level.

Taking your skills to a higher level will help in the end towards completing Manifestation and even the way you are able to meditate, focusing on the most important things all at the same time.

As mentioned before, affirming through faith, in particular that you can change the way you think and act, it can also make a difference in how you recover from certain downfalls. Here are a few examples of what can be said during your affirmations towards recovery that might shock you.

-Mental health *I will not sleep more than needed, I will get out of bed today, and I will not think of harmful thoughts and actions.*

-Smoking *I will quit smoking, it can be done with ease and joy, I will achieve this to keep my health.*

-Drinking *I will quit drinking, it can be done with happiness and understanding, I will do it to keep my health and sanity.*

By also using the guidelines found below paired with the ones earlier in this chapter, you can transform non-meaningful, negative, and self-harming affirmations into what we call mantras for manifesting a huge change in your life!

-Be in the here and now

Don't think of the future too far in advance, only what you would like for your future and the reasons you need that NOW. Start your affirmation by entering the present tense. Take the condition you desire and declare it to be already true, just like it was happening right now.

-Be positive and hopeful.

You can do this by using those words of joyful affirmations. Use those small and simple affirmations to keeps the focus and make sure you add emotions that are kind and positive.

-Be specific.

Short and sweet as said before. The right here is what I need and this is what I want, but need as in NEED. So specific that you say exactly what you think and therefore you receive. Shorter is better. Affirmations with fewer words are often easier to recall in the future or day to day especially in situations when you feel some stress or are in a hurry.

The best way to know that you have had a good and positive affirmation is when you feel a surge of energy which in turn will start to grown in the physical evidence that it has worked or is working.

To wrap this chapter up, a few more examples of positive affirmations are…

-I am celebrating feeling the goodness of my life.

-I am the perfect body weight and praise my figure for the joy it brings me.

-I am happy to be forty, this is the time of my life.

-I am enthralled to be flying in a plane for the first time.

-I am drawing happiness around me wherever I am.

-I am confident in the fact that my life is attracting truth and joy.

-I am positive that I am an honest and good person.

-I am feeling exhilarated and not tired and run down.

To conclude affirmations, remember the steps given to you and how affirmation can be a game changer is key. Stay positive and know that you are the best version of yourself when your affirmations affirm your character and the positivity that can now surround you.

Surrender yourself to the possibility that things can happen with the spoken word… they already do.

"I'm ugly," may not be true, but it has become the truth because you believe it to be. You may be believing a lie, but you believe it, nonetheless.

"I am beautiful," negates the above. It's as simple as that, make sure you know the power rests in you.

Now, you are even closer to achieving Manifestation, especially now that you know how to affirm your faith and the beliefs that are now your reality.

Chapter 5
What are the Seven Laws of Attraction?

Here the discussion of what the seven known laws for manifesting and attracting into your life are, and why you need them so the things you want will be unveiled. This chapter will cover what those seven laws are and how they can be adopted and utilized for small and long-term goal-smashing.

It is an amazing gift to manifest your desires using the power of your mind. This is an amazing and well needed gift in every human being, whether aware of it or not, or if you are using it or not.

The universal law of attraction helps you in harnessing this power and use it to your advantage.

There are twelve laws of the universe that tells us that our beliefs, thoughts, and feelings have a great influence on what we attract into our lives. By turning it around, we can attract what we want by influencing our thoughts and belief system.

The law of attraction contains seven laws… these are like sub-laws to the main twelve. They deal with various aspects of our mental state.

Since there is not much information you can learn here without first knowing the laws and why they are as such, we will delve right in.

The seven laws to attract, and their meanings and reasons they are needed are…

- The law of Manifestation.
    - This is the most familiar of all the laws of attraction.
    - The object of our constant focus will manifest in our lives.
    - Our thoughts and feelings are mirrored in the world around us.
    - This is the ability make our minds an incredibly powerful tool.
    - The more positivity we manage to infuse into the world, the more we get in the end.

On the other side of law number one… we need to be careful about the negativity that creeps into our minds occasionally. Like talked about in the affirmations chapter, if you put out negativity, then you get back negativity.

- The law of Magnetism.
    - This law helps us understand what has happened in our lives now and forever.
    - You need to know what the possibilities are for a positive future and believe it can happen.
    - It says that everything in our lives including the people, things, and circumstances are the result of our energy but put into the world and pulled from it.
    - We attract what we are. That is, we attract into our lives people, things, and events that have the same energy and intentions as ours.
    - We act like magnets.

You can use this law to get what you desire in your lives. Raising energy, you can manage to match up to the energy level of your desires. This results in Manifestation. This is a simple enough process in theory, but not-so-easy to practice.

With a good knowledge of your beliefs and desires, it is possible to change the way our mind works to manifest our desires.

- The law of unwavering desire.
    - This law explains why some of our desires remain unfulfilled.
    - As read before, desire is the basic foundation towards achieving Manifestation.
    - We may know what we want, but that thing is not what's right for us.
    - Or, we may know what we want, but that thing could not survive the process of Manifestation.
    - The purity of fear and presence of good intentions can see this law into light.

As we get older, our desires change and what we want to happen at that stage in the game is never the same as we age. When we are twenty, we may want to be flirty and free, but as age sets in, you may want stability.

The same can be said for any other affirmation, intention, or Manifestation we do. At ninety, we are not going to want to be award winning actresses, we are going to want to rest with our families around us.

- The law of delicate balance.
    - The workings of the universe, hang on a thin line.
    - This thin like is the delicate balance on which it can all come crashing down.
    - Humans also need to experience that balance within themselves.
    - As age, desires, and situations change, so does our energy and the vibrations we give off. Knowing when that is and what happens with age is key.

You can only live the life you are capable of living. At eighty, you can go skydiving, but should you? At twenty, you likely won't be satisfied staying home and sitting at the crocheting hook.

Know what you want and why it is the right time for it to happen, or when the right time will be.

- The law of harmony.
    - Harmony is the central theme of the universe.
    - If balance is at the heart of the universe, then harmony is it's core.
    - Energy can be felt through harmony from the universe to your very core.

Tapping into the harmony and power of the universe will give direct energy and power to yourself so you may see and achieve. This gives you more creative freedom, ability for abundance, and the chance to make your dreams come true.

- The law of right action.
    - Our actions and words have a butterfly effect on the world.
    - They come right back to us in the end.
    - This means, how we behave and treat others directly influences our own lives.
    - As said before, what goes out comes back to you… this is why negativity and negative affirmations and intentions have no place here.
    - By choosing the right path, offering a helping hand to the needy, or just by being a good human, you can attract more positivity and good things into your life.
    - Your behavior and actions are well within your control, even in the most trying circumstances.

- By choosing to be good, dignified, and honorable when you are naturally inclined to be angry and destructive, raises your energy levels in no time.

By boomeranging hate and destruction out, that's what you will receive in return. Remembering the tools you need to achieve Manifestation and knowing they grossly apply to this law is important.

Making sure you are pure in mind, body, and soul will see you this far. There is no way you can follow laws three through five, and that get you what you dream. It has to be all or nothing, much like getting rid of the negativity that has bounced back at you.

- The law of universal influence.
    - Humans play a huge part in the universe and how it responds to us.
    - Words and actions hurt the universe and it hurts all the good inside it.
    - Be aware of implications.
    - Expect punishment if negative behavior continues.

Everything in the universe is interlinked and in knowing that, you can see the importance of following the steps towards achieving our goals, and the laws needing to be followed.

The seven laws of attraction are the steppingstones towards Manifestation.

There's nothing quite like visualizing what you want out of life and using the power of your mind to turn that vision into a reality. And no matter where you are on your journey towards Manifestation, learning the Law of Attraction in basic terms, means a lot.

Now that you know there are seven Laws of Attraction you should have access to the right mindset, the right tools, and even the know-how, which you should be learning as you read.

Are you using the laws of attraction yet? If so, are you using them correctly? Unless you are an expert on the subject thus far, it's likely you're not.

Now that you have read the fundamental breakdown of all seven laws, what they mean, and how they should be used, here are some steps towards better practice towards achieving your desires… Manifestion.

By knowing all seven of the laws of attraction, you can gain a better understanding of the Law of Attraction and see how you can change your future. By changing the way you once thought and improving your lifestyle, you can learn how to be successful and be happier.

Many people may understand the concepts but have a hard time using it to their own benefit?

With these simple steps, you can create your own life and use the seven laws to your advantage.

-Ask for what you want from the Universe.

-Know that the universe has everything you can ever imagine, want, or dream, and it has an abundance of everything not imagined as well.

-Write down your desires and manifest them from the univers by focusing on each desire and letting it out.

Think of it as ordering clothing from a magazine. When you place the order and send it off, then you expect the order to be filled and come back to you in the time they say. That's exactly what you need to do… order from the Universe.

-Know that you will get what you want when it's the right time.

-Act like you already have what you want. (Name the thing and claim that it is here and yours already.)

-Put your creative mind into action, and start acting like you have what you want already.

-Know that what you want exists and it's coming to you, or that it has already gotten to you.

A great example of this is if you gave a few pounds to lose. You will become more active than before and find ways to exercise throughout your day, such as doing jumping jacks, walking, etc. When you walk around your house or do pushups on a set of stairs your body realizes that you have introduced something new, or something you haven't practiced in a while.

When you act that you already have what you want, you'll be able to feel it more and in turn send out the energy needed.

-Let go of judgment and negative ways of thinking.

-First accept that everything around you is simply things you have created or that have been created for you by your desires.

If you label things negative, you will create negative thoughts and feelings within you as you have read before. In doing that, it will work against you instead of help you. When you just let things go you will see that you'll have an easier time of creating what you want.

-Use your mind to its full potential, don't let it go to waste.

The mind is very powerful. It can influence your actions, what you do, how you think, it controls everything that goes on in your body. That part is the part that is able to create your ideal and through Manifestation, make it a reality.

Although it will require patience and persistence, training your mind to be aligned with your desires is well worth the end results.

-Control your own mind.

-Don't let negativity bring you down.

When you are in control of your own thought process you also have control of what your outer world will look like to you.

-Practice changing your negative thoughts to positive ones.

Thinking about getting what you want is one way to retrain and reprogram your mindset and the way you have thought for a long time. Using the laws of attraction can elevate that mindset and you can also start meditation at this point if you hadn't already been doing that.

-Meditate daily.

-Create routines to help you clear your mind and focus on what you want.

The Law of Attraction is really quite simple, and we use it every day, even without thinking . The law is constantly in motion, even if you don't realize it. When you're aware of it, though, you may think that it takes a lot of effort to get what you want, but just do what you've been doing your whole life: think!

If you "think" about it, you have always had a mind of your own in one way or another. You have been thinking about what it will be like when you get older, what you should have done or what you should do. Imagining the things that can't be seen or can't be, but you know is there. Think about what you want only, and you will see it reflected in your reality.

The benefits of meditation are endless, but the most important one that meditation offers is that it helps clear your mind. Clearing your thought process is important to manifesting the things you want in life, and using meditation will help you get the best out of the laws of attraction and what they mean for you.

Here are a few tips to help you use the laws of attraction and meditation together…

- Meditate daily.
    - Do this by getting yourself in the habit of daily meditation for at least ten minutes at a time.

- Practicing meditation to get your mind to stay calm and quiet all the time is essential to using the laws.
- Get negativity away for good.

When you start to meditate, you'll notice a lot of thoughts playing in the background much like the background music in a movie. Over time, you start to ignore the sounds playing behind the voices, and the same can be said for this… over time and with lots of practice, those thoughts will go away.

In order to keep the benefit of a clear mind, you must meditate daily.

- Meditate to acquire more patience.

With all the things you have to get done in a day, you can feel rushed and feel that you need to get everything done before you feel happy, the same can be said if you are a student and with homework and tests, it you have a job and with duties and tasks. However, happiness doesn't come from outside sources, but from inside yourself.

It also means that you're letting outside forces control how you feel when you feel rushed to complete tasks, thus meaning it is time to bring affirmations into play if you haven't yet or haven't in a while.

Meditation will help you to gain patience and give you more of it.

That's what you're doing with your mind when you meditate. This will help you have more patience in your daily life since you are taking time out of your busy day to meditate. With the patience gained from meditation, you should be able to be patient enough to wait for things that you want while practicing Manifestation and other activities that create an end result that must be waited on.

- Use meditation to amplify your visualizations.
    - Visualization is another great tool to bring to the table.
    - You'll be able to amplify your energy frequency.

When you practice meditation, you release all your thoughts and feelings, including negative ones… or rather you should, the capability is there. You will then be able to focus more on positive visualizations only.

This method is called imagery visualization. *Imagery visualization is like having a movie or music play in your head while you relax and/or meditate.*

Countless people use this method to achieve their goals and dreams since this type of meditation helps raise your energy to a higher level then before. It then sends out said stronger energy into the Universe.

The seven laws and meditation can be combined to help you accomplish all your goals and get what you want. The more you do use this dual method, the more powerful it will become for you.

Remember that the laws are as such… laws. It's up to you if you want to follow them or not, as it is if you follow others, but be warned… this only works for you in this way if goodness prevails and negativity is stifled.

Chapter 6
What Choices and Decisions are Considered Proactive?

Are you a proactive person?

Here we will be discussing the choices that one makes and how decisive action can be harnessed in order to take control over your own life and create a vision that is both tangible and real in your day to day living in order to be a proactive individual.

Here is a good example of a situation that you might need to be proactive in to give you an idea of what being a proactive individual might be… if you don't know already.

Think of it this way, just say you are attending a three-day function in a different city, and you book the air travel, arrange ground transportation for once you have arrived, and have booked the hotel room. Then, you might mentally walk through the three-day event, deciding in advance what you are going to wear at the various functions, which classes at the event you will attend, and who you will search for to maximize networking opportunities. In the process, you might decide that you might need business cards, writing materials, a briefcase for the information that you will be collecting at the exhibits and then casual clothes for the Saturday night barbecue they are going to have on day two.

This is the person who is proactive but think of it the other way. The individual going to the same event, but might not be as active in preparing for the it.

You have arrived by the graces of whoever you believe in. You caught a last minute flight, hopped a cab, and was lucky a room was available, although it wasn't the suite you would have preferred.

You get to the event and forget that you need something to write with. A few people always seem to have a spare pen to loan so no sweat… you'll ask around. Then you're knockoff Balenciaga pump broke a heal… it's okay, you know you're co-worker that you never talk to but know that's there has always got a safety pin to offer, a Band-Aid or pain killer when someone's in distress and shampoo when there's none in the hotel room… she may also have some glue to fix the shoe.

That co-worker who you barely like is who you always turn to when you need a hairdryer or a list of meeting rooms or change for the hotel vending machine. They are also the person who is selected as project managers that you lable as a kiss-up… They are organized, punctual, and productive – and respected by their managers and peers alike… they are PROACTIVE.

In knowing how to become the proactive person you wish to be… here are a few of the tools, strategies, and mindset that form a proactive person.

Those steps are…

-Setting goals/Make a plan.

People who are proactive hold planning sessions in which they plan for the future, plan what is needed for events, and even involve others in order to set specific goals for the future.

They not only put them in writing, along with deadline dates, they schedule time in their planners. In doing this, they are helping to create their own future.

-Block off time for important tasks and activities

By using calendars proactive people don't have a problem with knowing how to visualize the future, they are able to anticipate possible problems and act before they can occur.

Sometimes they can even act before there is a reason to, just because they are paing attention.

They may have to do some juggling in order to fit things in; but they never allow a priority task or activity be replaced without first rescheduling it to another time slot to do at a future date. A proactive person practicing proactive behaviors never replace a scheduled activity with a less important one.

-Use checklists.

People that make up checklists for all repetitive events or activities, such as meetings, travel, conferences, and the like are proactive in many ways. They attend workshops and events to learn how to make things better and learn how to make propper checklists.

These checklists are updated if necessary after each event.

If anything was missed, it is added to the list so that it won't be forgotten the next time.

-Review results.

This is self-explanatory. People who are proactive follow through with planned tasks and events, they follow up as well which allows for a good foundation towards learning Manifestation.

-Plan long-term.

By planning ahead it gives a proactive person time to gather the things they need for the event. They also can attain the money needed and be able to check ahead of time to make sure all aspects of the even have been handled.

These kinds of people don't struggle as much with the timeline of Manifestation. Not knowing when but knowing that it will happen.

-Always set deadlines.

This is a good thing when talking about time management. Setting small goals such as, I will gather my tools in the next two weeks. Or I will achieve meditation in three weeks.

If those times are not kept, then push back your deadline, but only in increments that are small.

Proactive people set deadlines for every planned activity.

They are aware of which activities will consume as much time as you have available for them. Setting deadlines both increases efficiency and prevents procrastination especially in reference to time management.

-Maintain the right attitude

Although there are certain tools and techniques that proactive people use, a massive portion of it is their attitude or state of mind. In theory that is the same state of mind required for Manifestation, so they can and should go hand in hand.

-Act inadvance of a future situation, rather than just reacting.

For example, the owner of a law firm may be trying to hire a new lawyer and buy new office supplies in anticipation of a surge in new business for the new lawyer. This is a proactive behavior.

A new school might open without children to fill it, but they are still going to make sure to have the classrooms set up and staff to open. They will have desks and smart boards, the books needed for the curriculum… that is a proactive move.

-Take control and causie something positive to happen.

Do this rather than allow negativity in. the individual that does not need to be asked to act, nor do they require detailed instructions is always best at this.

A good example of this proactive behavior is a child that comes home and does their homework right after school, they clean their room, do any chores they have, then they have the rest of the night and weekend to do what they want (within reason) this is a proactive child.

With this knowledge in mind, you might learn how you might go about shifting your own mindset from being reactive to proactive.

These ways are, but are not limited to…

- Take control of your own life.
- Accept that mistakes are inevitable.
- Get rid of the negative.
- Be the solution to your life.
- Be goal oriented.
- Seek out other proactive people.
- Know proper proactive behaviors.
- Don't sweat the small stuff.6
- Don't sit on the sidelines.
- Be the star of your own life.
- Don't give in to negativity.
- Celebrate your successes and small victories.
- Make sure you take time to reward yourself for a job well done.
- Seized the moment
- Make something positive happen.

So, now that you are ready to become proactive, not reactive, look within yourself to see what needs to be done to be the person you have always wanted to be.

Especially on this journey towards Manifestation and the hopes and wishes of your dreams.

Chapter 7

How Should I speak to Myself?

This chapter will focus on how one should treat themselves, speaks to themselves, and ultimately how they should see themselves. It will offer advice on how to prevent yourself from falling into stressful and depressing thought patterns and how to change your thinking, so that you do not become consumed with overthinking and disruptive or intrusive thoughts that are harmful to yourself and your Manifestation journey.

Below you will find a breakdown of the positive ways to learn to teach yourself how to converse with self on an inward level, and even more than that how to see ourselves for what we are worth, and how you should treat yourself inside and out. This plays a little on the spiritual and mental levels of learning towards Manifestation.

You will also learn the negative thought patterns that one can have as a human, and how easy it can be to fall into such a pattern.

Here are the positive ways to change the way you act towards yourself. As learned about previously, the way we think about ourselves or believe others about the way they think about us, will permanently depict our self-wroth and esteem, however, even though for many of us that is permanent, it can be reversed, but exploring some of the following steps towards finding the right way to love and treat yourself is key…

-How one should treat themselves.

Some of the most basic ways for treating yourself is as simple as not saying and believing in harmful words being spoken about you by others or yourself. Then in order to reverse those thoughts and feelings, it becomes important to practice you time… a time of day, week, or month that is set aside to do something that you love.

Here are a few examples of what can qualify as self-care, and giving yourself the time needed, and attention towards treating yourself better.

1. Go on a walk alone.

   As long as this does not produce depressing behavior, it can be beneficial to get your mind back on track.

2. Give yourself a face mask.

   This also includes but is not limited to anything that pampers you behind the closed doors of your powder room or bedroom.

3. Learn something new.

   This is a craft of some sort, new hobby, learn to make something new. What ever it is, make sure it makes you happy and you only do it for you.

   If you decide to sell your crafts, then make sure you know when enough is enough. It isn't fun any more when the supply can't meet the demand and you get overwhelmed.

4. Get a pet or plant that you can pay attention to that makes you happy.

   Think about the time and space you have, and if it would be fair to the animal or plant to come into your life.

Do you have enough time to take care for it and give it the life it deserves?

5. Redecorate your favorite room in the house, or space.

   This needs to be a space that is primarily yours. It's fine if you want to redo the family room, but it doesn't stay nice long and you lose the happy place you once had.

6. Purchase a ticket to your favorite play or sporting event.

   Go do something you wouldn't ordinarily do… take a friend or loved one, but only if you know they will not harm your progress.

7. Host a girl's only night, or a guy's night out.

   Depending on preference and gender, make an exclusive night for which ever group you prefer to hang with and make it fun.

   Remember if it's to help you, keep down on drinking excessively and any other activities that might negate the progress you are trying to make.

8. Benge watch that series you have been putting off.

   Only use this from time to time. There is nothing wrong with a good veg out in front of the booktuber… if, and that's a big if, you don't do it all the time.

   This must be a special thing to you and or you and your loved ones.

-How one should speak to themselves.

Speaking positively to yourself helps to keep your levels of serotonin high and it helps you not doubt who you are and what you are meant for in life. Some positive things you could continue to say to yourself are…

1. I am worth it.
2. I can do it.
3. I am good.
4. I am beautiful.
5. I am good enough for the job.

   These fall under affirmations and if you have come to this point and need a refresher of affirmations, feel free to back track a little to learn how they will help you.

-How one should see themselves.

This is a hard one for a lot of people, but can be done by learning who you are and studying until you know it by heart, you can do this by…

1. Knowing your strengths.

   Know what you can do and what parts of yourself are great attributes to the people around you and namely yourself.

2. Knowing your weaknesses.

   Know what you can't or shouldn't do, and why it can heart others and namely yourself.

3. Asking yourself questions that need an answer.

   Sometimes you realize that you have been leaving questions unanswered in your mind… some that are important to knot the answers to and others that are minute topics that don't matter in the end.

   They all matter though.

Leaving questions floating up there only clutters your mind and makes less room for things that make it easier to learn and allow new concepts in.

4. Try new things.

   This means to try that thing that you have always wanted to do. As long as it will bring no harm to you or others, then there is nothing that could go wrong by trying.

5. Remember old things.

   Sometimes as humans, we forget the old things we used to like to do, and in turn just don't do them anymore. After a while, those things are distant memories, or are forgotten altogether.

   For example. A young boy liked to ride horses when he was in school… he lived by a ranch and he loved to go there each day and ride. After a few years he was getting good, and won a contest barrel racing, but then his family had to move… he missed it at first, but as life went on and other things replaced his love for horses… it was gone… until one day he stumbles upon an old award from the race and boom it's there again.

   What should he do with that, let it fall to the side as a forgotten pastime that he loved, or pick it up as an adult and try over?

6. Put in the time needed.

   Nothing is ever done in moments and without time and effort put into it. The saying "Rome wasn't built in a day" latterly meant that. It wasn't built over night or rather in several nights.

   It took a lot of planning and work to get it to where it was at its peak… good things are worth waiting for.

7. Give to yourself.

   This is similar to the above section where giving to yourself so that you don't go mad is importation. This can be in the way of personal time, self-care, and even doing something you love.

-How to prevent yourself from falling into stressful and depressing thought patterns.

Thinking something once is sometimes enough to change your mental way of thinking for a long time but falling into a pattern of such thoughts can and is often detrimental. Some ways to escape those thought patterns are…

1. Review the way you feed your body.

   There are two ways we feed our body, one, through the things we digest in the way of food and drink, and second, through what we watch, read, subscribe ourselves to.

   If we learn to watch what we eat food wise when feeling low, we can often up our levels of proper endorphins and bring ourselves up naturally.

   On the other hand, changing from horror movies to rom-coms depending on how the horror movies treat you, may be a good move.

   Knowing what the move should be is the most important while dealing with what you feed your mind, body, and soul.

2. Work out.
   Again, this can mean two different things. The way we treat our body, and the activity level we should be up to at a certain age, time in our lives, etc. This doesn't mean that everyone needs to be a body builder, it simply means to take a walk, jog, sit and reach, whatever it takes for you to remind your body that you are still alive.
   Then, you need to exercise your mind and heart. This can be done by reading, studying, loving, and caring. Doing this positively can and does reverse depression and major forms of anxiety.
3. Change environments.
   Sometimes knowing if being someplace or around someone is toxic for you is the hardest but best first step you can take towards getting better.
4. Give to others.
   Like said in earlier chapters. Contributions to others is a tool that is needed in order to achieve the highest levels of Manifestation. Doing this for other reasons, such as dissolving the negative feelings within you by helping others helps you so much.
5. Create boundaries.
   Knowing when enough is enough and being able to tell people no, don't come up into my space, or can you step back I need a moment to focus, is key towards recovering from mental health issues.
6. Give yourself some quiet time.
   Just like knowing boundaries, knowing when to back off, or walk away for a short amount of time is important.
   For some people doing this for an extended period of time is also important depending on who or what they are separating themselves from.
7. Refocus.
   Getting back to what we once loved and the good people we used to be may help rid your mind of intrusive thinking surrounded by depression and anxiety.
8. Reconnect.
   Shortly after refocusing, you can reconnect with the positive things and people that used to be in your life. Those are often the things or people that can help bring you back from the spiral and into the real world that is your life.
9. Congratulate yourself and track your progress.
   When you realize you are getting back on track, give yourself a pat on the back. It's okay to feel good about yourself, but make sure to give others credit where credit is due… working towards a healthier you mentally is more important than anything you could do for yourself thus far.

-How to change your thinking.

One of the best things you can do for yourself while trying to change your thought process towards Manifestation is, take advantage to all the steps available for you and do as many as you possibly can.

The more steps you can complete, the better… a few of the steps are, but are not limited to…

1. Thinking the negative thoughts that we think on the daily, and then replace them with positivity.
   By thinking of the negative thoughts and then about how to negate them by your own words and actions, you have become the superstar of your own existence. This is so hard to do, but if you are here, then the next steps should be easy for you.
   If you haven't, then it's not all that hard if you are in the right mindset. First, you think about all the bad things that you and other people have said about you. "You are ugly," for example. Then negate that by an affirmation that you can learn to believe. "You are beautiful… I am beautiful." Soon the negation will be stronger than the negative words ever were.
2. Become your own best friend.
   This does not mean that a person can't have a best friend or loved ones that they trust, it simply means that you need to learn to become the one person you can trust to love you, before you can possibly even try to love other or expect their love in return.
3. Write down everything you think.
   This can be in the form of a journal or diary, simply write all thoughts and actions so they can be archived and looked at later, if anything so that you can see your progressions and how far you have come.
4. Find things for you to love.
   Find the things that you love and focus on that or them. A child, spouse, parent, the list goes on.
5. Make sure those things are healthy.
   Be sure that who or what you love is a good thing.
   For example, one might love wine, and in ease and accepting portion controll, it can be an alright thing to indulge in, but for that person who has abused the thing they love, it is no longer a good thing to love.
6. Ask more questions… the tougher the better.
   Like before, where it said to answer all questions, that is true, but you need to have the questions to answer. Making sure you ask the right ones and feel confident enough to answer them for yourself are two different things.
7. Stop believing all social media.
   This is the hardest one of all. Social media and the news while not practicing moderation is a touch one to filter out, but it can be done, by one, not believing everything that has been said, and by two, checking facts before you believe everything that has been said.

Then on the other hand, there are a few things that you might want to consider while changing your thought process. For some, you might not think you have bruised yourself inwardly, but you have. The following are a good depiction of things we as humans do on the daily, that count towards damaging our self-worth and esteem. Here you will learn the definitions of each thing and common ways you and others like you have most likely experienced these, even when you didn't think you had.

-Overthinking-to spend too much time analyzing and thinking about the same things over, and over again.

1. Double thinking about a project you know you have put your time and effort in, but not thinking it's good enough.

2. Thinking that a dress you have loved since you saw it in the store and finally bought after trying it on ten times will look horrible on you on the big day, even thought you have seen it on yourself and loved it on yourself.

3. Not thinking you are worth something you have tried so hard for just because others have said you weren't.

-Disruptive thoughts-stuck thoughts that cause great distress within you.

1. Having the right mind set, but in the middle of the big presentation, there is that still small NAGGING voice that won't calm down until it knows you are done.

2. Knowing that in the back of your mind you know you are going to fail at the recital, but also knowing at the forefront of your mind and heart that you have practiced your rear off, and this is going to happen and you're are going to be great.

-Intrusive thoughts-thoughts that pop up or push their way in while we are trying to think of something else, likely positive thoughts being overshadowed by negative thinking.

1. You have saved for the car of your dreams and go to buy it, but your friends, friend said you would look dumb in that kind of car. You pushed it to the back of your mind but boom it's back as you are about to hand over the money.

2. You have to drive into a big city for the first time ever. You have the confidence in yourself, but somewhere down the line, someone else didn't. As you are halfway down the road, the doubt the other person had for you, has now pushed your confidence to the side.

-Harmful thinking-are thoughts of harm on yourself or someone else… not necessarily thoughts of death, but thoughts of harm, perhaps not ever to be carried out, but thinking it, nonetheless.

1. I might as well disappear.

2. Not a soul wants me why should I want myself.

3. I am not worth this.

4. My life would be better if they would just take a long walk off a short pier.

5. They should reck off a cliff and we would all be happy.

-Depressive overload-when the above thought processes have overtaken your mind, not allowing room for anything else to come in, be it good or bad.

1. It started off a good day, I was prepared for the big test, had studied hard even, but then I began to doubt I could pass, then words that others had said pushed the confidence I once had away, and then I was convinced I would fail… so I failed, and now I am laying in the dark all alone, because if I failed that one, then I will fail them all, then the class, then school altogether, I am not worth the funding I got, I am a waste of a desk and chair.

It's easy to see that on the daily you think negatively about yourself due to things you have thought or said, or that others have thought or said, but knowing there are other things to override the bad with the good to give you the chance to succeed through Manifestation and in other aspects of life makes it all worthwhile.

Chapter 8
How do my Thoughts and Words Effect my Body?

In this chapter, you will learn how your thoughts and words can affect your physical body and how this can also cause damage to your mental outlook and your Manifestation journey. This chapter will also provide insight into how to change thoughts so that you can become the healthiest version of yourself both physically, emotionally, and mentally.

The best way to discover this is by breaking down the categories and giving examples of each one so that you may better understand what is needed to reach your goals towards a healthier body.

Did you know that a large portion of sickness are trauma, stress, anxiety, depression, and environment induced? Here are some examples of sicknesses that can be caused by each.

- Trauma.
  - Post-Traumatic Stress Disorder (PTSD is an after trauma response to certain situations that causes the body to react to the same or similar situations when prompted so.)
  - Acute Stress Disorder (ASD is major or nearly debilitating stressors that cause daily life to be difficult, and in most cases unable to endure.)
  - Adjustment disorder or trouble adjusting to normal situations. (This also includes transitional disorders where a person often has trouble adjusting to change, included but not limited to leaving the home to go to the car… this is more prevalent in children where it is presented as transitional dysplasia.)
  - Reactive attachment disorder. (This is attaching ones self to things and people in an unhealthy way.)
  - A significant decline in social engagements. (This is refusing to move or react around people and during some or all social situations.)
- Stress.
  - Heart disease. (Researchers have long suspected that the stressed-out, type A personality has a higher risk of high blood pressure and heart problems than any other.)
  - Asthma and breathing problems.
  - Obesity, bulimia, anorexia.
  - Diabetes and hypoglycemia.
  - Headaches and pressure in the head.
  - Depression and anxiety if left untreated.
  - Gastrointestinal problems, usually in the form of ulcers.
  - Alzheimer's and memory lose.
- Anxiety.
  - Mental health disorders.
  - Sever depressive disorder.
  - Substance misuse and abuse.
  - Chronic pain.

- Social isolation including but not limited to problems functioning at school and/or work.
- Depression.
  - In all honesty, there can be other health issues that are caused by depression, but already standing heath problems can and will, often times cause depression. It is important to keep yourself in check.
  - A host of other mental health issues.

- Environment.
  - Cancer.
  - Post-traumatic stress disorder.
  - Depression.
  - Certain traumas.

Now, you will learn how certain things you do to yourself can have effects on your body. You might not think about how possible it is that YOU might be the cause of some of your illnesses, but it is possible.

Here are a few ways that YOU may be affecting your health on a daily basis…

1. Your negative thoughts.
   a. Having a thought pattern that reflects negativity.
   b. Thinking the worst.
   c. Being a doom and gloom kind of thinker.
   d. Thinking that everyone is out to get you.
   e. Thinking that you will never succeed in anything because of past experiences.
2. Your negating words.
   a. Saying mean things to yourself, about yourself.
   b. Saying mean things to yourself, about others.
   c. Saying mean things to others, about yourself.
   d. Saying mean things to others, about them.
   e. Saying mantras or negative affirmations that soon become reality.
   f. Intentionally seting negative affirmations by your words that can turn into the inability to manifest.
3. Your bad actions.
   a. Doing things that will hurt others.
   b. Doing things that hurt yourself.
   c. Self-harm.
   d. Eating too much or eating too little.
   e. Not catering to an illness in the way you should… Ie: proper medications, diet, etc.

f. Partaking in the use of illegal drugs.
g. Partaking in the use of addictive items in excess.

4. Your low mental outlook.

a. Thinking that your depression defines you.
b. Allowing stress to turn to anxiety then turn to depression without asking for help.
c. Refusing help in any form.
d. Thinking you can do it alone.
e. Refusing that you have an issue when there is an issue that is evident.

Now that you have seen some of the things we do to ourself on a daily basis, here are several ways that you can negate the affects and change your mindset, and in turn, your health…

1. Cast away bad thoughts.
   a. Creating positive affirmations as talked about in previous chapters is key.
   b. Practicing those affirmations.
   c. For every bad thought you have, think ten positive ones.
2. Bring in new thoughts.
   a. If you haven't thought of positive thoughts to replace the negative with, ask others about things they see positive in you… write them down and say them over, and over again.
   b. Hold onto the positive thoughts until you believe them.
   c. If you can't think of positive thoughts about yourself, then think positively about others.
3. Sweeten your words.
   a. Think about the words you say to yourself and others and add honey. This does not mean butt-kisser type of words it means to use kind words.
   b. Remember the way you would like to be talked to and talk to others like that.
   c. Cut down on down words… Ie: shut up, hate, never, I can't… and the list goes on and on.
   d. Consider cutting down on profanity if you feel that contributes to the negative side of you.
4. Write everything down.
   a. With affirmations, writing them down helps.
   b. Write down the positive words and use them daily.
   c. Write down your negative thoughts and burn them as a way, to rid yourself of them. (Make sure you are in a safe environment for burning things)
   d. Write down your schedule and include time for yourself.
5. Refine your actions.
   a. Think about your negative actions and cut them away.
   b. Create positive actions to benefit others first, then yourself.

6. Define your reactions.
    a. Think of the way you react to situations and change the negative ones.
    b. Reactive with positivity first, so that you may learn a proper reaction to the situation in the future.
    c. React with positivity always… it makes you the bigger person.
7. Develop a positive mental outlook.
    a. Affirmations.
    b. Positive thinking.
    c. Positive talking.
    d. Positive actions.
    e. Dealing with your demons.
    f. Getting rid of all bad and replacing it with positivity.

By doing all these things, you can discover what illnesses that are within you are caused by YOU and ways to fix them. If you feed on your depression, even existing illnesses will worsen.

Sometimes the hardest thing we can do as humans when feeling down is thinking positively, but it is possible through the above means. Think therefore you can and will do what is needed to make you better.

Another thing to remember while recovering from illness, you are going to need people and activities to build you wellness up… here is a list of who and what those things might be.

1. People.
    a. Mental health personnel.

- This may be, but is not limited to councilors, therapists, and mental health hospital care specialists.

    b. Support groups.

- This is the groups of people who are dealing with the same illness and causes of illnesses than you are dealing with, or have been dealing with.

    c. Family.

- These are all the positive members/nontoxic members of your family that help build up who you are and not drain your being.
- Knowing what family to be around, and what family you should cut or take time away from is key for getting better.

    d. Friends.

- The same as family, you need to surround yourself with people who love and understand you, these are non-toxic people as well.
- Keep in mind that you don't need hundreds of people you call friends, you only need a few fthat you call best friend.

    e. Religious or Belief based teachers.

- This would be any teacher or leader of your faith. Even if you don't believe in anything, join together with others who feel the same way, teach one another how to meditate for calmness if not for anything else.
- If you have a pastor, preacher, leader of your church, this would be a good person to talk to, or have point out someone else that would be good to talk to.

2. Activities.

- Sports.
  - If you have a sport you like to play for the fun of it… play.
  - If you have a sport and can join a team of sorts… join.
  - If you have family's children that play, then go watch them.
  - If you like a certain sport and prefer to watch it professionally, then subscribe to a channel or to getting year-round tickets at the field, court, arena, etc.
- Family or Friends.
  - Birthday parties, baby showers, weddings, graduations, etc.
  - Attend anything with anyone that isn't toxic… you will regret not doing so later.
  - Have just because parties, create a theme and have them for the fun of it.
- Likes and Loves.
  - Do things you like to do… if you love to shop, then shop, if you like to eat out, then try new places. (Make sure whatever this is, you stay within your means.)
- Outdoor.
  - If you are able go for a walk, jog, hike, if you aren't, then go sit in your back yard, get pushed in a wheelchair to the top of a hill, or down the road, whatever it is, do it.
  - Ride in the car with the window down. Top down too if you can. Feel free once again.

- Craft or hobby related events.
  - If you like to do something as a craft or hobby, join local or online groups that share the love.
  - Also consider traveling to circles that love the same thing you do.
  - You can make long-lasting friends that like the same thing and might even be able to relate to how you are feeling.
- Religious or belief-based events.
  - This would be attending church if you go, religious based meetings.
  - Go to circles and clubs that carry your belief system.
  - Pagans have circles, as do Native Americans, Norse, etch… find who you are and do it on purpose.
- Personal preferences.
  - If nothing on this list fits you, formulate an activity that does.
  - Make it your own.

Also remember at the end of the day, unless you are contagiously sick, you should likely get out and do any of these things anyway. If you are in pain, do them with moderation, if you have stress, start with a time limit, but you will find that you will get better if you allow yourself the time and means to do so.

Illness might as well be a four-letter word. Knowing the triggers inside yourself and what causes them to be set off is important. This isn't the same for everyone, so knowing what your individual needs are and how to meet them will help you.

Knowing what you can do and what you should do are two different things, but one the other side of that knowing what you think you can do and what you think you should do are also different.

We all have levels of capability in our bodies, but some feel like they are unable to do half of what they could actually do IF they would work through the issues, even if it's pain.

A great example of this is a person who is significantly over weight… this is a detriment to your body in many ways, but this person isn't able to walk for miles, or even half a mile to start out with… but even if it's with the help of a walker or someone else, on day one they can walk around the house, on day two around the house and down the block, five days in they are walking up and down in front of their house four times and has dropped five pounds. Even if weight is not dropped, momentum, energy, and self-love can be obtained.

This same person in a month, can be walking a mile, has dropped twenty-five pounds, and feels better then they have in years.

The same can be said with any illness of the mind or body. Doing something until it feels good, even if it hurts to start with takes willpower, but you have it.

YOU HAVE IT!

If you feel no one has faith in you… you can. You can have faith in yourself on your goal towards Manifestation, and this is a large goal to meet before continuing.

Being healthy in your mind is so important, and it simply isn't happening unless your body is healthy as well. Being healthy in mind makes it that much easier to be healthy in your body as well.

Don't be the destruction of your own self… be the architect of your own life.

Chapter 9
What is Conscious Living?

This chapter will feature advice on what conscious living is and the various ways its practice can lead to healthier lives and better Manifestation success.

Conscious living involves doing things simply because you want to, because you are passionate, inspired, and driven towards a said goal and you know you can achieve it no matter what it takes. It also means thinking positively and rationally all of the time no matter what might stand in your way.

Everything that you do should be a conscious act of everything in your life culminated into one set of actions that is designed by you and for you to do better and be better.

Conscious living is all about being aware of your lifestyle and your surroundings, and then understanding that if that living is not a good life lived, then it is up to you to fix what is wrong with it and make it work for you. Living consciously is about being aware of every aspect of your life and giving it considered thought, not just a passing thought, but by thinking long and hard about how it will work for you and your Manifestation journey.

It takes a lot of thought and then actions towards said thought, to get to a place that is good for you. Finding that place is one of the first steps and a great tool to bring with you during your time of Manifestation.

It's about choosing to be mindful of matters both large and small even when everything affects you in various different ways. Concepts with deeper meaning are also sometimes neglected… it's easy when you are living a busy life to let said distractions take hold and be too prevalent in your day to day walk.

Some of the reasons of why you need to/should adopt a lifestyle of conscious living are…

- Peace of mind and growth during your life in many, different ways.
- Growing in the goodness that can be and should be a long and happy life.
- Becoming a person that both you and other people like to be around. (Remember that it doesn't matter what others think in the long run, but if you aren't a great person, then others aren't going to like to be around you, and that does reflect who you are to others.)
- It helps you take note of who else in your life is as proactive with the way they live and might be a good person to associate with.
- It helps you raise your children to be good people who live a proactive lifestyle and get things done without feeling like they need others to do things for them.
- It gets you a step closer to your journey towards Manifestation.

For many people, hearing the term 'conscious living' brings up images of the following things.

1. Hippies.
2. Dreadlocks.
3. Rastafarian lifestyle.
4. Drugs perhaps to bring on a euphoric experience.

Or even on the extreme other side of things, to live a conscious life to some can only be obtained by…

1. People that are fake.
2. People who pretend to live their life a certain way but don't… in reality.
3. Heads of churches, cults, and other religious groups.

This is a total misconception however on any level. You don't have to be a hippie, eat fruits and vegetables only, be the leader of a fundamental foundation… Anyone can practice living consciously, and all of us should do so… we are given the tools just as we are on our journey towards Manifestation.

Here are some things that can be a benefit while practicing conscious living.

- Environment.
  - The place that you feel the most at home and the people that you feel at home with.
- Relationships.
  - The people that we call friends or family that are not toxic for us.
- Physical.
  - The way that you feel in your body and mind. It can differ if you are living consciously.
- Mental.
  - You will feel better mentally, which will help with depression, anxiety, and stressors of all kind.

And it's not some deeply mystical or necessarily spiritual practice; it's more about being aware of how you live your life and treat the people about you. Understanding conscious living and implementing it into your lifestyle doesn't have to involve massive changes either.

As long as you have been following steps this far on your Manifestation journey you should be a good portions of the way ready to practice conscious living. There are some simple ways you can improve mindfulness and pay attention to the world around you.

What is Conscious Living?

That is a loaded question, there are so many basic explanations, but some of them can get confusing if you first don't understand.

Conscious living is all about being aware of the way in which your practice your lifestyle and the surroundings that you call your normal life. This also includes the people that are in your life and those that you call friends and family… permanent fixtures of your life.

There are many different levels of this that you can explore in order to understand this better. Life can be either very grand on a massive scale or small and minute like a grain of sand. The habits that people get into for many of us is to switch out during activities that are part of our daily routines. We don't focus our attention on seemingly insignificant parts of our lives, some of them come as merely habits and that's how most days go by.

Some of these basic habits are, but are not limited to…

1. Eating.
    a. For the most part, we all know that we should eat three meals a day that are balanced and healthy, for many, this does not need to be thought about, it just happens.
2. Cleaning.
    a. This is cleaning our environments.
    b. This is also cleaning ourselves.
3. Forming an opinion.
    a. This is any thought we formulate and/or execute during the day that we make sometimes without even thinking.
4. Sleeping.
    a. We all sleep, some more than others, some less… this is done every day, or should so that we can survive.
    b. This comes naturally and occurs as often as we allow it to.
    c. Sometimes if we stay up on purpose, our bodies will subconsciously stop us in our tracks so that we can recharge.
5. Dressing ourselves.
    a. If you get dressed daily to go to work or rather change your casual clothes to other casual clothes, it's still a natural thing to be done and we do it often, times without thinking.
    b. After cleaning or bathing, we change as well.

We do these things every day, but rarely give them more than a passing thought… unless we stop doing them for some reason or it becomes troublesome.

Some examples of something that is normal for us becoming troublesome enough to notice are...

1. Insomnia.
2. Distractive disorder.
3. Sudden PTSD.
4. Newly added stressors.

And the list could go on and on, but it included things that are noticeably off.

Living consciously is about being aware of *every* aspect of your life and giving it considered thought… assessing and being aware of your daily actions and activities. It's about *deciding* to be mindful of matters both large and small… as discussed earlier in the chapter, that could be the biggest happening in our life, to the smallest most insignificant.

Some concepts with deeper meaning are but are not limited to.

- Neglect of our families.
- Neglect of our friends.
- Neglect of finances.
- Deterioration of health.
- Lack of leisure time.
- Bad environment.
- Downfall of spirituality.

These are are all important to consider, and those who live consciously give these things more consideration and change their lifestyle accordingly. It's easy for those that try to live this way to change things back to the way they should be.

It's through the awareness of our lives that matters, it's then choosing to act responsibly based on this awareness to make the difference. We can think all day long about what could change things for the better, but then NOT doing it.

A great example of this is being aware of what we eat… that can lead to making food choices based on health and ethical concerns, which in turn becomes a part of conscious living.

This choice can benefit both the individual and the environment that they live in or want to live in.

The same can be said for most aspects of our lives.

By being aware of what we do and making conscious choices, it's possible for us to be our best and most responsible selves. Once we are to that point, our lives can excel to an all new high point.

Then again, you might still be wondering why you should consider couscous living and what you need in order to practice a lifestyle as such.

First off, practicing a lifestyle of living consciously can make us…

1. Cleaner.
2. Happier.
3. Healthier.
4. More successful.
5. Goal oriented.

Some things you might consider while thinking on this are…

1. It's not something that comes overnight.
2. The process to reach awareness and fulfillment takes time.
3. It also takes a lot of disciplined effort.

Here are some ways that you can take the above areas of your life and how they could potentially see improvements…

- Cleanliness.

- Keeping clean also makes sure that your area, body, home, and environment are prepared for higher being.

- Health.
  - By paying closer attention to how you treat your body, you can identify areas that need work and do what it takes to fix it.
  - Consciousness in this area can make you understand the impacts of what you eat, both on your health and your environment.
  - Enacting changes to your diet contributes greatly to living a healthy lifestyle. Not only this, but you will be more in tune with your body.
  - Also, as talked about in chapters above, what you put into your body can turn to something worse… much worse.
- Productivity.
  - Being aware of how you spend your time can and will make a significant difference on how productive you are.
  - This covers procrastination and time management… or the lack thereof.
  - Paying attention to what you say 'yes' and 'no' to can result in you making positive choices.
  - This can also be the positive and negative affirmations that we send out into the universe weather we know it or not… weather we mean it or not.
  - This action means you can dedicate more time to areas of your life that need some or a lot of important.
  - These can be…
    - Family.
    - Friends.
    - All relationships.
    - Self-betterment.
    - Environmental influences.
- Environment.
  - Many people fail to recognize that they have an impact on the world around them or that the world around them has an impact on them.
  - Whether it's humans actions towards the waste we produce, the food we consume, or the power we use, it all has an effect on our planet and even on a smaller scale, the area we directly live in.
  - Those who make a conscious choice to minimize their impact on the environment are helping make the world a better place.
  - Some ways to do this are…

- Living eco-friendly.
- Practice sustainable living.
- Recycle.
- Teach next generations to love.

- Self-love.
  - This is realizing you're your happiness and not so much the happiness of others is a vital yet often underappreciated part of our wellbeing.
  - It's possible to be unaware that we're unhappy if we don't practice a mindful approach to living our daily lives.
  - We can be "down" and not have known that we are because we have been for far too long.
  - Happiness is a basic requirement for a fulfilling life and living it to the fullest.
  - Practicing conscious living can help you realize…
    - How you want to live.
    - Who you want to be.
    - What your passions are.
    - What your greatest desires are.
    - Set goals.
    - Recognize the important things in life.

After reading the above ways to live the life that is conscious and full, it can be likely that you already live consciously in some areas of your life, perhaps without even realizing it. Many people are motivated by…

1. Friends.
2. Family.
3. Money.
4. Health.
5. A good existence.
6. Happiness.

However, to unlock your full potential, mindfulness and living consciously are necessary. There are a variety of things that can be done right now that will set you in the right direction.

-Ask important questions to those you know will have the right answers.

-Start by asking yourself some questions about your life and existence.

a. Do you like your job?
b. Do you feel happy?
c. Do you feel healthy?
d. Do you want to continue, on this journey?
e. Do you like the way your job is headed.
f. Do you have room for improvement?
g. Do you spend enough time with family and loved ones?

-If the answer to these questions is 'no' then you've identified some areas in which you can start being more aware.

-Reflect.

-Set some time privately aside each day to reflect on your life.

- Always meditate.

-Write in a journal or diary.

-Think deeply about the matters that are close to your heart.

-Decided on what's right.

-Review how you've spent your time that day, and where your time could be better spent tomorrow.

-Try better tomorrow.

-Make positive choices.

-Live the changes you see in yourself.

-Support the changes you see in others.

-You should set a goal.

-Follow your passion.

-Make daily reminders to take small steps towards your goals.

-Set affirmations.

-Expand your horizons.

-Read.

-Watch, and listen to a variety of different media to think about yourself and the world in a different way.

-Be who you know you are supposed to be.

Changing your lifestyle to one focused on living consciously takes time and effort. Remembering that it is a process that's more than worth the effort is best. Knowing that no matter how hard it feels sometimes, the greater good and the best outcome are far worth the struggles you may or may not have. With a greater understanding of yourself and your inner thoughts and feelings, you can take actions that benefit you and those around you.

Remembering that you are not the only one out in the world helps… again you don't do what you do to please others or even to gain their reaction, but you should stay mindful that you are not alone.

By leaning and remembering this, it allows you the opportunity to connect with yourself, your environment, and the people you care about, and it gives you true power over your life… perhaps this is something you have never had, or had at one point and didn't think you would ever have again.

Remember you are worth it and can do it… these are only baby steps towards the bigger picture.

Chapter 10
What is Power of Thought?

In this chapter you will learn a host of information about the power of our own thoughts and how shifting them at various moments can be beneficial to our immediate end results and the quality of our day, to day living.

The power of our thoughts can make or break the way we live our lives and who or what we surround ourselves with.

What people don't know is, that there's a secret that many people don't know when it comes to the process of thought. In fact, there is a large proportion of great historical, present thinkers, philosophers, and high achievers which have agreed to the fact that there is a universal truth. This secret and the truth behind it simply revolve around the simple idea…

You are what you think.

This is like the saying you are what you eat but this is taken to a whole new level. Thinking is far different than ingesting something, it is projecting something.

English philosopher James Allen wrote: "*As a man thinks, so he is; as he continues to think, so he remains.*"

Stoic and Roman emperor Marcus Aurelius wrote: "*A man's life is what his thoughts make of it.*"

Ralph Waldo Emerson said: *"A man is what he thinks about all day long."*

Author Earl Nightingale said: *"We become what we think about,"*

Mark Twain wrote: *"Life consists mainly of the storm of thoughts that is forever flowing through one's head."*

"If you only read things that everyone else is ready, you can only think what everyone else is thinking," was said by Haruki Marukami.

Coco Chanel said: "*The most courageous act is still to think for yourself aloud.*"

In the book "1984" by George Orwell, you will read "*but if thought corrupt language, language can also corrupt thought.*"

All these great minds, fashion designers, dystopian books, authors, and the like have obviously discovered the secret to living a happy, purposeful and productive life.

Here are a few other quotes about thought that might make you think… pun intended.

We live in a world of thought.

Our thoughts create our experiences, and thus, we experience what we think.

It is the quality of our thoughts, then, that create the quality of our life.

The universe doesn't give you what you ask for with your thoughts, it give you what you demand with your actions.

If your thinking of something, you might as well think big.

Who you think you are each day completely determines the universe you live in.

If you realized how powerful your thoughts are, you would never think a negative thought again.

When we're unhappy where we are in life, we seek to create change. So, we go about transforming our environment believing that doing so will create the necessary change we hope to see... not through the thoughts that we think, but by the actions that we do, but as said above in the quotes by famous people and general quotes… our thoughts manifest into actions.

Great examples of this are, but are not limited to the fact that…

- We buy things for a materialistic boost of happiness.
    - Because we THINK if we have the best or the newest, then we will feel happy about ourselves.
    - Because we THINK that others will like us better if we do.
- We travel to escape our problems.
    - Because we THINK our problems won't be waiting for us when we return.
    - Because we THINK happiness is somewhere else.
    - Because we THINK that if we go somewhere else, we can be someone else.
- We seek substances to numb the mind and help us forget.
    - Because we THINK that the high will hide the pain.
    - Because we THINK if we can forget for a moment, it can be forgotten for good.
    - Because we THINK if we just drink one more, do this one more time, act again in a way that once numbed the pain, it will happen the same way every time.
- We pretend so we don't remember that we are.
    - Because we THINK if we can be someone else, we don't have the problems that once attached themselves to us.
    - Because we THINK that if we fake happiness, then we are happy.
- We act like the present doesn't affect us in the least.
    - Because we THINK that now that we are older, we won't have as many issues.
    - Because we THINK that if we are here and now, the things of the past are gone forever.
    - Because we THINK that if we are here and now, the future stands still for us.
- We seem to put off the future in hopes that it won't come.
    - Because we THINK that as long as the future doesn't come, we don't have to adult or grow up.
    - Because we THINK that the future is scary and as long as we stay in the now, we are safe.
    - Because we THINK we aren't good enough for a happy future.
- We act happy when we really aren't.
    - Because we THINK if we act happy, we are.
    - Because we THINK if others think we are happy then the bad doesn't exist.

In so many ways our actions are based loosely on our thoughts and so therefore because we THINK therefore we are and do and will always be what we put out into the universe.

But of course, we fall back to where we had started: unhappy with where we are today. And so, the cycle repeats itself.

a. We buy.
b. We travel.

c. We forget.

d. We always focus on the *external* factors we need to alter in order to create better circumstances.

This happens because we falsely assume that change begins from the outside. In truth, the change starts from inside. The thought process stats as a subconscious trickle that then turns into verbal vomit that dictates everything.

Environment does play a large role in changing your circumstances, but it doesn't address the *fact that your thought process is* is the driver behind why you feel the way you do, and why you act in the way you have grown accustomed.

Here's what you need to realize thought in order to change the way you think, and by association, act.

- If you want to change the outside, you must first change the inside.
- You must change the attention of your thoughts because what you think directly influences how you feel.
- Know that how you feel directly influences how your body reacts.
- And as a chain reaction, how your body reacts directly influence how you behave.
- And then, how you behave comes to define who you are and what you experience in life.

"If you get the inside right, the outside will fall into place." Eckhart Tolle.

It all begins with your thoughts and our life experiences spring from the thoughts we actively engage in:

You are what you think.

And to comprehend the essence of this statement, you first need to understand the link between your thoughts, emotions, and behavior, or better yet the process from thoughts to actions.

This all begins with the power that you put behind your thoughts. This is a hard concept because you could be one of four kind of people…

1. Those that put little to no thought into the process of which they think, and therefore don't know how powerful their thinking can be.
2. Those who know that their thoughts can affect their life, but they don't care enough to practice mindful thinking.
3. Those that know, and work hard to think before speaking and acting.
4. Those that know and practice to the utmost, especially on their journey towards Manifestation.

Your thoughts are the main ingredient of the power inside you.

When you add to your thoughs…

- Focus.
- Emotions.
- Intellect.

- Consciousness.

Thoughts become powerful and can affect your reality.

The thoughts that pass through your mind are responsible for almost everything that happens in your life. You may not think of it that way, but it's true. Some good examples of thoughts to action on a daily basis are…

1. Because you THINK of putting your feet on the floor in the morning, you actually do, and that starts your day, no matter the outcome.
2. Because you THINK of applying for the new job, you may get it, then you will have a new job, and practice the duties that said new job require.
3. Because you THINK about trying for another child, put the try into action, you can reap the results of a positive pregnancy.

Each of those are examples of the formula *I think, I do, therefore it is,* process. Neuroscientists have discovered that repetitive thoughts form neural pathways as neurons that fire together get wired together.

Thus, the more a thought is reinforced through action and reaction, the stronger these neural pathways become and the more automatically they become our "go to" pattern of thinking, even if we don't consciously think about it that way.

Did you know however that you can change your thought process. If you find that you have trouble thinking, doing, and reacting to what you have done in a positive way, or if your thoughts reap negative repercussions, these are the ways to turn your thoughts into positivity.

This is needed to reach Manifestation, for without it, there is no way to do so.

1. TAKING BACK CONTROL.
   a. Mind control is a character strength that improves the quality of your life, you can control your own mind.
2. Be aware.
   a. Know that thoughts can have negative repercussions.
   b. Know if yours have or are having negative reactions towards others or yourself.
3. Be prepared.
   a. Be prepared for the repercussions of negativity in…
      A. Relationships.
      B. Jobs.
      C. School.
      D. Social life.
      E. Spiritual life.
      F. Happiness.
      G. Health.
      H. Wellbeing.

4. Name it.
    a. Be sure to name what you want out loud or in the form of affirmations.
    b. Be sure to name this every day until it becomes reality.
5. Claim it.
    a. Claim that you are worth the positivity.
    b. Claim that no matter how bad your thoughts get, you are worth the change you make in yourself and for yourself and others.
6. Don't fear.
    a. Don't be afraid of the change.
    b. Don't fear the positivity, bask in it.
7. Erase.
    a. Find ways to erase any bad that you have done via your thoughts.
    b. Find a way to erase any hurts caused to yourself and others.
8. Replace.
    a. Replace those thoughts and actions with good ones.
9. Have a reality check.
    a. Let it hit you in the face.
    b. Fall down but get back up again.
    c. Know that you are worth it, but don't get a big head.
10. Practice mindfulness.
    a. This is the best way for you to figure out how to practice positive thinking, manifest into positive actions.
11. Write it down.
    a. If you can't remember the steps or affirmations, write them down and use them over again.
12. Repeat.
    a. Keep going every day until it becomes second nature.
13. Know that it's your choice.
    a. It's your choice to do this.
    b. Only you can change.
    c. Only you can make the difference you want to see in you.
14. Know that your thoughts are not insignificant.
    a. They are important because you are interacting with a conscious Universe which not only "hears" what you say but more importantly knows what you feel and believe as well.
    b. You believe everything you say to yourself.

The Universe is always responding to your beliefs.
This is how your thoughts create your reality.

Since emotions and the body's reactions are triggered by the thoughts you give attention to, you are living in, and causing the others around you to live in a world of thought: Your thoughts create your experiences, and thus, you experience what you think… your environment becomes filled with the actions of your thoughts and the products of your actions.

Some things in life cause people to feel, these are called emotional reactions.

All emotions are a result of actions which are a result of thought and what stock we put into our own mind. Some things in life cause people to think, these are sometimes called logical or intellectual reactions. Through logical and intellectual reactions, life is divided between things that make you feel and things that make you think.

A study done stated that if part of your brain is being occupied by feeling, then it makes sense that you have less capacity for thought.

That is obvious if you take emotional extremes, such as crying, where people can barely think at all.

This however doesn't have to mean that emotional people are not intelligent people, and in most cases isn't the case, it just means that their brain doesn't perceive in the same way during the times in which they are emotional.

Emotion goes on and off for everyone, sometimes people cry, and sometimes they are completely serious and capable of anything intellectually.

Some things in life can identifiably cause more emotion than other things. Some examples of those are…

- Color.
    - Color causes more emotions than just neutrals do.
    - Red-one of the three primary hues is one of the most powerful emotional evoking colors.
    - Green-is another primary color that is one of the most calming and neutral of shades.
    - Blues-these are hues of serenity, peace, and security.
    - Purple-this mixes some of the warm and cool and evokes passions most of the time.
    - Yellow-is simply happy.
    - Orange-is harmonic.
    - Neutrals and browns-are the epitome of nature and are used abundantly in design they however only create a voided
- Things that are personal are emotional.
    - Home
    - A nostalgic location.
    - Your favorite book/movie/tv-show.
    - Food.
    - Personal items.

There are things that people like that cause thought. You could like something, and it causes you to think.

If you think about it, you may have previously thought that emotion was a feeling, not evoked through thought, but studies have shown that is not the case anymore. It proves that thought can level emotions where they stand or evoke them.

Before leaving the learning chapter on thought and how it can affect you, we hope you can close off your mind for a moment and think unilaterally about the way your thoughts can dictate your emotions.

Some examples for this are…

- Sadness.
    - You may already be feeling sad, but if you dwell on the source of your sadness via thought, then the emotion will escalate to a state of catatonic sadness that might be difficult to escape.
    - On the other hand, if you are sad, you can think about things that make you happy to reverse the emotion.
- Happiness.
    - If you are having a rough day, think on the happy things, and through the thought process, happiness occurs where it once was but a passing thought.
- Depression.
    - By using affirmations (THOUGHTS) of what you want for your life, you can reverse depression.
    - Also by negative thinking, you can enhance your depression and make it debilitating.
- Anger.
    - You can think about something you haven't thought of in a while and bring back the anger attached to it, this is a good example of how humans hold onto things such as anger for far too logn.
- Fear.
    - Fear is the biggest thought induced emotion ever. If you think too hard on passing thoughts fear can and will grow to the point you are afraid of your own shadow… literally.
- Excitement.
    - You can become excited about something by thinking, or over thinking about the thing in which you are excited about.
- Disgust.
    - This is something that feels more natural, but can increase the more you think about the thing or things that disgust you the most.
- Joy.
    - Think of this like happiness.
- Surprise.
    - Surprise is something that can and sometimes doesn't come from thought. If it's spur of the moment, then it often is a response to the moment, but if you have time to think about it, then thought can cause your surprise to grow.
    - Surprise while the thought process grows can easily turn to other emotions.
- Embarrassment.
    - This works very much like surprise does.
- Love.
    - The more you think about someone or something, the more love grows within you for that someone or something.
- Anxiety.
    - This works much like depression, or stress.
- Satisfaction.
    - Similar to happiness.
- Shame.

    - Shame is instantaneous sometimes, but with thinking about it over time, it can grow to the point of debilitation.
- Annoyance.
    - Similar, to the way disgust works.

A few other emotions that workt he same through though are…

- Envy.
- Confusion.
- Guilt.
- Boredom.
- Pride.
- Loneliness.
- Frustration.
- Jealousy.
- Awe.
- Gratitude.
- Shyness.
- Extrovert.

The next time you wonder how what you think reflects on your life, remember…

You are what you think.

Chapter 11
How Do I Increase the Level of my Vibrational Response?

This chapter will cover topics regarding elevation of your vibrational response to the universe and how this can help bring in a higher quality of people, opportunities and spaces in which you can expand.

By learning about vibrations and how they work for you both spiritually and for cleansing your mind, body, and spirit, you create or attract nothing in the sense of bringing something into existence that did not exist before.

It goes back to earlier reading about asking the universe but knowing it's already out there for you. You only have to believe that it's there and ask for it… or manifest it into reality.

You only shift your thoughts, emotions and physiology, altering your signature – you're feeling or state of being. In this sense, your signature is the vibrations that you send out into the universe that come back to you after bouncing off soothing and come back to you.

It's important to comprehend that all frequencies that can exist already exist; A frequency is the time, speed, and way that a vibration bounces back and forth between you and the universe. It's important to know that all frequency combinations or signatures of all possible realities that can exist do co-exist, simultaneously, right now in the moment that you are in.

This is referencing that all things are there for you to take with the permission of thc universe, you only have to ask and receive.

Vibrations are also sometimes referred to as the universal life energy. This is simply a method to describe your overall state of wellbeing through the vibrations that you send out or receive.

Higher vibrations on the other hand, are associated with…

1. Putting out empowering thoughts.
2. Having positive emotions.
3. Practicing good health.
4. Having strong spiritual awareness.

This is the hardest part of Manifestation for some people. However, in thinking about Manifestation and sending and receiving from the universe then you must believe to some degree that the universe is based on cosmic laws and phenomena. They are essentially of the nature of vibrations or motions of different kinds.

This is energy.

Everything in the universe is energy. Every

1. Matter.
2. Thought, as talked about in the previous chapter.
3. Belief.
4. Emotion.
5. Body.
6. Mind.

Vibrations operate at high and low frequencies, and this is true for the vibrations that occur within our beings too.

Lower vibrations of being are associated with…

1. Disempowering thoughts.
2. Bad vibes.
3. Un-belief.
4. Negative emotions.
5. Overly poor health.
6. A true lack of spiritual awareness.

Higher vibrations on the other hand, are associated with empowering thoughts such as…

1. Positive emotions.
2. Good health.
3. A strong spiritual awareness.
4. A good head on your shoulders.

The universe is created by vibration and is maintained by vibration.

Each vibration has its own individual wavelength which characterizes it and can identify it.

Vibrations of energy fields or aura…

- Every human being is surrounded by fa luminous invisible subtle energy field.
- This fields are what interpenetrates the physical body.
- It emits its own characteristic radiation or vibrations known as aura.

The aura is divided into several layers or bodies interpenetrating each other and surrounding each other in successive manner.

Each body is composed of finer substance with higher vibration than other that it surrounds and interpenetrates.

These might be…

1. Vibration.
2. Frequency.
3. Health

Vibrational frequency plays a wildly important role in the creation of our physical reality and the one we want to be our reality, even if it differs from the one, we have. This is because it allows energy to express itself into any form, including…

1. Molecules.
2. Atoms.
3. Planets.
4. Stars.
5. Biological life.
6. Non-biological lifc.
7. Diseases.

They each have their own energy or vibrational signature.

Understanding how energy frequency works is important for your well-being, because when your energy isn't vibrating correctly, you are more vulnerable to diseases and stress.

In 1992, Bruce Tainio of Tainio Technology, an independent division of Eastern State University in Cheny, Washington, built the first frequency monitor in the world. Tainio has determined that the average frequency of the human body during the daytime is 62-68 MHz. A healthy body frequency is 62-72 MHz.

This states that when the frequency drops, the immune system is compromised and often gets sick or detrimentally impaired.

According to their study, it says that…

1. Colds and Flu start at: 57-60 MHz.
2. Disease starts at: 58 MHz.
3. Candida overgrowth starts at: 55 MHz.
4. Receptive to Epstein Barr at: 52 MHz.
5. Receptive to Cancer at: 42 MHz.
6. Death begins at: 25 MHz.

These are all in reference to the vibrations we all give and if we believe this is true. Even if you don't believe, it is still feasible that it's true and can be as stated above… if that's the case, one might be able to predict their own death via *Vibration, Frequency and Disease.*

In theory and according to the practice, if you are able to keep your body's frequency above 62 MHz, you should not have to worry about getting sick… potentially ever.

To prevent your body's frequency from dropping to lower levels, avoid these things.

- Avoid eating junk food.
- Don't consume canned food.
- No processed food.
- Practice meditation on a regular basis because meditation increases the vibrational rate of your energy.

The pulsation rate of spiritual person's aura is 92-360 MHz. The aura of spiritual person vibrate or cause vibrations at a very high frequency compared to other persons.

A great example of this might be… a spiritual seeker has much developed higher subtle bodies and energetic vibrations, therefor, the seeker's aura vibrates at a much higher frequencies. While the aura of a normal human being pulsate at lower pace due to…

-Possible spiritual limitations.

-The normal person's material desires.

-Lust for things and people.

-The mental status of the "normal" person.

-Any emotional blockages.

The change may be positive, negative or neutral. Energy flows from a higher to lower voltage during vibration.

Some reasons why not harmonizing your vibrations with others around you might cause discord are…

-Not being within the same frequency.

-Not being able to synchronize harmonically.

-Becoming difficult to communicate.

-There are noticeable and very big difference in pulsation rates of the auras.

Intimacy requires vibrational fields of concerned persons to be in harmony. The ability to either pulsate in the same frequency range or to synchronize harmonics is necessary for communion.

This could be…

1. Spouse.
2. Friend.
3. Family.
4. Loved one.
5. Someone you work with.
6. A non-family member that you live with. Ie; a roommate.

Another great hindering factor of synchronizing auras and vibrations is that sometimes the high voltage pulsation of the spiritual person induces a series of vibrational changes in the aura of a non-spiritual persons.

The elevated flow of power running though the aura of the others person may release…

- Mental.
    - The mental status of you.
    - The mental status of the person you are trying to vibe with on any leve.
- Psychological.
    - The psychological level in which you place your trust.
    - The psychological level in which others place their trust in you.
- Emotional blocks.
    - This can come in about any way possible.
- Deep rooted anger.
    - Anger is the root of everything bad it if can't be delt with first.
- Fear.
    - Fear can be all consuming.
- Hatred.
    - Same for hatred as anger… you can't have either to send out positive vibrations.
- Sex.
    - If sex is just sex, then it may not allow for good vibrations in any way shape or form.
- Evil memories.
- Discord.
- Stress.
- Disharmony.
    - All the above are hard ones to have in your life to send vibrations to anyone, or to the universe for yourself.
    - These are all the negative… they can't be a part of a happy and healthy life.

It's important to avoid the negative things that can work it's way into your life so that you learn how to raise your vibration to match those around you, or adjust to the lower ones too. Those can either be the negative ones that you put out of your life, or the positive ones that you try to work into your life in a bigger way.

You might want to know how to raise your vibration to fight off negativity and bring in positivity.

Here are a few ways how you can start attracting more positive experiences and overall abundance in your life while letting go of the negative aspects all together.

Here are some ways to raise your vibration in positive and constructive ways.

1. Become conscious of your thoughts.
2. Know that everything you think, say or feel becomes your reality.
3. Learn that every thought that comes into your head has an impact on you. Just like in the previous chapter, this can be detrimental or a great way to negate negativitiy.
4. When you change those thoughts for the positive, your reality is likely to become positive too.
5. Find something beautiful and appreciate it.
6. Discover that beauty is all around you, yet so often we walk around with our blinkers on... appreciate the beauty.
7. Stop rushing for a moment and take the time to stand in the sun and appreciate your surroundings... what beauty you see in others and your surroundings can and often do reflect in you which negates negativity.
8. Be conscious of the foods you eat.
9. Learn and write down what foods vibrate at high frequencies, and the ones that vibrate at a lower. Some great examples of this are... broccoli has a high vibration as do blueberries; while Big Macs don't vibrate at all... nor do most processed foods.
10. If you are consuming foods covered in chemicals and pesticides, or foods found in plastic packaging, cans, etc, it will leave you vibrating lower.
11. Learn to love organic produce, food as nature intended it, and feel the high vibrations throughout your body.
12. Most importantly, pay attention to how eating certain foods make your body feel... you literally can make yourself sick by the foods that you eat.
13. Drink water.
14. Understand that water is a form of energetic life force. Drinking plenty of water water will help your body to flush out toxins and keep your energy levels and vibration high.
15. Meditate. At least ten minutes of meditation a day will help build your vibrations and ready you for Manifestation.
16. While meditating, sit in a comfortable position, close your eyes and breath in and out.
17. Don't rush through your days with a scattered brain leaving you in a state of anxiety and stress. Meditation helps to calm your spirit down and put you in a peaceful state of mind.
18. Be grateful.
19. Make a gratitude list. This can shift your vibrations from focusing on what you don't have to what is already a part of your life.
20. Practice acts of kindness.
21. Give to someone else without expecting anything in return.
22. Get your blood pumping. Vibration requires movement, the more you move the better your vibrations move.

Some more in depth ways to work on vibrations, particularly in a spiritual way are by...

- Checking your thoughts.
    - Make a conscious decision to check in and stop yourself when you feel the following.
        - Negativity.
        - Judgment.

        - Negative and critical thoughts come through.
    - This can be one of the hardest tasks, especially if you're a pessimistic person, but you will soon notice such a shift in your energy when you start to do it. Your vibrational energy will increase.
- If you use them as a conduit, then program your crystals.
    - If you're a fan of using crystal energy for energy, then here are a few of the crystals that can best be used for vibration work.
        - Citrine.
        - Clear quarts. (The best choice if only selecting one.)
        - Rose quarts.
        - Amethyst.
        - Tourmaline.
        - Tiger's eye.
    - Sometimes, however, your crystals will need reprogramming so they can send out the best possible energy for what you need… specifically in vibrational work.
    - After washing each crystal with salt and water, follow your heart or look up an online tutorial to reprogram them and set a new intention for each.
- Again, this is subject to beliefs, but oracle readings are good for vibrational work.
    - Make sure you take care and caution when picking your cards or going to someone to have a reading.
    - Oracle cards are slightly different to tarot, in the way that there's no set structure to them.
    - You can either pick one card to answer a question quickly and give you instant clarity.
    - You can pick two cards to indicate how you have been feeling and how you will feel about a situation.
    - Or, you can pick three cards to explain how you feel in the mind, body and soul.
- Again based on belief, you could take part in Shamanic Tapping to up your vibrations towards the act of Manifestation.
    - Shamanic tapping is a way of clearing your energetic paths and it's something that can up your vibrational pull.
    - This is part of the Law of Attraction as discussed in chapters above… if you need a refresher, see the chapter on attraction and the seven laws attached to it.
- Try scripting/writing.
    - Scripting is a way of journaling where you write as if you already have what you're wishing to attract.
    - This is a form of Manifestation or affirming that you WILL receive what it is your asking for.
        - A great example for this is, if talking about manifesting… Your dream home... Your journal becomes like as if you're writing your diary in this house… the minds eye, or third eye depending on how you believe.
            1. You could talk about how much you love going down into the open plan kitchen to make a coffee and how you have so much space to be able to invite friends over.
            2. You could write about how you're so happy in your master bedroom and how you love the colors you've chosen for the walls.

        3. You are a happy mother of three kids and the best wife a man could ask for… again this can be done when you are single.
    - These are all examples of things you wish to happen and because you have written hem down as such, you are manifesting them into reality.
    - Remember that in order for this to work with vibrations, you must be pure of mind, body, and soul as talked about in chapters one and two.
    - To help raise your vibrations within the Law of Attraction, you can…
        1. Act as if you already have what you're wishing for.
        2. Write a missive or practice scripting the reality.
        3. Affirming that it has already come true.
        4. Even dream it… it's nice to even daydream and feel excited about what it will be like when you get what you've asked the universe for.
- You should get moving to increase vibrations.
    - There are ways to raise your vibrations through getting moving.
        - Drink more water.
        - Exercise.
        - Walk as much as you can.
        - Eat high-frequency foods as talked about above.
        - Take a yoga class.
        - Meditate.
        - Dance around your house.
        - Or take a dance class.
    - Moving the body is a great way to get a hit of endorphins and feel less stressed.
- Practice social detoxing.
    - This is cutting out all the bad places and people you once had in your life.
    - Knowing that you can't visit the bars that you used to, not because of the drinking, but because you are hanging with bad people or doing things that wouldn't be something you would normally do.
    - This could even be going back to the places that you once liked to go and that made you happy in order to regain that happiness.
- Smile.
    - This could be something as simple as the following…
        1. Smile at a passerby.
        2. Smile when you don't feel like smiling.
        3. Smile at those that don't deserve your smile, this makes you the better person… not that is what you want to be, but you should always turn the other cheek, this is doing that… a smile and a walk away might be the exact thing needed to make the person or persons realize that even thought you are dying inside, they don't know that, so they think that their words and actions don't affect you.
- Share your journey.
        1. Find someone you like to talk to and tell them everything they are willing to here.
        2. Find others who have been through similar situations and talk about it.

3. Remember you can talk to all but don't make them think that what your going through good or bad is better or worse than their journey.

All in all, it's easy to gain positive vibration in life and to rid yourself form the negative ones, it's just up to you as to ho wand when you do it.

Chapter 12
What is Living with Intention?

This chapter is going to focus on how to live a life with intention, and what an intention is. That is, how to go about your daily tasks with the hope and focus to better yourself and the way you live daily by making choices with the intentional focus of being a better person every day that you live in every aspect.

Here you will also learn the proper way to set intentions towards meditation and practicing Manifestation.

Setting intentions is the act of stating what you intend to accomplish through your actions and putting it into the world, knowing it's out there to receive. It's a commitment to what you want the journey to be about as you move on or move up through your life… and even more so in your Manifestation journey.

When you are intentional about something, your focus is in the moment:

1. Who you are?
2. What you, want or need?
3. Why do you need it or want it?
4. What do you bclicvc?
5. How will you practice intention work?
6. How does it tie into your beliefs, hopes, dreams, and wants for the future?

Setting an intention is activating a part of your receptivity… receptivity is the way you receive things from around you and how you put yourself out into the receptors of others. This can be great sometimes particularly because you're allowing fate to happen to you… what the world has for you, you can and should receive, but if you know that you want to get somewhere, the power of setting an intention is going to help you get there… sometimes faster then should an intention never to have been made.

Here are the first steps or (start up) steps to considering making an intention.

- Picturing where you want to go.
- Know what you heart feels and going with it.
- Making sure what you do is good for you and those around you.

Intentions are a critically important step in creating the life you have always wanted or at very least the life you have dreamed of.

But think of it this way… if you've never dreamed them before, it can be daunting to imagine them happening.

Here are some sample intentions to inspire you to write your own down or say them in the way of affirmations and intentional Manifestations.

Overall Intention: these are basic intentions to benefit your every day life.

- I intend to experience greater levels of vibrations, fun, creativitiy.
- I intend to connect on a greater level.

- I intend to live my life with divine peace, prosperity, and abundance.
- I intend to practice safety, elegance, and ease.
- I intend to be healthy and practice healing.
- I intend to have divine grace, Divine guidance, joy, freedom, beauty, trust, wisdom and love.

Immediate Intentions: These are the ones that you want now, and you intend them into reality to help you in the here and now.

- I intend to live every waking minute of every day conscious, awake and aware of what and who is around me and what is out there for me.
- I intend to live in the present moment, while feeling as much joy as possible.
- I intend to move into a positive cash flow quickly.
- I intend to do everything magically, easily and joyfully.
- I intend to live the most beautiful life possible.
- I intend to harm nothing or no one and give benefit to all living creatures.
- I intend to allow the companies I keep to growing easily, elegantly and with a great deal of joy and love.
- I intend to grow into an inspiring, healing, love-filled, fun and phenomenally successful person with growth every day.
- I intend to create the most loving relationship possible with my friends and family. (remember these are not the toxic ones as talked about before.)
- I intend to support my children in separate but loving ways without enabling them.
- I intend to see them as strong, loving, capable, creative and successful people like they currently are, will always, and have always been.
- I intend to change each of my subconscious and unconscious beliefs, drives, patterns habits, projections, vibrations, affirmations, imprints and contracts that are keeping me from living the life I was born to live.

Relationship Intentions: these are the intentions that affect others that are a part of your life… partners, parents, children, family, friends, those you work with, teachers, and the like.

- I intend to cause a deeper and loving relationship with my partner. This is by providing greater levels of peace, safety, fun, freedom, sexuality, ease, joy, intimacy, vulnerability, trust, play, creativity, expansion, positive activation, tenderness and love for us both… this also includes but is not limited to adding any and all conversations needed between us for decisions made in and for the relationship.

- I intend to open my heart, as fully as possible, and feel my partner's love in return, even if I feel that I have not been worth love or had love that ruined me in my past.
- I intend for my partner and I to lovingly support each other in our individual dreams and goals no matter how big or small they might be, and never make a mockery of who they are, as I would want the same from them.
- I intend that my partner and I both feel deeply and richly loved and supported by the other. This also includes any and all children had between the union or outside the union that has joined in.
- I intend that my loved ones and I will enjoy each other's lives, friends, families, children, interests and passions, no matter what they might be as long as they don't bring in negativity.
- I intend to allow all freedom for each of us to enjoy our independent lives as well so that we can enrich ourselves and each other through these experiences.
- I intend that the communication between my partner and I be crystal clear, both with words and beyond words. This even works in the concepts of intentions of relationship boundaries, such as:

1. Brining in a third partner.
2. Swinging.
3. Polyamory.
4. Monogamy.
5. Abstaining until marriage.
6. How many children both parties want and compromising between the two.
7. If in-laws will be allowed to move in as they grow older.
8. What is intended to happen to shared things if death occurs… and yes, it is never to early to talk about this… you never know when the time might come.
9. Talking about what might happen if you separate, not expecting to, but just in case.
10. Discussing faithfulness and what you intend to get and give from the relationship.

- I intend to enjoy my relationship with my partner, allowing it to unfold and deepen with elegance and ease in the time needed to make it perfect.
- I intend that my loved ones and I will attempt to find easy compromises and meet each other's needs while honoring our own needs.
- I intend to peruse this, resulting in ideas and realities far better than either of us could originally conceive or create in our thoughts or dreams.
- I intend to, no matter what the challenge or opportunities are, that my partner and I face, to always remember to love.

Other Relationship Intentions: might extend further into more distant relationships… not simply partners… etc. This extends more so to children, friends, and family, extensions of your normal everyday relationships.

- I intend to deepen the loving, joyful and fulfilling relationship I have with each of my children.
- I intend to be the best parent I can be.
- I intend to act in a manner that my children need me to.
- I intend to positively support my children in living the lives they came here to live with as much ease, elegance and joy as possible.
- I intend to accept my children for the persons they intend to become.
- I intend to build loving relationships with as many of my partner's family and friends as possible, remembering that this may be harder because you haven't been in their lives for all of yours.
- I intend to develop friends… specifically those that I'm emotionally, spiritually, mentally, and physically tied to.
- I intend to create friends my partner and I both love to be with.
- I intend to accept the friends that he/she/they/them already have.
- I intend to introduce my friends to my partner only if they are not toxic in any way shape of form.
- I intend to create conscious, loving, interactive and supportive relationships.
- I intend to create a star family with angelic friends and unseen friends.
- I intend that all of my relationships develop greatly.
    1. Esoteric.
    2. Blood family.
    3. Work relationships.
    4. Community-based, acquaintances.
    5. Passing acquaintances.
- I intend to be filled with as much fun, joy, love, light, kindness and compassion as possible.
- I intend to make sure that my relationships are filled with as much fun, joy, love, light, kindness, and compassion as possible.
- I intend to lift those I connect with, however significantly or insignificantly, to greater levels of healing, loving and recognizing who they are to me and my journey towards Manifestation.

Work Intentions: are indentations set for your work family and environment, the way you intend to do your job both at work and at home with the duties you have on a day, to day basis.

- I intend every minute I work to be filled with fun.

- I intend to work with creativity.
- I intend to work with excitement, abundance, prosperity, and joy.
- I intend to service those associated with my job with positivity.
- I intend to create supportive, healthy and nurturing surroundings at work both with the people I work with and the environment in which I work.
- I intend to work with like-valued people, who I enjoy immensely and feel greatly supported by and cut those that create toxic relationships and environments.
- I intend to find meaning in my work.
- I intend to pay attention to everything, be it the broadest or tiniest details.
- I intend to remember that I am sending positive energy to the greater whole whenever I am only but a part.
- I intend to gratefully and gracefully perform my duties at work.
- I intend to work in the perfect timing, with joy and fun, and with the highest level of positive impact possible.

Physical Body Intentions: these are the intentions made about your own body inside and out, as well as what you will allow your body to do and partake in.

- I intend that my physical body is one hundred percent vital, healthy and filled with energy.
- I intend to keep my body weight at the range that is best for me.
- I intend to keep my body healthy and watch what I put into it and what comes out of it.

Spiritual Intentions: are the intents you set for yourself and your journey.

- I intend to strengthen my connection in the ways that best connect my beliefs.
- I intend to form a deeper and stronger bond on all levels with my unseen interties who will support me in this lifetime.
- I intend to investigate my beliefs.
- I intend to grow in said belief with the guidance of my spiritual beings and teachers.

Surroundings Intentions: are the intentions that have to do with what's around you.

Some good examples of this are:

1. Home.
2. Work.
3. Place of worship.
4. Your favorite coffee place.
5. School.

Mental & Emotional Intentions: are making the intentions for your mind in whatever way you need it.

- I intend to be a courageous adventurer and risk taker as long as it is safe and good for me.
- I intend to be confident about who I am.
- I intend to see beauty in everything.
- I intend to look for beauty everywhere I go and in whomever I'm with.

Creative Intentions: are the intentions that benefit your mind and body and the way you react to things around you.

Some of these things can be but aren't limited to:

1. Being open fully.
2. Explore the greatest depths of creativity possible.
3. Allow myself to express that creativity.

Financial Intentions: are all intentions associated with money and influential amounts of financial gain.

- I intend unlimited cash and resources flow into my life easily, abundantly and endlessly.
- I intend my financial abundance to provide greater and greater levels of security, freedom, ease and elegance.

Intentions for the Earth & Humanity: these are the intentions for the things around you.

Some examples of this might be…

1. The universe.
2. Your environment.
3. Your home.
4. Your town.
5. The state in which you live.

In learning the above intentions that you make, here are some prime examples of what you can expect day to day for the way you can live through intention.

-Every single morning you have two choices:

a. Continue to sleep with your dreams to see what else may come.
b. Or wake up and chase them to their fullest.

Below are some quotes from some famous and influential people that might help you see creating intentions in a better light. You will be left with these to reflect and hopefully create your own intentions.

"Intention is one of the most powerful forces there is. What you mean when you do a thing will always determine the outcome. The law creates the world," Brenna Yovanoff.

"Intention is not something you do, but rather a force that exists in the universe as an invisible field of energy- a power that can carry us. It's the difference between motivation and inspiration. Motivation is when you get hold of an idea and don't let go of it until you make it a reality. Inspiration is the reverse- when an idea gets hold of you and you feel compelled to let that impulse or energy carry you along. You get to a point where you realize that you're no longer in charge, that there's a driving force inside you that can't be stopped. Look at the great athletes, musicians, artists, and writers. They all tap into a source," Wayne Dyer.

"In the universe there is an immeasurable, indescribable force which shamans call intent and absolutely everything that exists in the entire cosmos is attached to intent by a connecting link," Carlos Castaneda.

"Every journey begins with the first step of articulating the intention, and then becoming the intention," Bryant McGill.

"A gift consists not in what is done or given, but in the intention of the giver or doer," Seneca.

"It is not good enough for things to be planned – they still have to be done; for the intention to become a reality, energy has to be launched into operation," Walt Kelly.

"You've got to know what you want. This is central to acting on your intentions. When you know what you want, you realize that all there is left then is time management. You'll manage your time to achieve your goals because you clearly know what you're trying to achieve in your life," Patch Adams.

"The more aware of your intentions and your experiences you become, the more you will be able to connect the two, and the more you will be able to create the experiences of your life consciously. This is the development of mastery. It is the creation of authentic power," Gary Zukav.

"Quality is never an accident; it is always the result of high intention, sincere effort, intelligent direction and skillful execution; it represents the wise choice of many alternatives," William A. Foster.

"Energy is directed by intention into action. If the action is not happening, if you're finding excuses to not do whatever you set out to do, revisit your intention. Perhaps you were not being honest with yourself. Where is your energy flowing instead? That is where your intention sits," Akiroq Brost.

"Guard your time fiercely. Be generous with it, but be intentional about it," David duChemin.

"Gratitude in advance is the most powerful creative force in the Universe," Neale Donald Walsh.

"As a single footstep will not make a path on the earth, so a single thought will not make a pathway in the mind. To make a deep physical path, we walk again and again. To make a deep mental path, we must think over and over the kind of thoughts we wish to dominate our lives," Wilfred Arlan Peterson, The Art of Living, Day by Day.

"Intention is more than wishful thinking—it's willful direction. It is a philosophy of the heart put into practice, a consistency of conscious patterns of thought, energy, and action. Through intention, we see more and create with more clarity, passion, and authenticity. Our attention then becomes a spotlight for every shred of supporting evidence that we're on the right path," Jennifer Williamson.

"I learned this, at least, by my experiment; that if one advances confidently in the direction of his dreams, and endeavors to live the life which he has imagined, he will meet with a success unexpected in common hours," Henry David Thoreau.

If you'd like more support cultivating a life lived well, check out more quotes and inspirational and individualized writings online and in other passages, but a good step towards the life well lived would be to write some or all of those quotes and others down and affirm that each day starts out by you saying and acting upon those intentions.

Intentions drive so much of what we bring into our lives and have always been the driving force behind the law of attraction and how we perceive our daily lives. As learned about in previous chapters, you should know that setting intentions is key to Manifestation.

They are also the key to manifesting anything we desire in life. Intentions allow us to ground our energy in what we would like to call into our future, whether it's a new moon, full moon, or new year.

You can put intentions out into the Universe by simply thinking a thought or going through a more in depth practice.

Here are a few things that you can put your intentions into…

1. Crystals.
2. Clothing.
3. Any aspect of your life.

Intentions will always shape our future reality even if it doesn't look how we expect it to, or what we feel it should look like.

When should you set intentions?

Really whenever you want! But here are some ideas for times of the year that pack a little extra punch:

- A new month, there are twelve of those a year.
- New moon, there are thirteen of those a year.
- Full moons, there are thirteen of those per year as well.
- Solstices, there are two of those per year, a winter and summer equinox.
- New year, there is only one new year a year.

It is sometimes best to work in the cycles of the moon. That way you can set an intention and see how it progresses and when that moon cycle comes back around, you will be able to see what has happened. Then it's a great reminder to revisit the intention you previously set to see if it happens.

Then you need to consider setting intentions towards Manifestation… this is important when on your journey towards setting your Manifestation goals.

Intentions act as a wonderful and needed tool to get your energy in the frequency of what you're trying to manifest… this is the same or similar to… releasing your vibrations.

1. You can set intentions anyway that feels right to you!
2. You can say them silently to yourself.
3. You can say them out loud.
4. You can write them down in a journal.
5. You can type them on a document.
6. You can write them fancy or plain.
7. Saying them to others.
8. Recording yourself.
9. Creating simple notes.
10. Draw what you feel, think, and say!

This is especially important since they don't need to be a long list of either verbal or written intentions. It's just 3-10 things you'd like to cultivate more of in your life or manifest in your life! This is like an affirmation but bigger.

Here are the steps you need to consider while trying to connect intentions to Manifestation.

- Set the stage.
- Connect with yourself!
- Get a yummy smelling candle or invoke smells to awaken your senses.
- Burn some sage or frankincense to cleanse the energy in your space.
- Pull out some crystals to help you with your intention setting.
- You can even draw yourself a cleansing bath and do them in the tub!
- Meditate! This will likely be in all steps towards most things in the reading towards achieving Manifestation.
- Create a mantra or anchoring theme.
    - For instance, maybe while you were "setting the stage" you chose to read a book that inspires you first in the theme or troupe of your intention.
    - Pull out the quote from the reading and write it down.
- Try an oracle deck to help let the Universe guide you in your intentions.
- Write! Again this is another step that is often talked about, but getting in the habit will help you in so many ways.
    - Just don't filter your thoughts, only write!
    - Take a few deep, cleansing breaths and put pen to paper.
    - Remember, this is for your eyes only, so there is NO need to censor yourself!
- Express yourself.
    - This is the way that you can show who you are.
    - Expressing yourself means to say or show one's thoughts and feelings in every sincle way you see fit.
- Revisit.
    - Revisit things from the past briefly so that you know where you came from and how far you have come.
    - Know the difference between who you were and who you are.

    - Know the difference between who you are and who you want to be.
- Reflect.
    - This is looking back on how far you have come and giving yourself the opportunity to pat yourself on the back, but not in a condescending way.
- Grow.
    - Knowing that there is always room to grow is important. When setting intentions, you may intend one thing today, allow growth and see that the intentions you had made are childish or selfish.
    - Growing for there and customizing your intentions is great.

In the end all you have to do is think the intention and follow the steps towards making those intentions a thing. Sending them into the environment, the universe, and beyond so that it can be heard and you can receive what has always been waiting there for you.

Intentions are the best step towards achieving your Manifestation goals.

Chapter 13
How Do I Break Negative Patterns?

In this chapter you will learn how to gain individual help, particularly with advice on how to break free of negative thinking, stop negative patterns from forming, and gain an extensive knowledge on how to break habitual negative recurrence. You will also learn how to diligently work toward your dreams while staying positive.

Here are those topics broke down so that you might better understand what they are and how they apply to you…

-Gain individual help for specific or specialized needs.

- Where you go for help will depend on what the problem is and who in your life has the problem.
- This will differ for an adult versus a child.
- Knowing the nature of the problem is often the best place to start.

When trying to gain help for any problem you have, particularly mental health issues is your local mental health organization, an expert on the subject, your religious guide, or just voicing your issues to your family and friends. For more severe issues, you can search for a local mental health affiliate and seek them out.

For mostly any issue you have no matter how big or small, your primary care doctor is also a good person to talk to if you think you may need to see somebody about anything that is bothering you.

If the issue is serious no matter the need, if they are unable to handle it, they can often, and will provide the name or a referral to a specialist that can help you more than your PCP can.

Here are some of the first steps however for finding help with your mental health… this includes…

1. Depression.
2. Anxiety.
3. Stress.
4. PTSD.
5. Suicidal thoughts.
6. Or basic thought confusion.

These steps are, but are not limited to…

-As stated above, you can get referrals from your family doctor.

-Gain referral from your spiritual leader or clergy.

-Gain advice from your local Mental Health offices.

-Seeing a mental health specialist. (Consider looking up more than a few names, so you can interview more than one person before choosing. This is not frowned upon… people will understand.)

-Your insurance company can provide a list of providers who are in your plan.

Your local health department is a good place to ask any questions you might have on any subject.

1. Pregnancy.

2. Immunizations.
3. Contraceptives.
4. Counseling.
5. Infant food assistance.

And the list can go on and on for the unlimited resources some of these places might have.

However, back to the topic of mental health, it is important to know that there are, a variation of mental health professionals that might work for your specific needs… here is a list that might help you better should you need a push towards ridding yourself from negativity towards your Manifestation goals.

- Child psychiatrist- A medical doctor specially trained in the diagnosis and treatment of emotional and behavioral problems in children between birth and the age of eighteen.
- Psychiatrist- Is a medical doctor with special training in the diagnosis and treatment of mental and emotional illnesses. Like other doctors, psychiatrists are qualified to prescribe medication for the needs of both adults and children.

- Clinical social worker- This is a counselor with a master's degree in social work trained to make diagnoses and provide individual and group counseling that can be specialized in one specific area of expertise.
- Psychologists- are professionals with a doctoral degree in psychology, two years of supervised professional experience, including a year-long internship from an approved internship and is trained to make diagnoses and provide individual and group therapy. They are well studied and often care for more severe cases, but they can not prescribe medication.
- Licensed counselor- this is a counselor with a master's degree in psychology, counseling or a related field, trained to diagnose and provide individual and group counseling.
- Mental health counselor- A counselor with a master's degree and several years of supervised clinical work experience trained to diagnose and provide individual on traumatic levels including abuse and PTSD.
- Alcohol and drug abuse counselors- are counselor with specific clinical training in alcohol and drug abuse trained to diagnoses and prevent further abuse.
- Marital and family therapists- are professionals with a master's degree, with special education and training in marital and family therapy trained to diagnose and provide people with the ability to cope, get through, or get over traumas of the past.
- Pastoral counselor- is a member of the clergy or person of your belief system with training in clinical pastoral education trained to diagnose and provide individual and group therapies through religious troupes.

-Gaining advice for needed subjects.

The above portion of the chapter will also help in finding educational information and material in order to help you make an decision on the help you need in order to get over your negativity and into the light of positivity… this is the only way that Manifestation can be practiced.

-Breaking free of negativity.

There are several ways of helping yourself break free from the negative lifestyle you have been living. Sometimes you might think that you haven't been living a lifetime in the wrong, but in reading the below material, you might just realize how much you have been missing by living life the way you have been for so long.

1. Re-visit nature.

To break a cycle of negativity, return to nature or go back there… if you haven't been a fan of the great outdoors, then go, try it out..

- Go for a walk.
- Sit outside.
- Take a drive.
- Go to the beach.
- Go on a hike.
- Take a swim in the backyard or public pool.
- Soak up the sun.

Ralph Waldo Emerson once wrote,
"In the woods, we return to reason and faith. There I feel that nothing can befall me in life, which nature cannot repair."

Choosing nature to help you escape the chaos and commotion of life is a great step towards gaining positivity and losing the negativity you have been keeping.

3. Look at the big picture.

If it has gotten to the point in your life that the present moment is burdened with unbearable pain and discontent, shift your perspective away from the here and now and onto the big picture. Focus on said picture and think about the benefits that are on their way by realizing that the big picture is all that matters.

After all, isn't Manifestation merely seeing the big picture and then believing that it can, therefore it is?

3. Surround yourself with the people you love and cut out all toxic folks from you're here and now.

Seek out the ones you love and who love you. Reach out to a friend or lover even a blood relative that you know you can trust! Turn the focus on them and see how it feels to surround yourself with outside considerations to break the negativity in your life.

4. Laugh as much as you possibly can.

Happiness, laughter, and smiles are enlivening and spirit-lifting as well as negativity crushing and toxicity detectors. They bring together people on a level much greater than we often fully appreciate. Laughter, happiness and smiling are great… we all naturally recognize, appreciate and connect through smiles and laughter… so speak the human language.

-Breaking free of negative thinking.

-Stopping negative patterns.

Reference the negative thinking chapter to learn more about how to break negative patterns especially through thought and thinking.

-Break habitual negative recurrences.

These are the things that happen over, and over again. What makes this such a bad negativity to have is that we sometimes become powerless to the holds of what thing that might be.

A great example of this is shopping.

One might not think of shopping as being something negative, but when it's to buy things you don't need or with money you don't have, then it both becomes negative and habitual.

It's hard to withstand the temptation we sometimes get from seeing something in our favorite color, style, collection, etc.... it's even harder to pass it by when we have the money for it, but that money might be credit that we don't need to use or bill money that will put you in the dark, but hey, you might look nice while sitting there in the pitch.

Anything that can become an addiction or produce addictive behavior falls to the category. May people thing that only drugs, alcohol, and cigarettes can be addictive, but your cellphone, computer, television, exercise (YES I SAID IT) and even shopping and beyond can become addictive to the negative side of what's good for you.

-How to diligently work towards your dreams.

The first thing to do is dream the dream. Everything begins in the heart and mind and everything has to start in the begining. Every great achievement began in the mind of one person and then was put out into the universe much like a Manifestation. What you dream, if you dare to dream it, you then believe that it is possible.

Once you have the dream in mind, then take some time to allow yourself to ask yourself what if...You want to be a dreamer and let your dreams come true, what if it came true. Dream of the possibilities for yourself, your family and for others.

If you had a dream that you let grow cold, re-ignite the dream! Fan the flames. Life is too short to let it go... think it, dream it, then do the next step.

Believe it. Your dreams need to be big and in order to do that, you need to be dreaming something that is seemingly beyond your capabilities but not at the same time. It also must be believable in the end.

If you dream about being a unicorn and state that one day you will be, now that isn't believable, is it? But if you state that you dream of dressing like, living like, and acting like a unicorn would in your dreams and from your own imagination, then you must be able to say that if a certain thing takes place, if others help, if you work hard enough, though it is a big dream, it can still be done... as silly as being a unicorn sounds.

Now, that's just an example, the same can be said about being a race car driver, ballerina, the president of the United States of America... think it, dream it, believe it... it's almost yours.

Another good example is- A person with no college education whatsoever can dream that they will build a fifry-million-a-year company. That is big, but believable, if the dream is acted upon and put out there.

A bad example of this would be- That a ninty-year-old with arthritis will someday run a marathon in under three hours. It is big all right, but also not so believable, at this rate, earning the above income for the elderly person might be more believable.

Also, remember that just because something isn't believable doesn't mean it can't happen.

The next step is to see it. This is the step of seeing and picturing yourself walking around the CEO of the office in your new twenty-two million corporate headquarters... that is also called visualization and something else that has been touched on previously.

Then once you can see it, then you need to tell it. One of the main reason most dreams never make it off the ground is due to the fact that people don't tell others what they are dreaming or that they believe it will come true.

They let it be a quiet dream that only lives inside of one's mind.

The one who wants to make their dreams come true must tell that dream to many people.

One reason this must happen is- As we continually say it, we begin to believe it more and more.

Then after we dream it, believe it, see it, and speak it, we must plan on it… plan that the dream will come true and prepare for it's eventual coming.

The old saying that you "get what you plan for" is so true when speaking of dreaming and Manifestation. Your dream won't just happen. You need to sit down on a regular basis, and plan out your strategy for achieving the dream.

After all that is said and done, you need to work it. Life isn't fun all the time and the human race hates the word work and even more so the action of doing it, but nothing is worth having unless you first earn it. Remembering that the successful are usually the hardest workers is important. While the rest of the world is sitting on their sofas watching reruns and Netflix originals, *regular* achievers and over achievers are working on their goals aka: their dreams coming true.

In the end it's up to you to enjoy it. When you have reached your goals and your dreams have come true, you have found yourself living your best life, be sure to enjoy it to it's fullest.

-How to do all this while staying positive.

In the end, it's all about staying positive to continue living a life worth living free of negativity and habitual negations of the reality you should be in.

Some of the habitual things you will learn to negate, but are not limited to are below, but it is important to know that they are all things that are commonly experienced by the human-race and can be broken if and only if you chose to start the process now.

Some of those are…

- Self-loathing- a strong dislike for who you are based on thoughts you have produced on your own or options you have formed simply by the words that others have spoken.
- Procrastination- taking far to long to start and finish a project be it timed for work or simply a task you have set for yourself.
- Stress eating- simply eating even when you are not hungry just because you are stressed, anxious, or nervous about something.
- Nail biting- biting your nails until there is nothing much left as a means to self-sooth or as a form of nervousness, release of tension.
- Association with naysayers- associating yourself with a person or persons who criticizes, object to, or are opposes most everything.
- Smoking- this is the habitual use of tobacco or marijuana in any way. (Your specific problematic and negative habitual level of smoking is left between you and your doctor, however a good example of when this is an issue is in times of cancer, needing a smoke when you don't have the money and doing anything you can to obtain said money, or using or obtaining in an illegal manner or way that is harmful to you or your loved ones. This can also include neglecting obligations simply to obtain.
- Excessive drinking- drinking and driving ever is an excessive drinking habit, although this means the action of drinking beyond your legal limit and preforming actions in public while intoxicated above said limit, as well as obtaining and drinking illegally due to age, action, or deed. (KNOW WHEN ENOUGH IS ENOUGH, this is important to keep away negative things caused by actions of yourself or others that may or will likely have a detrimental outcome on your future, relationships, and personal view of yourself, by yourself or others.)

- Eating too much- this is the act of eating more than your fill in order to alter your body image or the way you think about yourself or others, or also as a result of depression or stress. This can result in obesity and in extreme cases, death.
- Eating too little- the action of not eating enough in the fear that you might get fat or not look the way others or yourself, thinks your should… this can often lead to anorexia and/or bulimia and can result in death.
- Not exercising or moving properly- staying sedimentary is a fair way to assume that your body is or will soon shut down on itself causing obesity, immobility, incontinence, and the like. (You may think that sitting for eight hours without moving or getting up is alright, you are young and healthy, but with the chance of that becoming a habitual negative act, it is likely to become an issue in the long run… and soon.)
- Over exercising- abusing your body with too much exercise or diet. This can do the opposite of what you want… it can cause your body to become unhealthy and shut down resulting in the opposite of what you wanted happening.

Now that you have gotten to take a look at some ways to get your life back in a positive light, it's likely that you should write down some more ways to fix the habitual negative aspects of your life and learn to love who you are without the bad parts sneaking in to make you happy…

Because it isn't going to make you happy… ever!

Chapter 14
How do Meditation and Manifestation Work Together?

In this chapter you will be discovering how meditation also known as prayer, can help work with manifesting the life you hope to achieve. We will discuss what attributes help most when it comes to meditating and what practices are commonly found to induce the best manifesting power from within them.

As discussed in previous chapters, you can not achieve Manifestation without first meditating on the thing you wish to be manifest. There are other words that you might think of when thinking about how meditation can work for you or what other names it might have that you may already practice.

Here is a list of those so that you might better understand which ones you have already been doing, if any.

-Meditation: is the action or practice of meditating as well as a written or spoken discourse expressing considered thoughts on a subject, often for long periods of time or until one has achieved their goal.

-Praying: sending out thanks and wants into the universe or to the deity of your choice in order to be thankful or request something.

-Projecting: pushing a thought, dream, or idea out into the universe and projecting the perfect outcome. (Accepting that it's yours without yet having it but knowing its there for you for the taking.)

-Affirming: is simply putting out positivity while pushing away negativity in the hopes of receiving what the universe has for you.

-Contemplation: the action of looking thoughtfully at something for a long time while practicing deep reflective thought. This is also the state of thinking about or planning something in advance.

-Positive thought projections: are the practice of positive thinking. This just means that you approach unpleasantness in a more positive and productive way. You think the best is going to happen, not the worst. Positive thinking often starts with self-talk. Self-talk is the endless stream of unspoken thoughts that run through your head.

-Musing: is a period of reflection or thought. These thoughts and reflections are often characterized by the process it takes to achieve both the deep thought and reflection.

-Reflection: is serious thought or contemplation towards something needed and/or wanted.

-Deliberation: long and careful consideration or discussion. slow and careful movement or thought.

-Pondering: to think on something carefully and for long periods of time.

-Rumination: a deep or considered thought about something specific to a need or want you may have.

While some of these aren't exact matches for the above discussed methods of meditation, they are all good steps towards achieving a meditative state… or heightened state of being through meditation. All of these however can lead to meditation and then head straight for Manifestation.

Also, you will need to understand the basic components to meditation and how it works in order to achieve your highest understanding.

How does meditation work towards Manifestation?

There are several ways how you can use meditation for manifesting: Meditation helps you to identify your abundance blocks faster and to overcome some of them. Meditation makes you more aligned with the universe, and thus brings you into the flow state more easily. Meditation Strengthens Your Intuition. When you use meditation as part of your manifestation routine, you will begin to notice something pretty amazing… As time goes by, your connection with your higher self and source energy as a whole will grow stronger than ever before.

Meditation is a practice of consciously choosing to center yourself, to quiet your mind and find inner peace. Manifestation is very different. You don't need to meditate to manifest. Manifestation is the continuous process of creation.

How does meditation help you get the life you hope to achieve?

- By reducing stress.
  - Stress reduction is one of the most common reasons people try meditation and then they are shocked to find that it works.
- By controlling anxiety.
  - Anxiety can be easily piqued when out in public or in private. Learning to meditate to calm yourself in the moment can help you life the life worth living.
- By promoting emotional health all around.
  - Gaining positive emotional health and wellness is key in order to help yourself life a positive life and in the long run live the life of your dreams or the life you have always wanted.
  - People who can achieve this often make the best role models for people suffering from the same things as you used to after gaining highness through meditation and Manifestation.
- By enhancing self-awareness.
  - Self-awareness involves being aware of different aspects of yourself including.
    - Your traits.
    - Any good or bad behaviors
    - Your feelings and emotions.
  - Essentially, it is a psychological state in which oneself becomes the focus of attention.
- By lengthening your attention span.
  - A good example of this is test anxiety… if you have anxiety before a test, it is proven that if you step away a few moments before class and meditate, it can help you gain a higher understanding and steady your nerves to rid yourself from the test anxiety.
- By possibly reducing age-related memory loss.
  - This will benefit you when Dementia or Alzheimer's try to creep in. By keeping your mind fresh and young by meditating to achieve Manifestation or anything for that fact, you will stay younger in mind longer than others your age.
- By generating kindness for others and yourself.
  - This means that people will like to be around you and you might make others feel better by expressing yourself in a positive way.
- By possibly fighting addictions.
  - Through meditation you can learn to fight some simple addictions all the way to higher ones… some were talked about in the last chapter.
  - One of the things to remember is that you can also manifest these addictions away.
  - As well as affirm them away.

What are the positive attributes of meditation?

The mental health benefits of meditation include…

- Better focus.
- Better concentration.
- Improved self-awareness.
- Improved self-esteem.
- Lower levels of stress.
- Lower levels of anxiety.
- Fostering kindness.
- Improvement of tolerance of pain.
- Help fight substance abuse.

Here are some of the top benefits of meditation, while some of these are recaps from above, it's important to read the reiteration of the important factors that can help you achieve highness.

- Reduced inner and environmental stress.
- Helps achieve emotional balance.
- Increases focus on all levels.
- Reduces pain in your body and soul.
- Reduces anxiety on many levels.
- Increases creativity and artistic natures.
- Reduces depressive behaviors.
- Reduces depressive thoughts.
- Reduces depressive actions.
- Reduces the act of self-harm.
- Increased reflective memory.

How much should you meditate?

This differs from person to person… collectively you should consider it a minimum of thirty-minutes a day, although while attempting meditation towards Manifestation, you should work with it no less than an hour at a time in a serine place where you will have little to no distractions.

What practices are commonly found to induce the best Manifestation journey?

- Creating a vision board is a great first step towards seeing and believing during your meditation and Manifestation journey.
    - A vision board is a collage of images and words that should be displayed in a prominent place to remind you why you are doing what you are doing every day.
    - These boards should be filled with pertinent images and words that spark your motivation and remind you of your values, goals, and dreams towards Manifestation and life in general.
- Intention Journals.
    - These are another powerful Manifestation technique that comes from the intentions we set through written word.
    - These are simply journals that we put pen to in order to have our inner most desires, thoughts, and dreams written in reality.
- Belief assessments.

    - A belief assessment is used in the evidential reasoning approach for multi-criteria decision analysis to represent the performance of an alternative option on a criterion.
- Gratitude journals.
    - A gratitude journal is not unlike the diary you kept as a teenager, but instead of writing random thoughts about your day, you write about the things you're grateful and thankful for be it big or small.
- Bedtime reprogramming.
    - This is reprogramming your mind while you sleep in the hopes that the bad things from the day before will slip away and leave only the positivity and good things.
- Write a letter to your future self.
    - This is writing a letter at thirteen to open at eighteen or even older.
    - This can be as young as you would like to open as old as you would like.
    - A few examples of letters to your future self are…
    -

Dear Me of the Future,

Whatever you're doing right now, stop and take a walk, because I doubt you have gone for a good walk in a long while. That's it, take me with you and go the hell outside. While you are out there, find a pay phone, or the new aged phones of the future and call your parents… that is if they are both still there with us. We both know that Bindi Rodrigo's parents died in that crash last year and she and I, the past you, are only fifteen.

Take a moment and go have yourself a proper personal day… self-care is a thing now I hear, and you don't do enough of it, well because I know us. And don't you dare feel bad for taking the time for yourself… well, I mean us.

This year has been a crazy one. I learned what love really means, that was until Bobby Jessup broke up with us. Then I learned the lengths to which friendship can be tested when Susie Hathaway our best friend since preschool moved. Her mom says she will still get to visit, but only you will know if that happened.

I have lived in New York for fifteen years now, and I am ready to go to the mountains at this point… did we ever get to go? If not, can we?

Do we have a garden and goats and a fireplace yet, that was always my dream?

Have we gotten married, had children? I ask that though I'm not sure whether or not children are a thing I want, but it might be something we want now. After graduation… in three years, I plan on heading out on an epic backpacking trip… please tell me that we went and had the best time.

Know that whatever decisions you have made for us, it was the right one. We are here now and are exactly where we need to be.

A couple things to remember though as we get older.

I learned how to honor and treat my body well this year when Teddy Lee tried to touch me, and I hope we are still respecting it.

I learned how to honor and treat those around me when I saw Jenny Perry put her hands on that deaf girl in the halls last week, I should have stepped in… do we step in now?

I learned not to ever settle for the easy way out, that's because I cheated on that math test last month and got detention for the first time in our life… was it the last?

Remember that this current version of yourself loves you… And that's not going to change ever.

Love you in 1992.

Dear Future Self,

Remember your wedding day, I'm sure you do, it will be in ten days from now. It is exactly ten days from today and hard for me to believe. Ten days before you marry the love of your life, a woman who not only puts up with your quirks like our neurotic need to obsessively eat healthy and diet all the time. But she has found a way to laugh with you, especially when you measure the number of beans you put in your salad and obsess over your dress size.

You had a lot on your plate this year, and despite a few major meltdowns, being called bridezilla a time or two, and the few wedding dress nightmares you had, you survived it all, with the help of a few important people that I pray are still in your life.

You're getting ready to go home to see your family, and many of your closest friends and to me, this is pretty much the most fun ever and I hope you look back on this time with love… I pray we are still loved and are loving your wife at ten years down the road… you will be thirty-two when you read this, and Maddi will be thirty-six… I am sure she is just as beautiful as ever.

Tell your children you love them, a lot, I'm sure they are incredible humans and deserve to hear it… I know Maddi and I wanted many, let's hope we got that in our lives. Also, let them eat a piece of cake once in a while… God knows I don't and look how miserable I am… maybe you do now, and I hope you do… for sanities sake.

Remember to hang out with your mom as much as possible, words cannot describe what she has done for you over the years, and she was the first to accept you for who you are and who you love.

You probably work really hard, so this is an order: take a vacation with your wife, this month even. Book it today, but don't think too much about it, wherever you go will be perfect… be spontaneous… get a babysitter even.

I love you and I always will.

Vanessa Marks-Kissinger (I hope)

Dear Future Maria.

Take a breath. Look down at your two feet… you were always bad at that, seeing where you were in order to get to where you were going. Well do it now… Where are you at right now? Look around you. Do you see nature?

Go touch the leaves, feel the rain, pick a flower and deeply inhale its beautiful fragrance, because the place I am at right now is not a happy one. Do you hear birds like I hope you do? Stop and take a moment to go listen to their music, because not everyone is so fortunate enough to be able to hear and enjoy that experience… I pray that we still can.

Do you feel the sunshine on your skin? If not, go step outside and be grateful for the fact that it is constantly shining down on you, and that you are alive... I hope we are alive.

Go take a bite of something delicious and savor every moment with absolutely no concern around any kind of weight gain… pick something that we don't like now, but that you like in the future… that means that I like it now too.

Remember that not everyone is so privileged to have access to food. Do you remember taking a second lunch for Lacy Masson your whole third grade year… she vanished after that, but we fed her for a whole year, even added breakfast and snake items too. Mom was so good at making sure we were able to do that.

How have you been of service to others today like we were to her all those years ago?

You spent your whole childhood yearning to be an adult, impatiently waiting for the rite of passage that would grant you the maturity, respect, and validation you so desperately sought... has that even happened or was it all a misconception? Now that we are an adult, how do we feel… Mrs. Wall always said, that we would "all crave the sweetly uninhibited moments of play and lack of responsibility that childhood granted us. Life isn't a sprint, it's a long race and you're not in it just to win." She would add that we should "be gentle with ourselves. Be messy sometimes too." She was our art teacher and is suffering from cancer now… is she still alive?

I pray we have learned how to hug those around us, even though they say we have asperges, that doesn't mean we can't overcome the impossible. I hope we ask people how they are doing, and truly listen, we didn't get asked that often and not a soul seemed to listen to us… so I pray we have changed that for others.

I learned this year that money is just a number. It comes and it goes.

"Love is the true currency," mother would always tell us… she passed away today though.

When you open this, she will have been gone fifteen years… you will be twenty-five then, and I know it's still hard for you… it's killing me now.

No one lives forever so be sure to cherish every moment, and when they pass find comfort in knowing that we are simply souls within these bodies, and we will all be connected at some point again.

Another thing that mother always said was that… "Life is a gift, not something that is a given, so enjoy every second while you're here."

Love your ten-year-old self… Maria.

Hey, Future Self,

What's up! I can just see us now… Life has been interesting, crazy, fun, boring, unexpected, expected, and a lesson in opposition. We have been a bit of a dare devil in the fashion industry, and you started walking the catwalk like a champ.

Despite all the constant frustration, you've managed to wear glitter every damn day since today… because today is when I decided we were going to be killing it, and hey, that's kinda a victory, right, just last year we wore only black and grey.

You are confident and your clothes are on point, I am sure of it, because you have fashioned all of it. People are buying your shit and love the tones and tons of shiny stuff, colors, and general epic outfits in your online store.

By the time you read this, it will be twenty-thirty-two, and we will be pushing our flirty thirties… and you are fearless, I'm sure.

You've got the most epic dog by now, probably named Sweety, Pudden Pie, or Pippy. You have oh my god the sweetest friends… likely all girls because let's just face it, girls just wanna have fun. Oh, and an above average family, not including your extended family of course. Your probably married to a Rouxel, Jose, or Seth, and have two children planned for the future, but they haven't fit in yet… maybe.

You get to spend time outside in one of the most beautiful places on earth and you're in the best shape of your life thus far, so that's great to hear… we love Cali! We are stuck in Montana now, and as you know, little gay boys from tana tana ain't getting no love.

As you continue to age, you'll continue to get more awesome. Remember, the goal is to peak at 90 or later… I giggle to my eighteen year old self.

You've got a lot of time to be amazeballs.

Despite the frustrations of life, which you won't have many, you're on your way to making all your dreams come true… I hope… no, no, no, I just know it.

Now go on an epic vacation and buy a new outfit with your sweet bank account that you hopefully acquired by now. You've earned it. Drink mimosas on the beach and party till the cows come home, well, movie stars, I'm not in Montana anymore.

Keep killing it… your bad ass self from the past. Slay all the way.

PS. We are rich now, aren't we?

Dear Future Self,

Everything that has happened has led you to this moment. Don't change a thing. Everything worked out exactly as it should be. All the puzzle pieces fit, and all the paths make sense. All the people were meant to be. All the successes and failures and heartwarming and heartbreaking moments were all worth it.

No regrets Timothy. You were and are and have been and always will be yourself, and that's what matters above all.

Love, the Timmy of your past.

Deer Me.

I hopes you've gots lots of friends now and that's you have a good live. You are maybe a autrdonut now or maybe a supster model… be gweat in whutevah life yous in.

Love Bwian in the furst grade.

You see from the last example that you can start as young or as old as you would like, be who you want to be. Some of those were Manifestations of who you are confident that you will become, while others are hopeful missives to the self you are sure you will be.

Some of them are hard, like the one where she lost her mother, others funny like the man from Montana, it doesn't matter what you project, just get it down, seal it up, and read it years down the road to see how far you have come and what dreams have come true.

- Manifestation Affirmations.
    - Refer to the affirmations chapter to recall what these are and how you may use them.
- Always think outside the box.
    - This is self-explanatory as in it helps you think in ways different than you normally would.

What powers do you have within yourself?

- This refers to the power within yourself given by nature and the universe.
    - Some of the powers of the universe that can be tapped into by humans are…

Naturally, you may think of the given powers of the universe as in the scientific ones… here they are…

- Gravity.
    - is a natural phenomenon by which all things with mass or energy—including planets, stars, galaxies, and even light—are brought toward (or gravitate toward) one another.

- The weak force.

- Is a fundamental force of nature that underlies some forms of radioactivity, governs the decay of unstable subatomic particles such as mesons, and initiates the nuclear fusion reaction that fuels the Sun.

- Electromagnetism.
    - Is the interaction of electric currents or fields and magnetic fields.
- The strong force.
    - Is a force that binds quarks together in clusters to make more-familiar subatomic particles, such as protons and neutrons. It also holds together the atomic nucleus and underlies interactions between all particles containing quarks.
    - The strong force originates in a property known as color.

However, there are also the spiritual powers of the universe that are referenced in this reading. Those are.

- Faith.
    - Is the complete trust or confidence in someone or something, or strong belief in God or in the doctrines of a religion, based on spiritual apprehension rather than proof.
- Energy.
    - Is the capacity for doing work. It may exist in potential, kinetic, thermal, electrical, chemical, nuclear, or other various forms.
    - There are, moreover, heat and work.
    - There is also spiritual energy which is the connectivity that you have with the elements and the universe.
- Mindfulness.
    - Is the quality or state of being conscious or aware of something.
    - It can also be, a mental state achieved by focusing one's awareness on the present moment, while calmly acknowledging and accepting one's feelings, thoughts, and bodily sensations, used as a therapeutic technique.
- Concentration.
    - Is the action or power of focusing one's attention or mental effort.
    - It also means a close collection of something that can be collaborated and moved spiritually towards something good
- Wisdom.
    - Is the quality of having experience, knowledge, and good judgment; the quality of being wise.
    - It is also the soundness of an action or decision with regard to the application of experience, knowledge, and good judgment.
- Enlightenment.
    - is insightful and open-mindedness.

Knowing what it takes to meditate, especially towards Manifestation is important in order to grow in the understanding of what is out there for you and what you should already be asking for.

Chapter 15
What Creative Methods Can I Implement Right Now?

Creative outlets have been found to truly open the individual mind and in this chapter, you will learn about what options one might find to creatively express themselves and start their Manifestation journeys. Expressing oneself creatively is the best medicine for just about anything ailing you, sucking you dry, keeping you for doing tasks that you used to feel were easy or that you once loved.

Here is a list of creative methods that you can implement right now in order to gain positivity and get on the right track to a better you…

-Focus on the sun.

- Do things you love out in nature such as garden.
- Learn to hike long distances.
- Paint out in your yard.
- Practice sidewalk chalk drawing for others to appreciate.
- Become an outdoor tour guide in your free time.

Natural sunlight stimulates the production of Vitamin D, which elevates mood and makes people feel happier, healthier, and positive about themselves and their future. Ample access to natural sunlight can help alleviate depressive symptoms and uplift lonely, ill or aging people to the point they finally feel themselves again… even if it's only for a little while.

To capitalize on the positive powers of sunlight, open your curtains and open windows to let natural light into the rooms within your living space. Even if you don't want the windows open, make sure to clean the glass windows and remove obstructions that block light. This can also help make the room feel brighter and more positive as well as make it seem bigger.

-Find an activity that you used to do and miss.

1. If you used to jump rope, try it again, it will bring back childhood memories that may help in the logn run.
2. Take back up riding a bike, they say once you know how that you never forget.

Whatever you do, do it to the best of your ability. Think back at that one thing that brought you joy, but before you attempt it, make sure you body is in good enough shape to execute the activity.

-De clutter.

1. Get rid of things that have been sitting about for a long while.
2. Also make sure if it's not been used for six months or more… throw it out.

Clutter causes stress and nothing squashes positive energy quite like stress. In addition to being unpleasant to live with, clutter can often be dangerous in a home setting.

De-cluttering an area helps the space feel calmer and more open than it once had and also serves the utilitarian purpose of getting rid of things that are no longer needed.

This also helps with hoarding syndrome.

Even a simple step like de-cluttering a single drawer in the kitchen or bedroom can have a good effect on the positivity of a room or space that you are used to living in negatively.

Make sure that commonly used areas of your home are cleaned such as…

1. Your kitchen table.
2. All night stands.
3. The coffee table and end tables.
4. Any kitchen counters.
5. Any flat surface in your home.

Replace the clutter with the following items.

1. A jar of flowers.
2. A table covering.
3. Cherished family photos.
4. Plants of any kind.
5. A candle or scented burner.

-Find your green thumb.

1. Incorporating plants or flowers in your home helps to brighten the space and bring you serenity.

2. In addition to improving air quality, beautifying a space and adding personality to an area, living houseplants and fresh-cut flowers have also been shown to help with emotions and mental status.

Make sure to start out with easy-care plants like succulents or ferns and arrange them around the house in sunny windows and high-traffic areas. This is best if you have never tried to care for living plants before, or if you don't think you have found your green thumb yet.

- Paint your house inside or out.

1. Although some home situations may not allow this, sprucing up a room with paint is a wonderful way to make it feel clean.

2. Pick a color or colors that you as the occupant loves and paint while all other members of the house is away.

-Create and hang artwork.

1. Hanging meaningful artwork on the walls goes a long way toward inviting positive energy into the home that you live in.

2. Hang some of your favorite artwork in high-traffic areas and consider placing cards or drawings done by children, friends or even yourself in high traffic rooms.

-Brainstorming- is perhaps one of the most popular creative techniques you can use.

This is the most obvious creative techniques. A whiteboard hanging on your wall or a hand-held one is perfect for this. The basis of brainstorming is about creating ideas in a group setting.

This is you and at least one other person that you love and trust.

By brainstorming solutions to problems both big and small, you will be able to create the desired solution and execute it with ease.

-Negative brainstorming- is finding negative solutions to make sure you never use those solutions.

This is another example of creative techniques. It uses brainstorming to generate all those bad solutions to the problem and then see how those could be transformed into good solutions by negating them.

The method is a two-step process, that consists of generating the worst ideas first and then transforming them into good solutions to even the smallest problems.

A good example of this would be drunk driving. Knowing that if you drive while intoxicated, you could potentially harm or kill oneself or someone else, then being able to flip that and know that the best solution would be not to drive drunk at all, or simply not to drink based on personal preference.

-Play the insight game- it is a game about using moments of insight that you gain insight points for… one point per insight used in fact. You need to have at least one point every day, if not the game is over. That means that you must create positive insight to win the game every day of the week, month, year.

This will help you gain a better outlook on life.

The goal and the reward of this game is that you will improve your ability to see the big picture, process more complex problems and challenge your beliefs. You can do this by using pictures, recordings, writings, or whatever you want to put your insights on the board.

-Create mood boards- this is a type of collage that may consist of images, text, videos and samples of objects in a composition of the choice of the mood board creator in order to decide what moods you are in most of the time and how to negate them to better moods or how to better understand how we obtain the good ones.

-Play the random words game- by doing this, it encourages your imagination to create different perspectives and new angles on your idea or the problem you are facing in your life.

It is by far the simplest of all creative techniques and is widely used by people who need to create new ideas or small solutions to help make their life smoother and more positive.

-Create a story board- by doing this you can go back to the very beginning of something and see it through to the end.

Walt Disney and his staff developed a Story Board system in 1928. Disney wanted to achieve full animation and for this, he needed to produce a plethora of animated drawings.

Managing the thousands of drawings and the progress of a project was nearly impossible, so Disney had his artists pin up their drawings on the studio walls. This way, progress could be checked, and scenes added and discarded with ease.

The same thing can be done in your day to day life by using pictures and video to keep track of your life story.

-Practice metaphorical thinking- a metaphor is a thinking method which connects two universes of meaning.

A good example of this would be if the flow of time. Our mind tends to look for similarities. A road map is a model or metaphor of reality and useful for explaining things even today, even though some of it is more so based within technology.

-Create mind maps-

Mind maps developed by Tony Buzan are an effective technique of structuring information and note-taking. They are also useful during the brainstorming sessions.

To make a mind map you must start in the middle of the board with the main idea, invite your team and work in all directions, producing a growing and organized structure that will make sense to you and anyone helping you.

-Brain shifting- is one of creative techniques that is similar to mind mapping, but you should act as if you were someone else while doing it. The purpose is to create new ideas that you never thought about before.

No matter what you chose to help fill your time for the good, devote your energy to it and allow it to help you on your journey to a better you. By using Manifestation paired with any of the above activities, you are sure to manifest the best destiny for the person you are ready to become.

In the end, it's important to remember that creativity comes in so many ways. You can do something as small as draw a doodle, and as large as paint a grand painting fit for the biggest gallery in the world.

Some quotes to live by regarding creativity and their meaning are…

"The creative adult is the child who survived," by Ursula Leguin.

This means that if you can draw even the slightest amount of creativity that means that you were able to harness it from your childhood and bring it on into your adult life. Some people were not as fortunate to have been able to do this.

Dieter F Uchtdorf said, "the desire to create is one of the deepest yearnings of the human soul."

This is perhaps the truest quotes in the fact that some people live their entire lives not being able to be creative. Others struggle with trying one thing and failing and not wanting to try anything else in the off chance that they will fail with that as well. If you don't have a green thumb, it doesn't mean that you won't succeed at painting, and if you can't paint, it doesn't mean that you won't be a great writer.

If you don't try you will never know.

"Creativity doesn't wait for that perfect moment. It fashions its own perfect moments out of ordinary ones," was perfectly said by Bruce Garrabrandt.

One of the greatest art forms to use in this reference is the question mark challenge. Simply draw a question mark on a paper with whatever medium you prefer to use, and make it develop into something beautiful. Sometimes in taking the opportunity to draw or express yourself, some of your deepest and most inner thoughts and feelings come out.

Don't let this scare you. It simply means that you are allowing negativity to rise to the surface, escape, and be replaced with positive iti.

Pablo Picasso, perhaps the epitome of creative persons said, "everything you can imagine is real."

This doesn't mean that by imagining it, it becomes tangible… it means that the possibilities of you being creative, inventive, or things happening by your hand is possible. Allow this quote to inspire you along your Manifestation journey to realize that through Manifestation anything is possible.

It's out there, so take it it's for you.

"You can't use up creativity. The more you use the more you have," was spoke into existence by the great Maya Angelou.

Maya Angelou was perhaps one of the wisest women of her age. This simply means that you never run out of creativity you simply learn to create more things which gives you an arsenal of creativity to use in many difference outlets.

Albert Einstein, one of the worlds smartest and most creative men said, "creativity is intelligence having fun."

This is perhaps one of the most literal quotes meaning that even the smartest people can have fun through creativity and invention. But it doesn't necessarily take great intelligence to be creative or have fun. They go hand in hand which makes this quote even more powerful!

"To practice any art, no matter how well or badly, is a way to make your soul grow. So do it," Kurt Vonnegut.

This quote perhaps takes on the best meaning It means that no matter how good or how bad you think you are at something, simply doing it and having fun means that your soul will grow in happiness and positivity, shedding negativity and allowing good things to grow in its place. Just remember that just because you think something isn't good, doesn't mean that others won't enjoy it.

So, share your work no matter how good or bad you think it is.

"Creativity is inventing, experimenting, growing, taking risks, breaking rules, making mistakes, and having fun," said by Mary Lou Cook.

This quote is so eloquently put that it doesn't require much explanation. It doesn't mean do illegal things to reach your highest potential, it means to think outside of the box and do what feels right for you.

"The chief enemy of creativity is good sense," another quote by the one and only Pablo Picasso.

Again Picasso states so beautifully that sometimes thought and good sense gets in the way of what we know we are able to do. This falls under the category of overthinking and letting your mind wander. Sometimes putting thoughts to paper, canvas, or words to page is the most beneficial way to stifle negative overthinking.

And lastly, Edward de Bono said that "creativity involves breaking out of expected patterns in order to look at things in a different way."

Sometimes we need to step back from our normal and allowed new things in, in order to become the better version of ourselves. If you are expected to be one way, act one way, and do only certain things, it becomes mundane and humdrum and the monotony of it can become a negativity of its own.

By using any of these quotes and their meanings to form a positive way of thinking that is best for you and pairing them with the creativity of your choice, you have no choice but to live through positivity and with the knowledge that anything is possible for you.

Chapter 16
How can I Trust the Process?

In this chapter, you will discover the ways to regain your personal faith and to continue to keep that faith and trust in your manifesting journey as you work through everything that happens on a daily basis. It will help you to find ways to live in the present moment and be at peace with it instead of feeling worrisome, stressed and depressed.

Sometimes it is hard for us to experience our daily living and not worry about the bumpy parts that occur during the day. Thinking about what a day looks like, most of us think about getting up in the morning and the steps it takes to get in bed at night, however thinking of it differently might help you process the bad or negative parts of the day and make them good or positive for the future.

If we take the concept of a storyboard like discussed in the last chapter you can create a storyboard for your day. At the end of the day if you create the storyboard even if it's in your head then you are able to process what went on during the day that could have been prevented or could be changed in the future. This helps in order to create a positive day and positive environment for…

- Work.
- School.
- With you family.
- With your friends.
- In your home life.
- Out in the public.

Sometimes the basic steps through the day seem repetitive enough that we don't think about the small things that make our day different than the days before, but if we think about it as if we were altering small bits of the day in order to create the best life possible, then this chapter will help you formulate a plan to living positively through Manifestation and belief in yourself, your deity, and others!

Here you will…

- Discover the ways to regain your personal faith.
- Learn how to hold onto said faith.
- Have trust in your Manifestation journey.
- Live in the present moment.
- Be at peace with your wife.

Here you will discover what an average day should look like for a person either going to school or work and the steps you could take to fulfill the above processes in order to make your day the best day possible. Remember that good days, turn to good weeks, which turn to good month, which turn to good years.

Once your life circulates towards the good years category it becomes easier to live the positive life you've always wanted without fixating on the negative aspects even if they are small there's no use in sweating the small stuff. This will even help you be able to function during the bigger things that occur such as…

- The death of a family member.
- The death of a friend.
- The death of a pet.
- The loss of a job.
- A fleeting romance.
- The parting of a friendship.
- Someone you love moving away.
- Your children growing older and moving out.
- Your children getting married.
- Your children having children.
- Any kind of sickness.

Here are the daily routines of most people and the bumpy parts that could occur and how to negate them to a positive reality…

- Get out of bed.
    - When getting out of bed you may experience aches and pains that might throw a negative feeling or worry out into the atmosphere.
    - You might realize that you have woken up late because of the alarm not going off or you not hearing it which will also throw a damper on the start of your day.
        - The best way to process either of these outcomes is to simply get out of bed and move to the next step by listening to music, smiling, talking it over with a friend on the phone, jotting it down in a journal, meditating, manifesting, and saying daily affirmations.
- Take a shower, get dressed, get ready for your day.
    - While doing this you may realize that you are out of your favorite shampoo.
    - You might also realize that you have gotten your clothes wet while you are showering by an open end of the curtain.
    - Perhaps your hair is tangled, and it becomes difficult to brush or comb through.
        - The best way to negate the negative thoughts and feelings associated with this is to do the steps required to either go to your closet and get new clothes, ask someone to get them for you, or simply have a backup choice.
        - Also, take care of your hair and keep up with it.
        - This once you may need to use the shampoo you dislike, knowing you will go to the store and buy your favorite for further use and then making sure that you have it on hand from now on.
        - There are always ways of making that moment into something good so that it doesn't bother you as much the next time.
- Eat breakfast or get breakfast on your way to work or school.
    - You might realize that you were running too late for breakfast.
    - You may not have your favorite breakfast items on hand.
    - You might have burnt your breakfast in the hurry that you are in.

        - The best way to figure out how to process this for the future is by creating a list for the store so you make sure that you don't run out of the items that you like.
        - Make sure that you have quick items that you like on hand for those days that you are in a hurry.
        - Make sure that you set at least two days a week where you will cook a hot meal for yourself and set the alarm slightly earlier so that you will have enough time.

- Arrive at work or school.
    - Your vehicle might not have started.
    - Your bus, taxi, Uber, or the subway could be delayed.
    - A train might be on the tracks, or the line into your place of employment or school you attend is backed up for an unforeseen circumstance.
        - Some ways that you can get over these hurdles for the future in order to make your day positive is to make sure you leave early enough to avoid any of those unforeseen issues.
        - Always have a backup way for getting to where you are going.
        - Invest in a bicycle and a good pair of tennis shoes in case they are ever needed as a backup to your backup.
        - Be polite to anybody that is driving you or that is having a rough time so that in the future you can be treated the same way if you are ever experiencing something similar.

- Complete your day until lunch.
    - Up until lunch your computer might have had issues or be updating.
    - Your teacher or boss might be having a rough day which causes you and the rest of your fellow employees or students to have a rough day as well.
    - The copy machine might be jammed, or the projector may not work.
    - You are given an assignment either at work or school that you weren't expecting and you don't feel capable for.
        - A good way to see yourself through these circumstances in order to create a positive future for yourself is by giving yourself credit where credit is due. You are smart and you are capable of figuring out the assignment given to you.
        - Ask for help when you need it.
        - You may consider taking some courses on computer management so that in the future you might be the one able to help sometime by fixing the problem faster than it would have gotten done otherwise.
        - Always be prepared for downtime by bringing extra work or something for leisure if it's allowed so that you're not sitting and twiddling your thumbs.
        - Offer extra assistance to your boss or teacher so that they don't feel so overwhelmed with their workload. In doing this you may need to ignore comments by others that

say you are a suck up, or that you are trying to gain brownie points, this is just for the benefit of the person in charge that is having a rough day.

- Have lunch either at your workplace, school, or off campus of either.
  - You may realize that you don't have enough time or money for lunch.
  - Your favorite place might be closed for some reason.
  - While you were on lunch you spill something on your clothes that it is very noticeable.
    - Some ways to prepare for this would be to have a backup lunch with you in case any of these things happen. Keeping something small in your car that is not perishable and easy to grab would help with this. If you don't have a car throwing something in your bag that would hold you over would be beneficial and would help, by bringing positivity to your day.
    - Having a backup shirt or pair of pants in your locker or your desk drawer might help in case you spill something on yourself. This is generally a good thing to do even when you're not eating, messes happen.

- Complete your day until the end of the day.
  - It's very possible that what happened at the first part of the day could happen during the second half of the day.
    - Simply be prepared for anything. As the days goes on at the school or job you are at you will learn how to cope with the small negative occurrences so that you can turn them into positive happenings.
    - Just because something bad happens does not mean it should or is going to ruin your entire day, it simply means that you need to make small adjustments towards the positive path ahead of you.
- Return home.
  - Any of the things that happened on your way to work, or school could happen on your return home.
    - Being prepared for those things helps to negate the negativity and make it a more positive experience.
    - Having the exact same plans in line in case these things happen as you did on your way to work, or school is beneficial.
- Do your chores at home.
  - When you get home and it is time to do your chores you may be overwhelmed by the amount, of dishes, laundry, cooking, anything that is part of your chores that feels like it is entirely too much to conquer in one day.
  - You may not have the cooperation of others to complete their chores and feel like it is your responsibility to take on yours, and theirs in order to complete them so that it isn't as overwhelming or embarrassing should you have company.

        - Having a chore chart helps keep things organized. That way when somebody doesn't do what they are supposed to do it is clear that it was them that did not do it and that they cannot blame others.
        - Setting time limits and the amount, of chores is important so that it can keep down on stress.
        - Realizing that feeling overwhelmed is inevitable but making sure that it is completed so that it doesn't add on to the next days chores will help assure that it doesn't become an unmanageable mess.

- Do any work needed for work or school that needs to be completed the night before.
    - Now at home you may face distractions that you didn't have at school or work that makes it difficult to do your assignment at home.
        - Making sure that you have a proper workspace and that everyone understands that you are working on something important is helpful in keeping down on negativity and depression.
        - Also making sure that there is allotted time for everyone in your home in the evening is of the utmost importance. This does not mean broad spectrum it means allowing small amounts of time for each of your children, siblings, parents, loved ones, and/or spouses.
- Pick up, cook, prepare, and eat dinner.
- Gather supplies for the next day.
- Groom yourself in whatever way you desire.
    - The above three processes are much like the beginning of the day. It is possible that some of the things that might have happened then could happen now or if they didn't happen at the beginning of the day, it is very possible that they could happen here.
        - Being prepared with the backups that you had for the start of the day, or by making lists and charts, you can run your evening smoothly at home, be it your family's home where you are a child, teenager, or young adult, or your own where you are the adult who runs it alone or with the help of a spouse or loved one.
- Go to sleep.
    - This seems to be the most problematic for many people in the fact that you may have some difficulties falling asleep.
    - Some people also have trouble with their mind shutting off during this time which makes it stressful and can make you exhausted in the morning.
        - Some good things to keep in mind to help you sleep are making sure that the environment is comfortable for you.
        - You might consider looking into ASMR.
        - Make sure that your routine is similar each night so that your body can get into the habit of going to sleep at a certain time.
        - Also, make sure to have positive thoughts as you fall asleep so that your dreams and when you wake are full of positivity.

In wrapping up this chapter simply remember that there are small positive things that you can implement in your daily life that will negate the negative happenings that may occure, and make your life better. It is always good to remember to add meditation and prayer into your daily life wherever it feels the most comfortable, this will help bring positivity and light into your atmosphere. Also, it will allow your life to be surrounded by good things so that your days, weeks, months, and years feel better.

In the end remember that by following the steps and creating a better day for yourself and your loved ones, while practicing meditation, this is the best beginning to your Manifestation journey.

Chapter 17
When Will I Begin to See It?

This chapter will discuss the ways that you might begin to see your Manifestation pathway opening and the examples of how it is going to happen even if it seems delayed, or almost impossible. Sometimes when we manifest something so important to us, we tend to expect it right away, and when it doesn't occur here and now, we don't think it's going to happen at all. It's important to remember that if it doesn't happen right away that doesn't mean that it won't, it's just in the universe is timing and you will receive it still yet.

Receiving it however, will depend on the nature of your Manifestation. As discussed before if manifesting through negativity and putting it out into the universe, you will not receive what the universe has for you. Getting rid of the negativity and bringing in positivity is about the only way that you will receive what you manifest.

Now that you have gotten this far in your journey towards Manifestation, it is time to talk about how you can begin to practice and see the things that you're trying to manifest come to life. You have learned how to purify yourselves mind, body, and soul. You have learned about affirmations, intentions, vibrations, and projecting yourself and your thoughts out into the universe as well. Then you have also learned the benefits of Manifestation through meditation, meaning that you are ready to learn the process of Manifestation.

Here are some of the steps you can take in trying to create your Manifestation and in trying to hurry it along without upsetting the universe.

- Give yourself permission to want what you want.
    - Say to yourself that you want it, therefore you give yourself permission to want it, therefore you give yourself permission to receive it, therefore you have permitted yourself into your Manifestation.
- Remember when to bring in affirmation.
    - Remember that when negativity sneaks in to use your affirmations of faith and daily affirmations to build yourself back up and to prove to others that they cannot tear you down.
- Be willing to receive.
    - Make the universe aware that you are willing to receive what it has for you. Let the universe know that you are ready for what you have manifested to come true.
- Remember to set intentions.
    - Setting intentions is much like prayer or creating intentions for the future. This goes hand in hand with manifesting something into reality or something into a positive happening. Refer to the intentions chapter in order to better understand how this works.
- Be willing to doubt your doubts.

    - It is natural to doubt the process, but it is important to negate your doubts with doubting that the doubts will come true. That may be a hard pill to swallow however remembering to brainstorm negativity and negate it to positivity is much like using doubt to negate doubt.
- Pick and choose who you share your dreams with.
    - It's important that you have people in your life to share your aspirations with, however sharing them with toxic people or people who will downtrodden your hopes and dreams is a negative way of bringing someone in, in order to help you achieve your Manifestation goals. These people come in the form of hypocrites, naysayers, doubters, and people who are abusive to you mentally, physically, spiritually, and emotionally
- Be creative and use your creativity.
    - Use creativity to get back to positive living. Refer to two chapters past in order to figure out the best way to get back to a positive way of living that fits your needs.
- Do your best to keep your vibration up.
    - If you need help with this concept feel free to revisit the vibrations chapter in order to center yourself towards manifesting greatness.
- Project, project, project.
    - While projecting or projection is close to affirmation, intention, and Manifestation, it is important to constantly be projecting into the atmosphere and into the universe what is most desired. Also sending thanks into the universe for the universe and your deity is also important.
- Take inspired action.
    - By taking inspired action this is your proactive view and doing of what is needed in order to receive what you most desire.
- Strive to rise above jealousy.
    - Be sure that there is absolutely no way you have fallen upon jealousy towards other people who have already received their Manifestation. Here is the place that it is most important to remember that there is a time and a place for everything, and that no matter how long it takes your Manifestation will come true.
- Use a mantra to deal with your current less-than-ideal situation.
    - Remember that mantra say I will, I have, I am.

- Trust your soul's path.
    - Here it is important to refer to chapters one and two in order to make sure that your soul is spiritually bonded in order to achieve Manifestation of the purest kinds. This also means that your soul is cleansed to the point of purity in order to make sure that you are capable of, pushing your Manifestation out into the universe and getting it back in return and not allowing it to be rejected.
- Trust the universe.
    - I you don't have faith and trust in the universe then there is no way that what you manifest will come to fruition.

- Trust your deity.
  - If you have a deity and belief in said deity to help you in every way, then you must practice the utmost trust in him, her, they, or them.
- Meditate, meditate, meditate.
  - There is only so much that can be said about meditation… refer to past chapters on the subject to realize it's importance.
- Do your inner work.
  - By doing your inner works, you can assure that you are ready to receive.

Remembering that everything comes in good timing and that being patient, while hard, is the only thing you can do after a Manifestation has been released.

Chapter 18
What are some examples of successful manifesting?

In this chapter you will come to learnsome examples in the world of people who have been successful at manifestation and what has transpired in their individual lives as a result of that success. These will be mostly testimonials found in person and on the web that are easily looked up and discovered further.

Know that in no time, this could be you.

Note:

Some of the names and specific details have been changed for anonymity and plagiarism purposes, but the integrity of the stories are left for your benefit.

Beth's Story

One thing Beth has been trying to do less of is gripe about things. She is trying to learn to go with what's happening a lot more than she has in the past. It has been helping her relationship more, and it's helping her choose a lot more carefully where her time and energy is spent, as well as who her time is spent with.

Thoughts become things and this has been something that has stuck with her through her journey. She has found that she is talking to people about it including her children. She knows so many people who can benefit from thinking this way and it helps promote more positive thoughts than anything. She feels calmer now. As her and her hasband have talked before, the more positive she is the more she notices the negativity melting away. She knows she's not positive at all times, but she is currently working on this Manifestation.

Cloe's Story

Cloe was recently told that she has a negative outlook on life. She was shocked by this news and hated to hear that that was the kind of person she had become.

Her friend told her that everything positive that had happened she had a negative way of looking at it. In discussing with the same friends they had decided that a negative experience in her childhood had brought on this behavior.

The friend also had heard about manifesting your own destiny and creating the life that you deserve. Cloe thought it was a bit odd to think about things in the future and act like they had already happened, but after practicing a few affirmations, her negative outlook switched.

What the help of her friends and family she has a long way ahead of her, but she has started practicing meditation and is even feeling some of the heightened energy and hopes to achieve Manifestation soon.

John's Story

John's computer had recently gotten a virus that crippled the system. His computer was important to his career, yet he didn't have enough money to go out and buy a computer capable of doing what his job demanded of him. He had just recently had to replace the engine in one of his vehicles which took quite a bit of his money that he had saved up.

The computer needed, cost more than $2000, which made it impossible to buy for him when trying to replace it.

John had heard of the law of attraction, but had never used it before. After feeling discouraged and under attack because every solution he had found looked extremely tough or unattainable, he turned the computer off and went to do some meditation.

He began to focus on the need for a new computer, not really understanding what manifesting to reality meant. He was well aware of what the law of attraction could do for him and what Manifestation meant, he also meditated often which helped. Eventually John put out in the universe that he needed a new computer and that he believed he would get one no matter what, it would be his. He knew he didn't have the means or the money to attain it, yet he believed.

The next day as a bonus for working so hard, his boss, not knowing that he had an problem with his computer, issued him a new one as a payment for hard work received.

Rebecca's Story

Rebecca began using meditation as well as a few other techniques that she had learned through various workshops and teachings. The more that she learned and discovered the more she practiced it and the more she saw results. Before learning these techniques however, she had began to have a rather addictive behavior of spending money she didn't have in the shops and boutiques in the town she lived in.

Retail therapy had become a big deal in her life to help cope with some past traumas and that became problematic when she both ran out of money and the need for the items she was picking up.

She found that her mind was led to specific clothing stores which had the ideal selection that she liked the most and that best fit for her, which appealed to her the most.

At her lowest Rebecca had lost some income due to a job cut in her company. She hadn't lost her job just simply was cut down on hours and it became an even bigger issue that she used money for frivolous items. During one of her shopping's excursions she had found the flyer for enlightened meditation and yoga, a class taught at her local rec center.

What she took that class she was hooked and began taking more and more period now, she is able to process her need for retail therapy by meditating an manifesting that what she needs will come to her rather than what she doesn't need will be bought with the money that she doesn't have.

Ian's Story

Ian didn't know if what had been meant to happen, had happened due to Manifestation, or if it just sort of happened, but eventually he surmised that Manifestation was the only explanation. It was a sort of an accidental practicing although he had heavy knowledge of it from years before when he had taken a philosophy of religion course in college.

He felt that his desires were somewhat vain, but during deep meditation one day he projected thoughts into the universe and received them within forty-eight hours. The first one was rather silly in his opinion, although he had wished for a six-pack stomach, he didn't think it would come easily without hard work and dedication, none of which he thought he had time for being a sophomore at the university and working thirty-hours a week. The next day however his mother came home with an ab and back machine that made his transformation that much easier.

During his weekends home from school he would use the machine which would give him motivation then to go to the gym during the week when he had the time at university.

He hadn't specifically asked for the machine and sort of in a silly way asked for the abs, but he was able to obtain them, nonetheless.

The second thing that happened to him, through meditation and Manifestation was the fact that he had wanted his father to be free of Indonesia to come and be with his mother, siblings, and him in the

United States. The paperwork had been many years in the making and the day after he manifested this thought into the universe, the papers were approved, and his father was home within a week.

Usha's Story

Usha had spent many years in an abusive relationship, she didn't feel like she had the means to get out of, and because of her nationality and religious practices, she knew that her husband would win in court. It was often difficult for women of her caliber to even get the papers submitted, let alone see them signed or to be carried out with the outcome of divorce. There were no children involved in this relationship which helped, but it still made things hard on her when the abuses would happen.

After talking with a friend, another female, she was encouraged to the point of filing the paperwork. Although she doubted that it would get through to even the first process at court, she hoped that it would. Her friend advised her to project it into the universe during her daily meditation, which she practiced at least four times a day.

Since meditation was already a daily practice in her life, it was easy to obtain the heightened level of concentration that she was used to. While there, she sent into the universe that she knew that her papers would get signed, and that she would be free from her abusive husband one day soon.

It's fair to mention at this point that she had moved in with the friend in the hopes that while the papers were being processed her husband couldn't find her and abuse her further.

She was shocked however when six days later, she had gotten news that her court papers were signed and were being processed in her favor. She is now a free woman!

Jackey's Story

Jackey had wanted to become more in tune with the people around him, in doing so, Jack knew that there might be consequences to those requests, but he felt like he needed the closeness to his society, nature, and the universe in order to become a better person.

After a week of manifesting in meditation he began, to notice a stronger connection to those around him. He could finish peoples sentences and was doing it more often. He knew what people were thinking and was able to aid them before it was even spoken.

Through this he felt like his awareness of reality had been heightened and he was able to get up easier in the morning. He also was able to function more in society which was something he had issues with before. More and more people were commenting on their connectivity with him, which made him happy because he knew they were happy in return.

All in all Jack had become a nicer person, and he hoped that others had as much success as he had had and soon he became a teacher of Manifestation and meditation.

Jack called it the circle of his spiritual life.

Devon's Story

Devon got his English essay done! AND despite not being prepared for the presentation he had to do, his English teacher thought it was outstanding! It was a big deal for him to get the thing done let alone be able to submit it and a teacher like it. He wasn't particularly lazy, he only had ample amounts of time to do it, but his anxiety would get the better of him every time. He would stare at the computer screen aimlessly, watching the cursor blink, blink, blink until his brain would shut down.

Not to mention that he had gotten a B on the whole thing when he was sure that he was going to fail!

His success had come from speaking with a psychology professor in his high school. He had found out that through projection an affirmation he could manifest what grade he wanted and how well he did on tests, essays, basic school work and everything beyond that.

He soon became a spokesperson for his class helping them to attain the same results. Eventually he became a straight A student and gained the knowledge from the work he had done.

Quin's Story

Quin's first request was still out there manifesting in the atmosphere when her second one for a smoother road on transition to new energy had come forth.

She was still waiting for her first to happen, but she was more than excited to step into the new role of her second Manifestation. She was much more at peace and content with herself and knew that perhaps she could ask for more Manifestations. She eventually began to ask for money, to further her education, for healing, and an additional energy boost. Little by little some of these things came through, while others waited a little longer.

Quinn began to realize the importance of being patient and she basked in the greatness of the gifts she had been given and did not feel jealous of others who had gotten theirs first. She didn't doubt that the other thing she had asked for would come, because she knew that they would.

Manifestation!

In learning some of these successful stories of manifesting something and receiving it, it is hoped that you will be able to take this knowledge and move beyond the here and now and into something great. Remember never to be jealous, remember to be patient, and good things are worth waiting for… and everything that you ask for as long as it is done so in the right way will come to fruition in its own time.

Chapter 19
What can I do when manifestation seems to be taking a long time or not working?

This chapter will help you learn how to focus one's mind when you begin to feel restless or feel like your attempts to manifest are not occurring. It will help to refocus the mind so that you can intentionally and clearly mediate and seek out what will make you feel the most fulfilled as the person in charge of your life.

Sometimes when you feel like your Manifestation is taking longer than you thought it would, it is easy to feel restless and sometimes think that it won't occur for you at all. Keeping in mind that you should always remember that you did once believe in the fact that it would come to fruition therefore you should continue to believe that it will… this is important.

Some of the best things that you could do while feeling impatient is to meditate and further manifest patience and understanding because those might be things that would come a little quicker for you. Remembering some of the success stories from the previous chapter will also help allow you to indicate where you are seeing smaller Manifestations come through while your bigger ones are still in waiting.

Some ways of helping your mind stay focused are…

- Remembering to do your creative activities.
    - By remembering to do creative activities that you love you will then be able to solely focus your mind on one subject so that it doesn't bounce back and forth between the worry an uncertainty that you may be experiencing.
    - By keeping creative you also keep young, vibrant, your memory on top of its game, and you keep positivity at the forefront of your life.
    - One last thing to remember while bringing in the creativity is that you can share it by putting it out and that by obtaining more creativity and things that you are learning how to do with it… it becomes an arsenal or your toolbox to increase your level of creativity or to teach others how to do that activity.
        - A good example of this is knitting, sewing, crocheting, or any other activity that is teachable once you become a master of it you then can teach others which then becomes a creative outlet of its own.
        - This could also be like teaching your children how to ride a bike when you had learned how to ride one long years ago. This could potentially bring up positive childhood memories which will create a bond between you and your own children.
        - If you don't have your own children at this point, bringing in activities such as skateboarding, inline skating, jumping on a trampoline in a special way, using a Pogo stick, hula hooping, these are all things that if you knew how to do them as a child you will likely know how to do them now, bringing them to a niece, nephew,

or neighborhood child, and teaching them also works as a great outlet towards being patient for future outcomes.

- Keeping your mind fresh on one subject that you desire.
    - This is particularly important to those the like one specific subject such as reading, writing, mathematics, or anything that can be a singular subject. Keeping that singular subject to the forefront of your mind while letting the doubts and worry subside is also a good positive outlet.
    - As crazy as it sounds to some people particularly those that don't like mathematics, doing math problems for those that do, is a positive outlet for the stress and worry, also if you are a fan of reading, sitting down with a good book, magazine, anything that you can find that you would particularly like to read, is a positive way to reinforce your mind and to set back the worry and anxiety of not receiving your Manifestation yet.
        - Keep in mind that if reading or doing mathematics, or whatever singular subject you choose becomes boring for you, you can seek out a child or children or even young adults that struggles in that subject that you can tutor or teach or pass on your knowledge that might also work for you in waiting and being patient. It helps to keep your mind off of things while focusing singularly on something while also helping somebody in need. This will help in waiting and also counts towards keeping your mind body and soul cleansed and positive.
- Learning patients Through watching younger children.
    - Sometimes as adults we become the most impatient versions of ourselves, this does not help while practicing or manifesting in any way shape or form. Sometimes sitting back and watching a child play… noting their unbridled attention towards something and the fact that they almost always are patient and loving is a good way to rekindle that within yourself.
    - Sometimes we get frustrated with people with disabilities, elderly people, people who don't understand the way that we do, but children have that… unfocused and unwavering patients that will see that person that is struggling completely through. As adults it's hard to forget what we need to do in order to bring back those patients, but by watching the children you will remember how easy it can be.
    - This will also bring you back to a time before you learned how to be callous due to bullying, abuse, traumas and other situations.
        - A great example of this is a child on a playground playing with another child with autism. The first child doesn't realize yet that that second child is "tarnished" in some way. As an adult it's easy to get that mentality that a child that is disabled is somehow "tarnished." But, as bad as that sounds, if you think about it, it is possible to get that mentality without even trying. Watching that child play with the other child will then bring back the idea that we once had the patience to do so ourselves.
        - Another good example of this is working with ill or aging parents. Our parents once took care of us in whatever capacity that they were able to, it may be possible or

probable that you will have to do the same for them in the future, sometimes by doing this it becomes super frustrating not knowing how things need to be particularly done for that individual, it makes you feel defeated, learning the patience through a child also makes you more equipped to be patient yourself.

- Practice yoga.
  - Yoga can perhaps be one of the most stimulating activities that you can do. As simple as it seems stretching and moving your body in minute ways can also help you formulate a good meditation routine. In keeping up your meditation routine you will then focus less on what hasn't come to fruition through Manifestation an focus more on your body, your breathing, and how you feel inwardly and outwardly.
- Practice Taekwondo.
  - Taekwondo is one of those activities that is both physically straining but mentally straining as well. Not straining in a negative way but a positive way. It allows your body to feel free and in control at the same time allowing you to push aside those negative and worrisome thoughts and bring forth something that is positive. This is also a great way to learn self-defense and a way to learn how to defend others that might need it. That will also come in handy in the future and it makes you feel positive about doing something proactive while you are being patient and waiting for your Manifestation to come true.
  - Also, in doing that the universe recognizes that you are doing something proactive therefore it may see fit to push along your Manifestation.
    - A great example of this is making sure that you do the things in your life that is needed to keep on track such as volunteer, work with the community, weed out all the negativity in your life. Being able to defend in the time of need or even eventually learning how to teach self-defense is a wonderful way to keep on the path towards becoming a better you.
- Visit nature.
  - By visiting nature, you are soaking up the sun which brings in the vitamin DS spoke about in previous chapters. You are allowing nature to heal your mind body and soul in so many, different ways. Allow it to touch you as you might touch it smelling roses, feeling the grass beneath your feet, breathing in the clear clean air of where you might be.
- Pick up old positive habits to replace the negative worry that is now infiltrating your mind body and soul.
  - While you are waiting and feeling somewhat impatient, now is a good time to pick up old positive habits that you might have once had that you then replaced with the practice of meditation and Manifestation. Know that this is a good way of bringing back in those intentions, affirmations, projections, and anything that will help you just push your feelings out into the universe, letting it know that you are absolutely ready for your dream to come true or your Manifestation to occur.

Sometimes it's hard to remember to be patient and to look for those still small signs that we should step into the reality that is meant for us. Through Manifestation it is important that we calm down, breathe, and implement the above actions in order to get through the time period that we are in. Another things human's do not like to do is wait. We are a rushed type of people, and we want things to happen now, and in the time present opposed to waiting for them to come in the future.

Learn to be that, waiting person who is proactive and patient even though you once weren't, it's possible to become that person now.

Chapter 20
Am I Now a Master of Manifestation?

Here we will recap everything already covered in the nineteen chapters prior to the ending chapter and you will be able to take the knowledge gathered from this book to develop your own methods to create the life you want most for yourself. While it is impossible to become an ultimate master of everything, there is always more to learn, you should have the equipment and tools needed to achieve your dreams, hopes, and aspirations.

Here is a recap of what each chapter presented to you and how you can use them towards becoming the best version of yourself on your Manifestation journey...

- In chapter one you learned what Manifestation is.
    - You discovered the steps required in order to purify yourself your mind, body, and soul both spiritually and mentally in order to prepare for your manifestation journey.
- In chapter two, you learned how to begin your journey.
    - Here you learned that there are steps needed to take in order to prepare yourself for the Manifestation journey.
    - You also learned that it isn't so easy to attain and with negativity it's near impossible to manifest anything.
- In chapter three you discovered the best way to manifest.
    - Here you learned what you needed to be doing in order to begin your journey. You learned that it isn't something that you can just pick up and do, you have to prepare yourself and you have to prepare the world around you in order to achieve it.
    - This is where you learned that getting rid of negativity is of the upmost importance and replacing it with positivity is the most important thing in order to begin this journey.
- In chapter four you learned about what affirmations are.
    - You learned that there are daily affirmations such as "I will have a great day" and "I am going to pass the test."
    - There are also affirmations of faith such as "I believe the universe has something to offer me," and "I believe my deity is all knowing and therefore will provide through manifestation."
- Chapter five covered the Laws of Attraction.
    - Here one should have discovered that there are in fact seven Laws of Attraction.
    - You should have also learned that you must follow all seven laws in order to achieve Manifestation.
- Chapter six presented what choices and decisions you could make that are considered proactive?
    - Being proactive is important towards reaching your goals and making sure that your dreams and affirmations are projected into reality.

- In chapter eight you discovered how the way that you speak to yourself can affect your body and your mind.
  - Here you learned that certain circumstances or the way that you talk to yourself or the way that you let other people talk to you can make your body reflect negatively through illness and depression.
  - Sometimes this can be reflected as hypochondria, while other times there are legitimate illnesses and pain set into your body due to the fact that you have allowed negativity to be at the forefront of your life.
  - And as hard as this pill is to swallow, it may be your fault due to the negative way that you are speaking to yourself, again because you have heard that so many times and believe it, or you dis-like something about yourself, therefore you project the negative thoughts and words and began to believe it even more.
  - Just because it's spoken does not mean it's real.
- In chapter nine we discussed what conscious living is and how important it is to your development.
  - Being a person who lives consciously helps with the environment, the way things occur in your personal environment, and the way that you react to situations around you.
  - Remembering that conscious living does not mean being a hippie, a vegetarian, vegan, it simply means being conscious and aware of the way that you are projecting and the way that you are living your life.
- The power of thought and how it can affect you was discussed in chapter ten.
  - You learned that thinking and thought are powerful tools or weapons depending on how you use them. In thinking negatively it becomes a weapon against your further development and thinking positively it becomes a tool to use towards your Manifestation journey.
- Chapter eleven discussed how you can increase the level of your vibrational response?
  - Here you learned how to measure vibrations in various different ways bringing in the aspects of negativity and positivity.
- In chapter twelve, you discovered what living with intention means.
  - Here you learned how to make and create intentions and project them into the universe much like you would during the process of manifesting something into reality.
- Chapter thirteen perhaps brought on the most important topic which was how to break negative patterns in your life.
  - Again, this reinforces that by having negativity in your life the positive aspects and outcomes are impossible due to the overshadowing of the darkness versus the light virtues in your life.
  - It also talked about how easy it is to negate the negativity and push it towards a positive light.
- Then in chapter fourteen it discussed how meditation and Manifestation work together.

    - You learned that they go hand in hand while helping you achieve your Manifestation goals. You also learned that while you were able to meditate without practicing Manifestation it is near impossible to manifest without meditation.
- In chapter fifteen you learned what creative methods you could implement in order to have a successful positive outlook.
    - These are the ones that you can do now. It's important not to have to wait for your creative outlet finding what you can do here and now not in the future so much, is important while still focusing on what you'd like to do in the future.
    - That part is alright, but you need something now!
- Chapter seventeen perhaps brought on the most difficult aspects of trusting the process and believing that it will come to fruition.
    - Believing and knowing are two different things this is trusting that you know what you believe in will happen but also be patient while doing it.
- Chapter seventeen was on when you would begin to see your manifestations come to light.
    - In this chapter you learned that in due time it will be possible to see what you have manifested come true, and that it’s important to practice patience and understanding.
- Chapters eighteen and nineteen were on what some examples of successful Manifestation are and what you can personally do when you feel like your Manifestation seems to be taking a long time or not working.

It's always important to remember that no matter what step you are in the process, that you are taking baby steps forward on your journey towards manifesting your destiny.

Just because it isn't happening in the timely fashion that you feel it should doesn't mean it won't, believing is everything and faith is the key. Remember to keep your mind and your body turned and tuned towards the spiritual and mental aspects keeping your thought process and your mental health at the utmost high.

Even when you feel down there are various ways of making sure that you can lift yourself back up… affirmation is one of the biggest in this department in making sure that your mental health status stays on a positive level. All in all it's important that you remember that you can't skip any steps on your journey, it's important also to recall the steps that you have taken and maybe re-practice them or revisit them when necessary or until you get them right for you.

That concludes this journey of awareness towards Manifestation, remembering that you are the worker of your own destiny by using your deity, the environment, nature, and ultimately the universe will help you achieve most anything you can think as long as you believe it.

Meditations, Affirmations, and Hypnosis for Wealth, Abundance, and Law of Attraction

With the out breath, releasing the negative belief that the rich are evil
With the in breath, connecting with divine abundance, inviting it into your life
With the out breath, releasing the negative belief that money is what others have
With the in breath, connecting with divine abundance, inviting it into your life
With the out breath, releasing the negative belief that you don't deserve to be rich
With the in breath, connecting with divine abundance, inviting it into your life
With the out breath, releasing the negative belief that it's not right to be rich when there are poor people

Feeling light in your body
A wave of relaxation sweeping over you
Like a weight has been lifted off you
And now connecting with these words
Repeating them silently in your mind
And really absorbing their energy
Becoming one with them

I tap into the power of divine abundance
Divine abundance cannot be taken away from me
I am an extension of the universe
I attract divine abundance into my life
I am open to receiving
I am grateful for all that I receive
I am the master of my destiny
I am in control of all my thoughts, words, and actions
The universe bestows on me wealth and abundance
I feel worthy of receiving
Divine abundance is present in all my financial affairs
There is enough for everyone
There is no lack
I speak only positive words for my relationship with money
All my thoughts about money are positive
All my ideas and beliefs about money are positive
I am grateful for all the abundance that currently exists in my life
My life is a creation of the universe
I am ready to receive more financial wealth than I have ever received before
I ask the universe to fill my life with its abundance
I ask the universe to fulfill all my desires about material success
I claim my right on divine abundance

As we near the end of this meditation
Place both your hands on your heart
And say to yourself silently in your mind
I am ready to receive wealth and abundance
I am ready to receive wealth and abundance
I am ready to receive wealth and abundance

Bring your awareness back towards your body
Take a moment to feel gratitude for yourself
And whenever you feel ready
Open your eyes

Thank you for being here today

2. Practice for manifesting wealth into your life (15 minutes)

Our practice today is for manifesting wealth into your life

We'll start with just as you are in this moment
You could be seated, cross legged on a cushion or a couch
You could be sitting on a chair, with your feet resting on the floor
Or you could be lying down with your arms stretched by your side
Listen to how your body feels and choose your most comfortable position

Once you settle down and come into a space where you feel relaxed and easy
You may gently close your eyes
I invite you now to notice your breath
Noticing the quality of your breath
Simply feeling how your breath is today
Is it shallow or deep?
Is it long or short?
Is it even or broken?

(Pause)

Simply sitting and noticing
Noticing how effortlessly a breath flows inside us
And how naturally a breath flows outside from us
Noticing also the coolness of the in breath
And the warmth of the out breath
Noticing the sensation of the in breath when it first enters the nose
And the sensation of the out breath when it leaves the nose

I invite you now to take your attention to your body
See if there is any tension that you are holding anywhere in your body
Send your breath to that part of your body and soften it
Notice where in your body stress has stored up
As you breathe out, release that stress
Making new space in your body
Breathing in relaxing, softening
Breathing out releasing, letting go

As your body becomes more and more relaxed
Feel a sense of calm and peace take over your whole being
In this space, in this time, I invite you to imagine being surrounded by golden light
A waterfall of golden light washing over you
Your whole body soaking in this golden light
Allowing it to take over your consciousness
Moving it in all directions inside of you

Trusting this light
Putting your faith in it
And as you do so, slowly begin to deepen your exhale
Making your exhale longer than your inhale
Breathe in through your nose
And now slowly, slowly, release the breath
Let it all go out
Breathe in through your nose
And as you release the breath, let go of all your worries and anxieties about money
Let the waterfall of golden light wash them away
Making space in your body and mind for all the money that you have ever conceived of
Follow this cycle of breath a few times
As you breathe in, inhale golden light into your body
As you breathe out, let go of all your negative beliefs about money
Surrender them to the waterfall of golden light
Making new space in your body, in your mind
In that new space, breathe in golden light
And once again, as you breathe out, let go of everything that is stagnating, that no longer serves you

Trusting that you are ready
Trusting that you will receive
That you are receiving
Trusting that you are supported
That you are guided
The only thing that you need to do is open yourself to receive it
Trusting in your being
Trusting in your power
Trusting in your potential
And putting your faith in the divine power of the universe
Reconnecting with the breath
And breathing in joy
Breathing out fear
Breathing in security
Breathing out anxiety
Breathing in luxury
Breathing out lack
Breathing in all your desires
Breathing out any worries

As you come towards the end of this meditation practice, keep the golden light within you through the day and through the night
Let your breath be your guide
Let your breath remind you that all that is yours will come to you
Let your breath reassure you that there is abundance for you
And keep the magic words with you
Know that you can trust

Know that you are safe
Know that you are supported
Know that you are protected

And bring into your heart
The feeling of gratitude for all that you have
And for all that is coming towards you
Allowing your heart to feel love
For everything and everyone there is
And believing that it is easy to receive money
It is easy to receive abundance
And that it is there for you

Whenever you feel ready, you can gently bring yourself back to the space around you
Thank you for practicing with me today
May love and light be with you

3. Using Goal Setting to Manifest Wealth and Abundance (40 minutes)

Hello and welcome to this meditation for setting your goals in order to manifest wealth and abundance

Before we begin, let's make sure you are comfortable
Wiggling if you feel like
And sitting or lying down really comfortably
All you need to do now is listen to my voice
And let your mind take you on our journey together

Gently close your eyes
The first thing we'll do is take a few breaths together
In your own time
Breathing in
And breathing out
Breathing in
And breathing out
One more time
Breathing in
And breathing out
If at any time you feel that your mind is thinking about other things
You can do this simple thing of paying attention to your breath
So, when other thoughts come, as we just did
Begin to notice yourself breathing
Breathing in
And breathing out
Breathing in
And breathing out

Now I want you to imagine a place where you feel safe
This place could be one you are familiar with or maybe it exists only in your imagination
But you feel really safe here
It could be inside a house, perhaps your own house, a bedroom
It could be one in nature, the mountains maybe, or at the beach, in a forest
Closed or open
Wherever you feel safe and supported
And I want you to imagine yourself in this place
Take a moment here and visualize yourself
Find yourself in this place
And soak in the peace and serenity of this place
Soak in its healing energy
And know that anytime you feel uncomfortable or restless
You can come back to this place
This is your sanctuary
You are safe here

I am now going to count down from 10 to 1
And with each exhale
You are going to move deeper and deeper into a state of complete relaxation
With each exhale
You will be leaving behind all memories of who you are
And begin to exist only in this present moment
So, take a nice, deep breath in
And 10
Exhale
As you exhale find yourself sinking deeper into the surface you are on
Again, a nice, deep breath in
And 9
Exhale
Finding relaxation here in this moment, finding peace
A nice, deep breath in
And 8
Exhale
Releasing any tension that you might be holding in your body, letting all of that go
Breathing in again, nice, deep breath
And 7
Exhale
Releasing any fears that you might be holding, letting all of them go
Breathing in a nice, deep breath
And 6
Exhale
Opening your body, opening your mind to this process
A nice, deep breath in
And 5
Exhale
Letting go of beliefs that hold you back, of worries and tensions
Breathing in a nice, deep breath
And 4
Exhale
Releasing all negativity, releasing everything that doesn't serve you any longer
Breathing in a nice, deep breath
And 3
Exhale
Letting go of the past and the future and arriving fully here, in this moment
Breathing in a nice, deep breath
And 2
Freeing yourself from anything that holds you back, that doesn't allow you to be yourself
One last time, breathing in a nice, deep breath
And 1
Arriving with your true self in this moment
Finding yourself completely relaxed
Your body heavy and grounded

Your mind completely free

And once again establishing the connection with your breath
Breathing in
And breathing out
Being fully present
And staying with my voice

I invite you now to think about money
And the fact that like everything else
Money is also a form of energy
Our natural state of being is abundance
Abundance is all around us
How we think about money creates energy
It influences are experience with money
When we set a goal for what we want
We send a message to the universe
A message that has clarity
The universe does not judge
It simply provides to you what you ask of it
Without judgment, without bias, without taking away from someone
Because the universe is abundance

I would like you to take this time
And think about your goal regarding money
Take a few moments here
And very specifically
Set your money goals
Once you have your desired goal
Repeat it three times in your mind
And let it become fully alive in your mind
Visualize it coming true
How does it feel?
Notice the minutest details
Where do you live?
Who are the people around you?
What is the environment like?
What you are wearing?
What are the changes you have made to your lifestyle?
Do you feel happier?
Do you feel more accomplished?
Do you feel and look healthier?
Are you taking better care of yourself?
Are you enjoying life more?
Feel these emotions in your body
How does it feel inside of you?

Take a few moments to relish this feeling
Relish this time when all your desired money goals have come true
How would you describe in three words how you are feeling?
How would you describe your relationship with money?
And as you find happiness, peace, and joy in this feeling
I would like you to set an intention
A strong and committed intention that this is your money goal
This is what you want to manifest
And that you will take all the necessary steps to get here
With the belief that the universe will support you in your journey
That you are being guided
That you will attract the right people who will help you achieve this goal
And you will attract all the right experiences
And that all the knowledge that you need is coming to you
You are manifesting through your actions
Through the small and big decisions that you take
Through each action that you perform towards your desired money goal
And through the clarity that you have gained about your goal
Your clarity acting like a catalyst
Turning your dreams into reality
Turning your potentials into action
Turning your worries into building blocks
And you trust and you believe

I invite you now to see this new you
Confident
Shining in your own light
Feeling free and standing tall
With all of this energy, this positivity
Noticing all of these changes
In your body
In your mind
In your energy
And in your heart
Notice how you feel right now
Notice this change
See the glorious you
Integrate with it
Take your time and really feel this coming together

And I want you now to place both your hands over your heart
And feel gratitude
Gratitude for this wealth and abundance
And for the confidence that you have found
The self assurance
Feel all of that in your heart

And connect with your breath
Taking a nice deep breath in
And slowly exhaling
A nice deep breath in
And slowly exhaling

As we come to the end of this practice
Bring some movement back in your fingertips
Wiggle your toes
And find the connection to your body
Noticing your body in this time space and reality
When you feel ready
Gently open your eyes
Thank you for being here today

4. Practice for Believing in your ability to create wealth and abundance (15 minutes)

Hello dear friend
Our practice today is designed for helping you find the belief that you can create wealth and abundance for yourself and for the world around you
It is meant for those times when we need some support to build our belief in us, our trust in us

Let's begin
Come into a comfortable seated position
Either on a chair or on the floor
Making sure that the spine is erect and tall
Allowing the eyes to close
Softening the jaws
Widening the eyebrows
Softening the face like it is at the beginning of a smile
Releasing any tension in the shoulders
Letting the shoulders go
Noticing the back
Noticing the chest area
Consciously relaxing
Consciously releasing
Noticing the arms and hands
Moving down to the abdomen
The pelvis
Down to the hips
The thighs, legs, feet
Breathing into the whole of your body
Releasing
Relaxing
And now working with the breath
Deep inhale
Hold for a moment
Slow exhale
A few more times
Deep inhale
Pause for just a moment
Slow exhale
Sending your breath into your body
Following the whole cycle of breath
Noticing how the breath enters the body
Noticing the pause of the breath
And noticing it as it leaves from the body

Taking awareness to the mind now
Observe if there are any thoughts that are present in your mind
Acknowledge them
And with love and kindness
Let them go
If they come again
Just let them be
Acknowledge them
And with love and kindness
Let them go

Self-belief is often all that we need to move from failure to success
Holding this faith in your heart
We'll begin the practice of affirmations
Affirmations are like votes of confidence we give to ourselves
Used regularly, they help to reprogram our subconscious mind
And help us achieve whatever it is we desire
You can repeat these words either silently in your mind or out loud
What is important is to make these words your reality, really believing in them, in their power

I believe in myself
I believe that I possess unlimited potential to create wealth and abundance
I believe that I possess infinite courage and wisdom to attract money into my life
I believe that I can have all the things I desire
I believe that I can achieve all the goals and dreams I have for my life

I believe in myself
I believe that I am the creator of my destiny
I believe that I am the writer of my destiny
I believe that I have the potential to succeed
I believe that I have the power to inspire others

I believe in myself
I believe that I have the power to transform any situation in life and use it for my growth
I believe that I have the confidence to go for my desires around wealth and money
I believe that I have the resilience to never give up on my goals
I believe that I have all the inner resources I need to achieve my goals and live the life that I desire

I believe in myself
I believe in my self-worth and I have high self-esteem
I believe that my life has purpose and my goals lead me towards my purpose
I believe that I can do anything I put my heart and mind to
I believe that I deserve all the wonderful things in life including my money goals

I believe in myself

I believe that I am worthy of success, wealth, and abundance
I believe that I am special and that there is no one else like me
I believe in my power to create the life that I desire
I believe that I am enough

I want you now to bring your awareness back to your breath
Breathing in
And breathing out
And taking a few moments here to really soak in all that you have experienced

Breathing with me a few more times
Breathing in
And breathing out
Breathing in
And breathing out
As we come to the end of this meditation
I want you to know that you can come back to this practice whenever you wish to
Every time that you listen to it
It will help you reprogram your mind
So you can replace the thoughts and beliefs that limit you
With positive thoughts that will enable you to become your best self

And taking your awareness now to your body and the surface on which you rest
To the space around you
And to this moment in time
As you do so
Give thanks to yourself for making this effort for yourself
Wiggle your toes and fingers
And when you feel ready, open your eyes

Thank you for joining me in this practice
Have a wonderful day

5. Practice to help you accept your desire for money (20 minutes)

Welcome to this guided practice to help you establish your desire for money

To begin
Find a comfortable place to sit or lie down
Somewhere you feel really easy and cozy
And make sure you are warm
And that your body is open
Your arms are uncrossed and are resting by your side if you are lying down, or on your knees or thighs if you are sitting
Taking attention to the breath
Observing your breath as you breathe in and breathe out
Deepening your breath a bit
Breathing in slowly
Holding the breath there for 4 3 2 1
And breathing out even slower
Breathing in slowly
Holding the breath there for 4 3 2 1
And breathing out even slower
We'll do this one more time
Breathing in slowly
Holding the breath there for 4 3 2 1
And breathing out even slower
Relaxing your body now
Taking awareness to how your body feels
Noticing your head and your face
Widening your eyebrows
Relaxing your jaws
Noticing your neck and shoulders
Releasing your shoulders
Letting them go
Moving down now to your chest
Noticing how your heart feels
Releasing any negative emotions you hold there
Noticing your arms and hands
Your fingers and the tips of your fingers
Observing how they feel
If there are any sensations present
If your hands feel cold or warm
And moving to your abdomen
Noticing how your belly feels
If it feels stiff
Or if there is any tightness in that area
Softening your belly

And relaxing all the internal organs in your abdomen
Moving to your hips
Noticing the places where your hips make contact with the surface you are on
Relaxing them
And noticing your legs now
Your thighs, your calves, ankles, your feet, your toes
Noticing how your legs feel today
If there are any sensations that you feel
Any pain, any tightness
Relaxing your legs
And taking your attention to your whole body
Scanning your body to see how it feels
Right from your head to your toes
And if there's any place that does not feel so good
Sending it healing energy
Breathing in and sending healing energy into that part
Breathing out releasing any tension, any pain, any stress
Breathing in and sending healing energy into that part
Breathing out releasing any tension, any pain, any stress

You feel light in your whole body
Really calm and relaxed
It is like you are covered in a blanket of deep relaxation
And from this space of comfort and ease
You listen to my voice and stay with my voice
The more you pay attention to my voice
The deeper is the relaxation that you experience

Most of us have a desire for money
Yet what most of us lack is an access to tools that can help us manifest money
The first step to manifesting what we truly desire
Is to establish that desire
The universe does not differentiate between the rich and the poor
The universe simply listens
And provides us with what we ask from it
When we have more money
We can also use it better to help others
And to create abundance not just for ourselves
But for those around us

In this practice we establish our truth
We no longer run from it
We assert it
We become proud of it
This truth is our desire for money
There is no guilt in wanting more money

There is no shame in desiring more money
The universe does not take from someone to give to us
The universe is abundant
It does not lack
It has enough for everyone, and more
Our only job is to make sure our hands are open to receive
And our hearts and minds are open to receive
I would like you to take a few moments
And feel this desire for money coming up inside you
Where in your body do you feel this desire?
What is the colour of this desire?
What is its shape and texture and size?
What is the intensity of this desire?
Is it warm or cold?
How does this desire feel?
Let it take its complete form inside of you

And now accept this desire
Make it part of your being
See it merging with you
This form assimilating inside of you
Like a seed
A seed of joy and of growth
The process of your abundance begins here
With this seed of desire
Watch it take its root inside you
Plant it firmly within you
Put faith in it
And hope and love and kindness
At the same time believing in your worth
In the fact that you are enough

As you see this seed grow inside of you
Feel yourself growing with it
Feel how confident you are
How happy
Feel how deep this love is that you feel for yourself and for the entire world
Your desires are met
Your dreams are fulfilled
You have money
All the money that you have ever wanted
And it feels good
You can have all those things that you have ever wanted
You can create all the experiences that you have ever wanted
All you need to do is stay connected to your desire
And respect it at all times

Never feeling that it is too much
Never getting overwhelmed by it
But knowing that money is here for you
You simply have to keep your doors open
Never letting doubt come in the way
Never letting fear come in the way
Doing away with any limitations you set on yourself
And becoming the most powerful, confident, happy you

Hold on to these thoughts
Believing that you are becoming more abundant with every breath
Allow love and compassion to pour into your whole body
Feeling gratitude fill up your whole body
And for the last few times
Taking awareness to your breath
Breathing in
And breathing out
Breathing in
And breathing out

As we approach the end of this meditation
Remember that you are abundant
Whenever you feel ready
Gently open your eyes and come back to the room
May love and light be with you

6. Visualization practice for attracting wealth and abundance into your life (20 minutes)

Welcome to this visualization practice for attracting wealth and abundance into your life
Thank you for being here today
This visualization is designed to help you find a new language to connect with the energy of wealth and abundance and invite it into your life

Let us take a moment to settle into this space
You are here now - safe, supported, and comfortable
Whether you are seated or lying down
Know that you are held

Gently close your eyes
Let your awareness travel to your body
Notice if there is any tension that you are holding in your body
Notice your shoulders, your face, your jaws
Release any tension back to the earth

Now take your awareness to how you are feeling at this moment
If there are any worries or thoughts, allow them all to be
You are ok

Taking your awareness to your breath
Breathe into your body
Deep breath in
Feel your belly rising
Deep breath out with a long sigh
Two more times
Deep breath in through the nose
Deep breath out from the mouth
Feel yourself relax with every breath
Deep breath in filling up your belly
Deep breath out, letting everything go
You feel completely relaxed

And now returning to the natural rhythm of your breath
Simply noticing the breath
Breathing in
And breathing out
Breathing in
And breathing out
And as you breathe
Feeling the light of love fill up your heart

If it feels comfortable
Rest one hand gently on your heart
Allow yourself to take this time for yourself
While you are here, if at any time thoughts arise, don't judge yourself
Simply bring your awareness back to the sound of my voice

Let's begin by visualizing golden light
Coming out from the core of the earth
And entering into your body from the soles of your feet
Making its way through your body
Through all your organs, your bones, your cells
Till it reaches the crown of your head
And from there it makes its way up towards the universe
See this golden light travel all the way up to the stars and the sun
Visualize yourself in this web of light
Taking in light from the core of the earth
Seeing it pass through your body
And going out into the universe
Continuing to stay connected with your breath
Feeling the earth supporting you, holding you
And the sky protecting you, securing you
Allow this light to clear away any beliefs you might be holding about lack of money
And as it passes through your body
Allow it to soften any places in your body where you might be holding resistance
Feel this connection
Feel the relaxation that has taken over you

Feel connected to the energy of abundance
Releasing your fears about money with every breath
Releasing your resistance to receive money with every breath
Surrendering to the idea that there is abundance for you
That there is as much money available for you as you have ever desired
And that it is easy and effortless to attract this money into your life
Money is making its way into your life
Wealth is flowing into your life

I invite you now for our practice of affirmations that will help you reprogram your subconscious mind and change the way you think about money
They help you shift your vibration
And connect with the universal energy of abundance
This is a simple practice
I say these affirmations and you repeat them after me
You can say these affirmations out loud, whisper them, or repeat them silently in your mind
Whatever feels best to you today

I am abundant
I have as much money as I ever need
I am a money magnet
Money flows into my life easily and effortlessly
I release all my negative beliefs about money
I no longer think negatively about money
The more money I have the more I can help others
I align myself with the vibration of money
I am the creator of my own destiny
I constantly attract the right opportunities to create more wealth
I constantly attract the right people who help me in my journey
I never have to worry about money again
I have more money than I could ever need
I am worthy of being rich
I am worthy of money and wealth
I am deserving of prosperity
I am deserving of abundance
There is no lack of money in the universe
Money is an unlimited resource
I am wealthy
I am abundant
I am happy

I would like you to take a moment
And visualize how it would feel to be wealthy
Paint this picture in your mind's eye
Let every little detail come to life
What does your life look like?
Where do you live?
Who are the people in your life?
What does success feel like?
How do you dress up?
What are your emotions?

As we near the end of this practice
Allow this energy to seep deeply into your body
Breathe into the feeling of financial freedom
And taking just a few more moments
To simply be here with your breath
And observing the breath
Breathing in, I know that I am breathing in
Breathing out, I know that I am breathing out
Breathing in, I know that I am breathing in
Breathing out, I know that I am breathing out

Gently bringing some movement to the toes and fingers

And perhaps inviting a light stretch
Taking a moment to feel gratitude for this body
And for this day
When you feel ready
Opening your eyes

Thank you for being here today

7. Practice for discovering the secret to wealth and abundance (40 minutes)

Welcome to this guided meditation for helping you find the secret to wealth and abundance
Through this practice
We overcome the roadblock to manifesting wealth and abundance into our lives

It is advisable that you do not listen to this recording while you are driving or operating machinery
And that you are in a place where you won't be disturbed for the next 30 minutes or so
To begin
Find a comfortable place to sit or lie down
Somewhere you feel really easy and safe
And make sure you are warm
And that your body is open
Your arms are uncrossed and are resting by your side if you are lying down, or on your knees or thighs if you are sitting
Taking attention to the breath
Observing your breath as you breathe in and breathe out
Deepening your breath a bit
Breathing in slowly
Holding the breath there for 4 3 2 1
And breathing out even slower
Breathing in slowly
Holding the breath there for 4 3 2 1
And breathing out even slower
We'll do this one more time
Breathing in slowly
Holding the breath there for 4 3 2 1
And breathing out even slower
Relaxing your body now
Taking awareness to how your body feels
Noticing your head and your face
Widening your eyebrows
Relaxing your jaws
Noticing your neck and shoulders
Releasing your shoulders
Letting them go
Moving down now to your chest
Noticing how your heart feels
Releasing any negative emotions you hold there
Noticing your arms and hands
Your fingers and the tips of your fingers
Observing how they feel
If there are any sensations present
If your hands feel cold or warm
And moving to your abdomen

Noticing how your belly feels
If it feels stiff
Or if there is any tightness in that area
Softening your belly
And relaxing all the internal organs in your abdomen
Moving to your hips
Noticing the places where your hips make contact with the surface you are on
Relaxing them
And noticing your legs now
Your thighs, your calves, ankles, your feet, your toes
Noticing how your legs feel today
If there are any sensations that you feel
Any pain, any tightness
Relaxing your legs
And taking your attention to your whole body
Scanning your body to see how it feels
Right from your head to your toes
And if there's any place that does not feel so good
Sending it healing energy
Breathing in and sending healing energy into that part
Breathing out releasing any tension, any pain, any stress
Breathing in and sending healing energy into that part
Breathing out releasing any tension, any pain, any stress

You feel light in your whole body
Really calm and relaxed
It is like you are covered in a blanket of deep relaxation
And from this space of comfort and ease
You listen to my voice and stay with my voice
The more you pay attention to my voice
The deeper is the relaxation that you experience

I want you to come on a journey with me
Imagine being in a garden
It's a warm day
The sun is smiling at you
And you can hear the chirping of the birds in the trees around you
The sound of a river flowing somewhere in the distance
You continue to walk towards the river by following its sound
You can hear the sound becoming louder and louder
And as you come close to the river
You see a bridge
Across the bridge you can see someone standing
Someone who has the kindest face
And the warmest smile
You feel that you want to meet them

And you start to walk towards the bridge
To reach the other end
And meet this person
As you get to the bridge
You are filled with anticipation
And you take the first step on the bridge
And the next and the next
Just a few more to go
5
4
3
2
1
You are now facing this person that you saw from across the bridge
And they smile at you
You feel so safe with them
You feel as if they understand you
That you can be yourself with them
They ask you if you would like to walk with them
And you say yes
So now you are walking with them on this other side of the beautiful garden
With lots of trees and lovely flowers and soft, green grass under your feet
You can smell the moist earth beneath you and you sometimes get a whiff from the flowers
You feel so relaxed
And so one with yourself in this moment
Take a few moments here to feel the safety, the comfort, and the ease

I would now like you to think of a very specific question to this person related to money and wealth in your life
The more specific it is, the better it would be
It could be anything like
How I need to be?
What I need to do?
In order to have what I want to have

Take a few moments to think of your question
This is the voice of your soul
Go ahead and ask whatever it is that you need to know
And once you do
Listen to what they have to say

(Pause)

As you find your answer
And say thank you
This person with you

They show you some pictures
You see yourself rich and wealthy
You are successful
You have all the things that you have desired
You look fit, healthy, and happy
You have a beautiful energy around you
Looking at those pictures
You realise that you are so happy in those moments
So light and joyful
So confident and self-assured
And then you see some other pictures
Of times when you were feeling lack
When you wanted a life that felt out of reach
So your energy was depleted
And there was a feeling of overwhelm
That you did not know what to do
You did not know how to change your situation
you could not find the means to earn more money
And seeing these other pictures starts to bring up all kinds of emotions in you
I would like you to connect to these emotions that are coming up
How are you feeling?
How does not having enough money make you feel?
What does it bring up in you?
Does it bring up guilt or helplessness?
Does it bring up sadness or frustration?
I want you to take a few moments to observe these emotions that are coming up

The person with you
They ask you to hand over all of those pictures in the most caring and non-judgmental way
The pictures that do not make you feel worthy and successful
As you hand over the pictures you feel all of these negative emotions leaving from you
As if they were tied to past memories
Now that you have given those pictures away
You suddenly find yourself free from your own judgments
You are free from your excuses and your fears and your doubts
You are free from the burden of expectations you put on yourself
There is new space in you, in your body, in your mind that you can fill with positive thoughts
Thoughts that will inspire you
Thoughts that make you feel good about yourself
And you know that you can start fresh whenever you choose to
In this space that is freed in your body and mind
You send these messages to yourself

I want you to repeat these messages to yourself silently in your mind
And I want you to accept them as your truth

I believe in myself
I believe in my ability to create a life of my dreams
I am the master of my destiny
I make the impossible possible
I am disciplined
I practice a morning ritual
I am focused
I achieve my goals
It is easy for my to see opportunities everywhere
It is easy for me to use those opportunities for creating the best outcomes
I am decisive
I am a leader
I live my life with courage
I am extremely successful
I attract money easily and effortlessly
I am full of energy
I am unstoppable
I constantly learn and grow
I think big
I am resourceful
I am creating the life of my dreams
I am rich
I am grateful for all in my life
I love my life

You find yourself walking towards the same bridge that you had crossed
And the person with you
They say it's time for them to go
But you can cross the bridge and meet them anytime that you wish you
They will always be there for you
To help and support you

As you take the first step on the bridge to come back to where you were
You feel joy and love and so much gratitude in your heart
You are walking on the bridge now
And with each step that you take
You feel more and more motivated
More and more determined
And you are filled with inspiration and enthusiasm and energy
The last few steps now before you reach the garden
1
2
3
4
5
As you step into the garden

You start to run along the path
And with each step you see signs of abundance everywhere
You see the abundance in nature
Everything is thriving, flourishing, and growing
It is as if you are rediscovering how wonderful life is
How much there is for everyone
Running with abandon
The wind at your back
And the sun upon your face
(Pause)

I want you now to bring your awareness back to your breath
Breathing in
And breathing out
And taking a few moments here to really soak in all that you have experienced

Breathing with me a few more times
Breathing in
And breathing out
Breathing in
And breathing out
As we come to the end of this meditation
I want you to know that you can come back to this practice whenever you wish to
Every time that you listen to it
It will help you overcome any obstacle that you are facing
It will help you reprogram your mind
So you can replace the thoughts and beliefs that limit you
With positive thoughts that will enable you to become your best self

And taking your awareness now to your body and the surface on which you rest
To the space around you
And to this moment in time
As you do so
Give thanks to yourself for making this effort for yourself
Wiggle your toes and fingers
And when you feel ready, open your eyes

Thank you for joining me in this practice
Have a wonderful day

8. Affirmations for attracting wealth and abundance into your life (20 minutes)

Welcome to this practice of affirmations for attracting wealth and abundance into your life

Energy flows to where attention goes
Our reality is a sum total of our thoughts
When we have doubts and fears
When we look at our lives from a place of lack
We make that as our truth and start manifesting that as our reality
In the same way, when we trust
When we can look at creation as kind, sustainable, nurturing
When we can put our faith in the universe for always supporting us, guiding us
Those take shape into becoming our reality
Affirmations help us to replace our negative thoughts with positive ones
They help us retrain our minds to make a fresh start
To begin
Find a comfortable place to sit or lie down
Make sure you are warm
And that your body is open
Your arms uncrossed
Taking attention to the breath
Observing your breath as you breathe in and breathe out
And when you feel settled
Deepening your breath a bit
Breathing in slowly
Holding the breath there for just a moment or two
And breathing out even slower
Breathing in slowly
Holding the breath there for a moment or two
And breathing out even slower
We'll do this one more time
Breathing in slowly
Holding the breath there for a moment or two
And breathing out even slower
Relaxing your body now
Taking awareness to how your body feels
Widening your eyebrows
Relaxing your jaws
Releasing your shoulders
Letting them go
Moving down now to your chest
Noticing how your heart feels
Releasing any negative emotions you hold there
And moving to your abdomen
Noticing how your belly feels

If it feels stiff
Or if there is any tightness in that area
Softening your belly
And relaxing all the internal organs in your abdomen
And if there's any place that does not feel so good
Sending it healing energy
Breathing in and sending healing energy into that part
Breathing out releasing any tension, any pain, any stress
Breathing in and sending healing energy into that part
Breathing out releasing any tension, any pain, any stress

As I say these words
Connect with their energy
And imagine every word you say as if it were coming to life in front of you

Today I choose abundance
I am aligned with the energy of abundance
The essence of my true nature is abundance
The abundance of the universe is flowing into my life
Abundance flows easily and effortlessly into my life
Abundance is my birthright
Freedom is my birthright
Abundance is freedom

Today I choose money
New avenues of money are opening up for me
The universe is opening new doors for me to make money
I release all judgments around money
I am worthy of making money from different sources
Unexpected opportunities are coming my way to make money
Money flows into my life easily and effortlessly
I know there is an unlimited supply of money in the world

There is a constant flow of money
Today I choose this flow
I am open to receiving all the money life offers me
I open to the flow of money to meet all my needs and wants
I am a magnet for money
Money is a blessing that I choose
Money comes back to me time and time again
New opportunities of making money present themselves to me every day

Today I embrace new avenues of extra income
I expand my definition of abundance
Abundance is flowing into my life in expected and unexpected ways
I am willing to receive new avenues of abundance

I open myself to allow more possibilities and more opportunities into my life
I welcome the abundance of the universe into my life
I open myself to more flow and to more forms of wealth
I welcome unlimited sources of abundance into my life

Today I choose faith
I have complete faith in my life to be full of wealth
Money is the least of my worries
My bank account is abundant
Money is flowing easily into my bank account
With the extra money, I help others and myself
With the extra money, I create a beautiful life for myself
I enjoy buying beautiful things for myself and others
There is always enough money
I like my life

Today I choose flow
I know this flow is abundance
My nature is flow
My soul is flow
I know money is flowing
There is money and more money in my life every day
I am exceeding my expectations with the money coming into my life
I am one with this flow
I know money is a great blessing
My soul is abundance
Abundance is my nature

Today I activate my inner potential
I have so much inner potential within me
People trust me for my abilities and skills
There are no limits to my potential
I do my best at every task that I undertake
I am living to my fullest potential
My true potential is manifesting in the form of more money into my life
I explore limitless possibilities
I am open to opportunities that deepen my skills, talents, and abilities
I easily attract all the money I want in my life
I have many skills, qualities, and traits within me that attract abundance
I follow my heart
I am successful
I grow and I flourish

I am bright and talented
I am strong and courageous
I am generous and resourceful

I am creative and passionate
I am knowledgeable and focused
I am visionary and intuitive
I am abundant
Bringing your awareness back to the sounds around you, to your breath, and to your body
Gently moving your toes and fingers
And when you feel ready
Slowly opening your eyes

9. Practice to develop self-worth in order to feel deserving of Wealth and Abundance (20 minutes)

Manifesting wealth and abundance into our lives starts from a strong sense of self-worth
This practice is meant to do just that
To cultivate in you a deep and abiding sense of self-worth

Let's settle down somewhere quiet and comfortable
If you feel like lying down, make sure you are warm and cozy
Or you could even sit on a cushion or on a chair
Wiggle all the parts of your body that want to move
And then when you feel ready
Softly close your eyes
You already feel a bit calm and relaxed
The first thing we'll do is make friends with our breath
We'll notice a few things about the breath
How does it come inside
Where does it go
And how does it leave
Watch your breath
Isn't it amazing how your breath always knows what to do
How to come in
Where to go
How to leave
Let's see if we can make the breath longer
So take a deep breath in through the nose
Watch it go into your belly
And let it out slowly through the nose
One more time
Deep breath in through the nose
Fill up your belly
Slow breath out through the nose
Good

We are now ready to go on a little adventure
We'll take a walk inside a beautiful forest
The forest is waking up to a new day
There are animals and flowers and plants and trees
You can see exotic colors all around you
The warm rays of the sun are falling on your face
As you walk, you can feel the soft carpet of the moss under your feet
You can hear the sounds of birds
And all of this lovely wildlife
Is sending loving and kind energy in to you

You feel deeply connected to the earth
A part of the wonderful universe
All you see around you is abundance
And the thriving of life in its many forms
You are amazed at how rich nature is
While walking through the forest
You hear the sound of a waterfall
And you make your way towards it
When you reach there
You are delighted by how beautiful everything looks
You make some space near the stream and sit there
Feeling safe and protected
While you sit there
A beautiful golden colored fish comes close to you
You follow it around with your gaze
And you realize that it is talking to you
It asks you to follow it inside the stream
And within a few steps you are inside the water
As you begin to float on your back
You feel completely relaxed
Free from any worries or concerns
The fish starts talking to you
It says that we are afraid of not being enough
We are afraid of not having enough
We don't feel strong or capable to achieve our dreams
We fear
We hold this fear in our body
All of these negative thoughts blocking us from being true to ourselves
All our past memories holding us back from claiming our glorious future
We forget that we are born out of divinity
We forget that we are living this life for a reason
The hurts of our past experiences
We use them as our shields
To protect ourselves from being hurt again
So we use the negative words that were spoken against us
Or the disappointments that we experienced
As our armor
We create our identities that tell us we are not good enough
We are not sufficient
We lack
We are not worthy

Over time
It becomes difficult to even imagine that wonderful things can happen to us
We find it difficult to even paint in our minds a picture of wealth and richness
And believe in our self-worth

Change the narrative around our self-identity
The fish asks you to release the old
Let it sink down from your body into the earth
Letting all of those judgments about yourself
Leave you from your conscious and unconscious self

You feel so light
In this lightness
Feel the golden light that is radiating from the fish
And breathe it in
This gentle and loving light
Soak it in
This is divine energy
It encompasses you
Travels though your body
And fills you with clean and positive energy
And you release
You release all the pain that is there in your heart
You release your disappointments
You release the suffering
The feeling of being unseen, unheard, unloved
The feeling of not having enough money
You release the feeling of being insufficient
Your bank account being insufficient
For feeling that good things were meant for other people
For people who were more fortunate
Take a deep breath in
And as you breathe out
Release all of these feelings of lack that you are holding

And one more time
As you breathe in
I would like you to feel magnificent
Feel that you are shining
That this golden light is coming from inside of you
That you are the core
You are the earth and the sky and the oceans
You are a paradise
You are the light that brings joy
You are here to share this light with others
You are wealth
You are abundance
You claim this for yourself
You are a celebration of this universe
All your dreams are real
All your dreams are worthy

You are the gift
You are prosperity
You are happiness
You are shining
Shining freely
You are love

You stay here in this feeling for a few moments
Before you realize that it is time to go
You slowly rise up and come out of that stream
You say thank you to the beautiful fish
And make your way back to the here and now

Connecting to your breath one more time
The natural rhythm of your breath
Breathing in
And breathing out
Breathing in
And breathing out
And let gratitude for this healing light from the universe fill your body, heart, and mind
Taking a moment to be in this light
Holding it inside you
Breathing in this light
Breathing it all in
And holding it there
And as you exhale
Releasing everything that does not serve you
Letting all of it go

(Pause)

Bringing awareness back to the body
Notice the parts of the body that make contact with the surface you are on
Wiggling the toes and fingers and finding movement in your body
And when you feel ready
Gently open your eyes

May the light be with you

10. Quick Practice to manifest abundance now (15 minutes)

Welcome to this quick meditation for manifesting abundance
Let us begin by setting an intention
A powerful intention to manifest abundance in our lives
To manifest the money that we desire
To manifest the success and life that we dream of
And to make it real
To make it come alive in our reality

To prepare ourselves for this meditation
We can come into a comfortable seated position
With the back straight and self-supported
Legs either crossed or feet placed firmly on the floor
Or we can do this lying down on the back
Relaxed and comfortable
If it feels ok, allowing the eyes to close
And now watching the breath
Watching the miracle of our breath
How it goes in and out effortlessly
Observing the rhythm of our breath

Noticing our body
With each in breath sending love to the body
With each out breath relaxing the body
With each in breath sending gratitude to the body
With each out breath relaxing the body
With each in breath sending healing energy to the body
With each out breath relaxing the body

And now that you are present here with your whole being
I invite you to think of what abundance means to you?
What does being rich look like?
How would you like abundance to manifest in your life?
Think of the wealth that you would like
Think of how much money would you like to be there in your bank account
Think of what being successful would look like?
Think of all the things you would like in your life
Or anything else that would make you feel that you have made it
That you are prosperous and abundant
That you are safe and secure

And now I would like you to think about the negative beliefs that you hold about being abundant
The beliefs that stop you from being courageous
That stop you from being honest to even express what you want

Think about all the judgments you hold around abundance
Think about your fears
Think about your insecurities
About your negative beliefs and associations
How do you feel about people who are rich?
How do you view them?
Do they come across as evil?
Does money come across as evil?
Are there any judgments that you hold about being rich?

I want you to invite all your judgments, all your negative beliefs to appear before you right now
Take you time and let all of them appear
And now imagine a large pit of fire ahead of you
I would like you to through these judgments and all of these negative beliefs that are holding you back
Into this fire
One at a time
Burn all the negativity
Burn every judgment
Burn every limiting belief that does not serve your best interest
Take all the time that you need
There is no rush
Watch as your body and mind clear up and create new space

And in this new space in your body and mind
I would like you to fill it up with positivity and courage
With the belief that you are worthy
I want you to think about everything that you are grateful for
All the abundance that you already have in your life
All the things and the resources
And also all the people you are grateful for
For what they bring to your life
For how they help you
Let your heart fill up with gratitude, love, and appreciation

Keeping this feeling of gratitude alive in your heart
I want you to again imagine everything that you wish to manifest in your life
All the money, the wealth, and the things
Everything that would make you feel abundant
And this time when you imagine
Bring up your courage
Not holding yourself back
Not thinking anything is too much
Feel the freedom, the joy, and the enthusiasm rising up inside of you
And feel that you are worthy
You are worthy of receiving abundance
You deserve to be abundant and to feel abundant

And now you are ready to receive
You are open to the gifts from the universe
You are worthy

I want you to repeat these words silently in your mind or out loud three times
I have faith in myself
I have faith in myself
I have faith in myself
I have faith in the universe
I have faith in the universe
I have faith in the universe
Everything that I desire comes to me
Everything that I desire comes to me
Everything that I desire comes to me
The universe takes care of me
The universe takes care of me
The universe takes care of me
I already have inside of me all that I need
I already have inside of me all that I need
I already have inside of me all that I need
I am complete
I am complete
I am complete
I am enough
I am enough
I am enough
I am worthy
I am worthy
I am worthy

I want you now to reconnect to your breath
Breathing in
And breathing out
Breathing in
And breathing out
Breathing in
And breathing out
Bring your awareness back to your body
And gently wiggle your fingers and toes
When you feel ready, open your eyes
Thanks for joining me today

11. Practice for Healing your Relationship with Money (45 minutes)

I welcome you today to this guided journey of healing your relationship with money
Money is one of the things that's so integral to our existence
Our relationship with money starts developing at a very early age and is influenced over the years by factors like our culture, our experiences, and our emotions
And there are phases in our lives when money becomes more than just a means to survive
It sometimes becomes our refuge and sometimes our enemy
This journey that we take today will help us alter the programming of our minds to heal this relationship that we have developed with money and make it beautiful and fulfilling

During this practice, which lasts for about 30 minutes or so
If at any time you feel that you feel overwhelmed and would like to pause, please feel free to do so
You can always come back to this recording when you feel more ready

So to begin I invite you to come into a comfortable position
You could lie down on your back with your arms resting by your side
Or if it feels better, you could be seated with your back supported
Make sure you are warm and that your body is open, arms uncrossed
And once you feel settled here
Allow your eyes to gently close
Taking your awareness to your breath
Observing the breath coming in and going out
Simply noticing how it feels
The sensation of breathing in, the breath coming in through your nostrils
Making contact with your body
And how it fills up your belly
When you breathe out, the sensation of the breath leaving from your nostrils
Emptying you out
And notice the difference in temperature of the in breath and the out breath
Sensing all of it
Following the complete cycle of your breath
And notice how you feel a deep wave of relaxation washing over you
From your head to your toe
As you breathe in and breathe out
Finding yourself more and more relaxed
More and more calm and peaceful
Staying with your breath
Breathing in
And breathing out
Relaxing further with this breath
Breathing in
And breathing out

I want you to imagine yourself on the top of a staircase

A beautiful staircase with 10 steps
And each time that you exhale
You take one step down this staircase
And with each step that you take down the staircase
You allow your body and your mind to become more and more relaxed
So taking in a nice deep breath
And 10
Exhale
You notice your shoulders
You release all the burdens that you have been carrying on your shoulders
Letting all of them go
And feeling light now
Taking in a nice deep breath
And 9
Exhale
You notice your jaws
You release the tension that you hold in your jaws
All the anger, all the stress
Unclenching your jaws and breaking into something like the beginning of a smile
Taking a nice deep breath in
And 8
Exhale
You notice your belly
You release any negativity, any stress, any emotions that you were holding here
You release all of those from your belly
Taking in another nice deep breath
And 7
Exhale
You notice your chest area, you notice your heart
And you release any grief that you hold there
Any difficult emotions
Letting them all go
Once again, taking a nice deep breath in
And 6
Exhale
You notice your mind
And any thoughts that are there, any worries, any tensions
You surrender them, you surrender them to this moment
Freeing yourself
Taking a nice deep breath in
And 5
Exhale
You notice your whole body
You notice how light it feels
Like you could fly
Without a worry in the world

Just being yourself
Taking a nice deep breath in
And 4
Exhale
You sink deeper and deeper into this state of relaxation
This state where you are here only with your breath
And with the sound of my voice
Once again, taking a nice deep breath in
And 3
Exhale
You surrender yourself to this moment
Becoming one with the moment
Feeling safe here, feeling protected
Taking in a nice deep breath
And 2
Exhale
You allow my voice to take over everything else
You allow these words to go deep inside your brain so you can restore your true self
One more time, taking in a nice deep breath
And 1
Exhale
You are here now
You are here with yourself
Your higher self
Your true nature

All you need to do now is stay with my voice as you begin to deeply absorb these messages

Allow yourself now to travel with my voice
And in your mind's eye, visualize yourself walking along a beach
The sand feels soft under your feet
You can feel the warmth of the sun on you
You can hear the sound of waves
You can see the waves as you walk
You see them rise and fall
You see them come up towards you and then go back again
This beach is the beach of abundance
It is the representation of all that you need to rich, wealthy, and abundant

Often times the only thing that is holding us back is how we talk to ourselves about money
And the beliefs that we hold about being rich
As you walk on this beach
I would like you to trust that you are supported and protected in this journey
That you are already abundant
And that you have everything inside of you that you have ever wanted
With this belief in you

Take a step forward
As your foot makes contact with the soft, wet sand and leaves a footprint
Imagine that footprint to be a judgment that you have been holding about money
And that has been limiting you
Stopping you from manifesting money into your life
Perhaps you can relate with these words
Money is evil
The rich are bad people
Money is what the more fortunate have
Money is for others
I don't deserve to be rich
I don't have it in me to be rich
It is not right to be rich when there are poor people
If I become rich, there will be others who become poor
With each step that you take
You leave behind a belief
Watch them disappear as the waves wash over them
Merging into the vastness of the ocean
Leaving behind no trace
All of these beliefs disappearing from your conscious and unconscious mind
And creating a new lightness in you
You becoming free
You shedding off that baggage
That extra weight that you have been carrying

There is new space in your body and in your mind
The space that was previously occupied with judgments and negative beliefs
As the rays of the sun shine upon you
You feel its light
You feel its warmth
And you feel its energy
You feel the touch of the breeze on your skin
You feel the touch of salt as you breathe in the air
You smell the salt of the ocean
You listen to all of these different sounds
The birds and the waves
Almost like an orchestra
And you see all the different colors
The blues and the greys and the silver and golden hues
As you feel more and more relaxed
You feel like lying down on the beach
And as you lie down
You find yourself relaxing even further
We will now replace these old beliefs with positive affirmations
You can either say these words out loud or repeat them silently in your mind, whatever feels best to you today

They help your brain to rewire and develop new patterns of thinking
The trick is to believe in them
Allowing them to travel deep within all levels of your consciousness
So they become your truth

My potential income is unlimited
I deserve to be financially secure
I use my money for the greatest good
My financial situation is improving every day
I have many gifts to share and I share these gifts
The universe provides to me whatever I need
My actions create constant prosperity in my life
My family and I are financially secure
My life is opening itself to receiving the abundance of the universe
I am free from debt and liabilities
I am attracting new opportunities to make more money

I am surrounded by abundance
I have complete faith in my ability to make more and more money
Money is a constant in my life and I rejoice in that feeling
Whatever I spend comes back to me multiplied
I find money easily
Money finds me easily
I am ready to welcome more money into my life
I am tuned in to the frequency of money
I make good use of the money that comes to me
New sources of income constantly come into my life
I have more than enough money
I am at peace with money

Through my work I can tap into the infinite abundance in the universe for my own goals and desires
Unimaginable sources of income are opening in my life
I love creating value for myself and for others
Life has bestowed on me money
I am making more money than I ever have
I have gratitude for all that I have
Every day my life is attracting more and more money
I see the beauty and abundance in the universe and in everything around me
I release all my inhibitions about money
I use my blessings to create a positive change in the world
The inflow of money starts with an appreciation of all that I already have
I release all my resistance towards money
Money comes to me easily and effortlessly
I am grateful for the money that I have and that comes to me
I operate from a place of love and compassion

I welcome money in my life
There are many paths to abundance
I make choices in line with my highest good
I welcome good fortune in my life
What I focus on grows
I choose abundance
I choose joy
I choose love
I choose happiness
I choose wealth
I choose success
I choose money
I choose my dreams
My life is rich with opportunity
I am open to receive

Abundance is a natural flow of the universe
All of nature is abundant
All of nature is abundance
My nature is abundance
Abundance increases in my life manifolds
I am an abundance magnet
I am a great treasure house
There is more wealth within me than I could possibly know in one lifetime
I choose this abundance now in this lifetime
I take steps to allow more money in my life
I ma open to new avenues of money
Abundance finds different ways to make its way into my life
I enjoy receiving as much as I enjoy giving
I balance giving and receiving
I deserve money
I open my heart to money
Abundance is the way
I am wealthy in so many ways
All my goals point to great abundance
There are many different channels of abundance opening to me now

All good things await me
I gratefully accept the money and wealth the universe wishes to give to me
I attract my highest good
Doors open for me in ways I could never have expected
I give and receive generously
Life is a miracle
I am a miracle
I am the creator of my destiny
I attract miracles

I am always in the right place at the right time
Life supports me
Life supports my abundance
Life supports my success
Life is generous in so many ways
I am thankful for all the blessings I receive
As I receive the blessings they multiply within me
My soul is abundance
My nature is pure abundance

As you sit here letting these words sink in
You think about your soul's mission
The reason why you are doing what you are doing
There arises faith and confidence in you
That as long as you are true to your path
True to your soul's journey
The universe will protect and support you
I invite you to place a hand over your heart centre
And connect with the feeling of love
Love towards your purpose in this life
Towards your being
And with this love
Find courage in your heart
And patience
And the willingness and trust for life to unfold in the most wonderful and abundant manner
Allowing your life to take its course in a way to give you a sense of stability, safety, and security
Believing that irrespective of how much time it takes
It is there for you
It is worth every bit of it
It is worth all the effort

Allow yourself to feel gratitude
Let it fill your body and heart
Feel gratitude for the present moment
For all your experiences that have brought you to this moment
And for all the abundance in the universe that lies ahead for you
With this feeling deep inside of you
Allow yourself to come back to the here and now
Gently wiggling your toes and fingers
And when you feel ready
Opening your eyes

11. Law of Attraction practice for manifesting wealth and abundance (50 minutes)

Hello and welcome to this Law of Attraction practice to manifest wealth and abundance in your life
There are often these times we find ourselves drawn to the same thought
When we are feeling unsure about the future
Perhaps a bit anxious or angry
Or perhaps feeling frustrated or lonely
When we feel helpless with our situation regarding money
This meditation is what can soothe you and give you comfort
This practice is your friend
It will not only help you manifest more wealth and abundance into your life
It will also help you relax and ease your concerns about money
Through this practice you will learn to free yourself from the false comfort, the false friendship of negative thoughts that you use to protect yourself
It will help you reprogram your subconscious mind to make choices that support you to manifest your greatest good
And to become successful, abundant, and happy

To begin this practice
I invite you to take your most comfortable position
Either sitting or lying down
And as you settle into this space
Bring your awareness to your breath
Taking a nice deep breath in
And exhaling slowly and fully
Breathing in letting the breath fill you
Breathing out letting all of it go
If you haven't already
Allowing your eyes to close
And allowing your body to surrender
To relax and let go
If at any time thoughts come and distract you
Not fighting them
Not attaching to them
But simply acknowledging their presence
Watching them come and go
And bringing awareness back to the sound of my voice
And to your delicious breathing
Your breath soothing you and relaxing you
Simply being here and breathing
Breathing in
And breathing out
Breathing in

And breathing out

I want you now to imagine a place where you feel safe
It could be a place that you are familiar with or something that you can make up in your imagination
It could be indoors like a room
Or outdoors like a garden or beach or in the hills
And sense and visualize yourself in this place
Feeling safe and protected
Take a few moments to just soak in this feeling
Finding your sanctuary here, your refuge
And as you arrive here in this place with all your being
Imagine a healing white light from the universe
Shining over your body
Breathing in, allowing the healing light to enter you
And sending it to your head and your face
Relaxing all the muscles here
Softening these parts of your body
And as you breathe out
Releasing any pain here, any tension or stress, any judgments for your head and face
Healing them
Breathing in, allowing the healing light to enter you
And sending it to your neck and shoulders
Relaxing all the muscles here
Softening these parts of your body
And as you breathe out
Releasing any pain here, any tension or stress, any judgments for your neck and shoulders
Healing them
Breathing in, allowing this healing light to enter you
And sending it to your chest and torso
Relaxing all the muscles here
Softening these parts of your body
And as you breathe out
Releasing any pain here, any tension or stress, any judgments for your chest and torso
Healing them
Breathing in, allowing this healing light to enter you
And sending it to your back and your hips
Relaxing all the muscles here
Softening these parts of your body
And as you breathe out
Releasing any pain here, any tension or stress, any judgments for your back and hips
Healing them
Breathing in, allowing this healing light to enter you
And sending it to your arms and legs
Relaxing all the muscles here
Softening these parts of your body
And as you breathe out

Releasing any pain here, any tension or stress, any judgments for your arms and legs
Healing them
Breathing in, allowing this healing light to enter you
And sending it to your belly
Relaxing all the muscles here
Softening your belly
And as you breathe out
Releasing any pain here, any tension or stress, any judgments for your belly
Healing it
Healing the whole of your body
Notice how light you feel in your body
Like a heavy burden has been lifted off you
Feeling a sense of freedom and release

From this place of freedom and lightness
I want you to invite before you the energy of money, the energy of abundance that exists in the universe
Inviting it to sit across you
And I want you to talk to it
Like you would talk to someone you know deeply and intimately
In these words that follow
I want you to surrender your whole self
And just allow yourself to be with my voice
As you listen to these words, allow them to become real in front of you
Bringing them to life
Let's begin

I am open to things being easier in my life
I am open to witness the miracles of the universe
I trust that whatever is happening is happening for the highest good
I believe that the world is inherently abundant
There is enough abundance in the world for everyone
I trust that benefits that I cannot see are accumulating in my life
I have faith that this too shall pass

I trust in my ability to climb this mountain
My dreams are on their way to being fulfilled
New opportunities are coming to me
I have gratitude for these times as they are giving me a chance to reset
I attract situations that are for my highest good
I choose abundance for me and the people around me
Success is here, knocking on my door

I have the courage to overcome anything
I know this is a phase that is testing my faith
My faith is strong and unshakable
My determination is amazing. I have tremendous inner force

I have the courage to keep going
I am moving towards success and prosperity
I have what it takes to win in any situation

The universe works in mysterious way
Even if there are things I don't understand, I know that they are the best for me
I will always have enough for all my wants and needs
I trust the process. I trust how life unfolds
I am at peace with my life. I love my life
Each day, I add value to my life
Each day, I add abundance to my life
Each day, I wake up feeling positive about what likes ahead
Each night, I go to bed with gratitude in my heart
My circumstances are changing for the better
I receive whatever I ask for
I overcome setbacks with courage and grace
My life is rich in opportunities
Everything I do is leading me towards success

I choose to feel happy, content, and fulfilled
Every day I grow stronger and stronger
Every day my faith in my abilities strengthens
I remain focused on my goals
Success and money are coming into my life
Prosperity and wealth are coming into my life
Things are getting better and better

There is nothing that can stop me
No challenge is too big for me
Challenges bring out the best in me
Everything I deserve is coming my way
I deserve the best that life has to offer
I am in harmony with the energy of abundance
I am attracting new opportunities into my life everyday

The universe always has my back
My circumstances are changing in my favour
New and positive energy is entering my life
Whatever changes are happening, are happening for my best
Things are getting better and better
Everything is aligning for my highest good
Blessings are coming my way

I deserve the best that life has to offer
I can do anything I want to do. No challenge is too big for me
Something wonderful is going to happen in my life

I am about to experience the magic of this universe
All my dreams are manifesting in my reality
I am ready to convert everything to success
I am strong and determined
It is ok to pause and allow life to take its course
I am compassionate towards my own self
I love myself unconditionally
I allow myself time to rest and relax
I feel happy and calm and peaceful
I nourish my body mind and spirit everyday
I am capable of much more than I can ever imagine

My biggest priority right now is my well-being
Only when I take care of myself can I take care of others
My actions inspire everyone around me
I ask for help when I need it
I trust myself. I trust my life
There is immense value in my efforts
All my efforts create unimaginable benefits

My journey is unique and special
My journey is blessed by the universe
I have the ability to quiet my mind
I focus on the positive in my life
What I focus on grows, and I focus on prosperity
I am worthy of prosperity and wealth
I deserve money and new opportunities

I am learning new things every day
These times are a wonderful opportunity for me to grow in different ways
I feel resilient and strong. I feel bold and courageous
I am discovering my own strengths
I am discovering the generosity of nature. I am discovering the abundance in nature
I am part of this abundance
I am nourished by this abundance

I cherish and value the person I am
I can rise up from anything
I always live in the moment
I release any thoughts about the future
My present is everything and my biggest asset
I focus on making my present the best time
I go easy on myself. I love myself

I trust in divine timing
I know that nothing is permanent

I know that I always have a choice
I think positive thoughts. My thoughts create my reality
Everywhere I see there is abundance. This abundance magnifies in my life
Abundance and prosperity are coming my way
Money and wealth are coming my way
I invite miracles in my life
Success, money, and happiness come easily to me
I trust the timing of my life
I trust that everything that is happening is happening for my highest good
I am open to receiving financial blessings
I feel good about myself and my life
My income is increasing every month

I take care of all my needs
I wake up feeling positive and motivated
I go to bed grateful and calm
I am filled with a sense of achievement
My life has a purpose and I am achieving it
I am the best version of myself
My positive energy is attracting incredible benefits to my life

People trust me for my abilities and skills
I do my best at every task that I undertake
I am living to my fullest potential
My true potential is manifesting in the form of more money into my life
I easily attract all the money I want in my life
My potential income is unlimited
I use my money for the greatest good

I give my best in whatever I do
I am appreciated and valued for what I do
I make money doing things I love
I make more money than I can spend
Even when I am sleeping, the universe is working to bring more money into my life
Multiple channels have opened to send money into my life
My life is safe and secure

My savings are increasing rapidly
I am relaxed about money
I am enjoying the extra money in my life
I enjoy earning money
I enjoy spending money
I feel secure about money
I will always have enough money

I am receiving blessings from above

I am receiving financial abundance from above
Each day is a day full of new opportunities
Each day I receive seen and unseen benefits
Each day I receive seen and unseen blessings
New doors are opening in my life
New opportunities are coming my way

I am proud of myself and what I have accomplished
I have come a long way. I am riding this wave
I choose faith over everything else
I am the strongest person I know
Everything I need is within me
My goals and dreams are coming true
The wheels of fortune are turning in my favour

Abundance surrounds me every day
Today is rich with opportunities
Money flows freely and abundantly into my life
Resources flow freely and abundantly into my life
My new ideas always lead to prosperity and success
I am always taking action towards success
The positive advantage is always mine
I am grateful to the universe for everything it has provided me

The universe protects me. The universe cares for me
Abundance is unlimited. I live in abundance
I am financially safe and secure. I am always protected
Life loves me. I love life
I am being supported in my journey
I follow the signs of the universe
I am being led to the path of my highest good

There is nothing that I cannot achieve
Everything always goes well for me
Everything is taken care of
I have nothing to worry about
I am in perfect balance. I live in perfect harmony
I feel more secure everyday. I feel safer everyday
Everything around me is beautiful

All is well in my life. So be it.

Take a few moments here to let these thoughts deeply embed in your subconscious mind
Feeling held here
Feeling supported
Feel the protective energy of the universe shielding you

Transforming you
Helping you make your choice
And continue to breathe deeply
Breathing in
And breathing out
Staying with the cycle of your breath
Feel the energy of this new path that you have chosen
Feel how it wants to embrace you
This path of wholeness, this path of abundance and of joy and of freedom
Sense how grounded you feel here
How complete and fulfilled
And how grateful

Take a moment now to thank yourself for choosing to heal
For the effects of this practice to really embed in your subconscious mind, for the words of this practice to reprogram your subconscious mind
Gently remind yourself to listen to this recording every day for the next 21 days
With each passing day
You will become more and more familiar with your true self
It will reveal its beauty, its truth to you

As we now come to the end of this practice
Gently bring your awareness back to this time and space
Wiggling your toes and fingers
Giving yourself a light stretch
Opening your eyes if they feel ready
And stepping back into the world with love and kindness
Until next time

Law Of Attraction- Get Your Ex Back & Manifesting True Love: Manifestation Techniques, Guided Meditations, Hypnosis& Affirmations for Attracting Your Soul Mate / Twin Flame

By Spiritual Awakening Academy

Table of Contents

Intro

Love is a word that holds meaning differently from person to person. For some, love may mean a simple kiss on the cheek in the morning, for others, it means a massive gesture that shows intent, for some it is the simple phrase *I love you.* No matter the definition or the connotation, there are very few that don't feel love on some fronts be it little or grand.

It does not need to be springtime for us to feel as if love were somehow in the air like we have been programed to think. It seems like love is always present no matter what, everywhere and with everyone... well, besides for some of us that is. Those of us that are destined to be loveless or at least in our own hearts and minds be left that way.

Then, for those of us that are that was, we are forced to watch on as couples strut about the park together holding hands, and all of our friends have managed to meet "the one", their soulmate, or twin flame. It can get to the point where if you receive another wedding invitation in the mail you will lose your mind. If you have never been happy for the couple, sad for yourself, and mad about the lack of love in your life all at once, then you may never understand... but something tells me that on some small level, you do.

Why is this thing called love so messy and difficult?

And does it have to be messy and difficult at all?

That would seem like a cruel joke if it was, wouldn't it? To think that love has to be difficult, or that there is no way to obtain it without a struggle. So, what is everyone else doing that some of us are not? Maybe others are just "different", or "lucky"?

Can it be that easy?

The truth is no one is different than the next person... we are all gifted with the same capacity to receive the same gifts as the next Tom, Dick, or Harry. We are all composed of the same essence, which happens to be the very thing that we are looking for in another person or waiting on them to find it in us.

The main problem with that essence is that we are all given is, but we sometimes don't keep it on display for others to easily find.

A great example of this would be:

- Every woman on Earth for the rest of time is given a crystal rose and that is their "Love Essence."
- Every man on Earth for the rest of time is given a diamond plated Babe Ruth baseball card and that is their "Love Essence."
    - Over time, some of those men and woman have put their cards and roses on display for the world to see and they hold on tight to it. But they share it while keeping it in their presence.
        - This is the best way so that they can find true love, a twin flame, or survive breakups.
        - They always keep their gift while sharing it with others as they share theirs with you.
    - There are those that hide their gifts fearful that others might take it from them.
        - For these, it's hard to find their gift or love to see if it's even available or if they are an approachable match.

- There are those that after lending it out once or twice, or sharing it, they break it, so it won't work for them.
    - These are the ones who have gotten hurt by lending or sharing their gift and then got rid of it never to love again.
    - And even after that person decides to find love again, it takes a lot to mend the broken pieces.
- Then there are the ones that keep the gift behind bars, built walls, have put it away under lock and key.
    - They often don't ever allow love to come in, or rather don't let people chip at that wall for a long while.
    - And for those, if the wall has been chipped away at to the point of exposing the gift, then if they are hurt again, the wall only gets built stronger and higher than before.

Love is a fickle thing and to know in which of those categories you belong is important in order to discover how far you need to go in order to make yourself ready for love the first time or love again.

And as far as luck goes, there is no such thing either. How could there be when each one of us is constantly creating the universe around us?

To assume luck exists it would have to discount manifestation, and if you have come here, you have at least a working knowledge ow what manifestation is and or the way it has worked for others and how you wish it will work for you.

Putting to practice the principles in this book you will become one of the so-called "lucky" ones as well, living a love-filled life that you could not have ever predicted. With the Law of Attraction, there are not victims and victors so to say, as compared to a winning person and a losing person, we are all on the same playing field and the universe is an equal opportunity employer.

Ie: the gifts of a crystal rose and the diamond baseball card. We have all been given the gift of love, it is just up to us as to who gets to see it, how it's used, or if it is ever given or received.

And once you put to practice the Law of Attraction, you will be grateful for the love that you receive but at the same time, you will see how easy finding love really is, and that it was only you that was ever making it difficult to begin with.

As we seem to be the only worst enemies that we as humans have. Mankind is its own downfall, especially in the department of love.

But even with knowing this, life can still seem like a struggle. It is especially frustrating when we see others around us living it with relative ease- you know, the people who...

- Never seem to have a hard time with making money.
    - They are smart with their spending.
    - They know what they want in their lives.
    - They know how to save and invest in what they have money wise.
    - Or in some cases they have a rich parent or spouse which can make it easier on them financially.
- Never seem to struggle with making friends.
    - Always hanging with their groups of friends.
    - Never has to search for someone to talk to.
    - Always doing something with someone.
- Never have a hard time in the love department.

    - Always dating someone.
    - Always announcing the next step in their life with their loved one.
- Never seem to have a bad day.
    - Can go to work or school and come home, get work at home done, and seems to still have time.
    - They are the ones that seem to do it all right with little to no effort on their part.

Despite what social media portrays, these types of individuals are quite rare.
Social media is good at depicting people as having:

- Money.
    - Those who have inherited their rights.
    - Those who have fought for their earnings.
    - Those who have brought their selves up by their bootstraps.
- Good fashion sense.
    - These people always seem to walk out of their closet looking fabulous.
    - Those two always have the best manicure, the best hair, the best accessories.
    - Those who never struggle from wearing hand me downs or shopping at thrift stores.
- Expensive taste.
    - Those that only like the best.
    - Those that go to the most expensive restaurants, most expensive stores, and most expensive locations!
- Luxury items.
    - People who can only stay in the most expensive hotels.
    - Those who ride in limousines.
    - Those who take private jets.
- Someone always on their arm.
    - A spouse.
    - A fiancé.
    - A boyfriend or girlfriend.
    - Eye candy.
- Vacationing all the time.
    - Traveling the world.
    - Traveling the states.
    - Going wherever and whenever they want.
- New cars, new apartments, and new pets.
    - Those that seem to change their personal items like they change their underwear.
    - Those that gain new items without regard to cost.
- Everything and anything they want.
    - Those who purchase everything they want instead of everything they need and some of what they want.

Truth be told those are all materialistic and fabricated views of human existence. In today's society one might think they need all of the above in order to find love. Or two love themselves. Knowing that this belongs to the smallest fraction of humans in existence, will help ground you an order to enlightening you on what is real and what isn't in the realm of love.

The truth is that we all have had struggles in one or more areas of our lives at some point, and while in the thick of it, things can feel almost hopeless like we will never be able to obtain that thing we want- in this case, love. We begin to question ourselves and our worth.

We think thoughts such as:

- "Well, maybe love is just not in the cards for me."
    - We do everything but throw in the towel because deep down we know that there is hope if we could only find it and clench onto it.
- "Maybe I should have settled for my ex because obviously I am not getting any better."
    - People say this with total disregard to their past relationship with their ex. Not even considering the reasons they broke up in the first place.
    - Sometimes even forgetting abuse is and ill treatment.
- "I will never be like my best friend Kindra because I don't have enough _____."
    - Never compare yourself to someone else because you are not that person. Sure, you may have the same capacity and capability for love but remembering the categories from above and how we all handle the essence of love differently, you are your own person.
    - You can just about substitute the blank for anything, money, success, upbringing, and in between.

Can you think of an area in your life where you struggled but do not anymore? If so, something must have happened to allow things to flow more easily, almost like something just "clicked". Did you do it through sheer willpower and the ego, or was it granted to you by some outside force? More than likely, it was something that happened internally- a shift.

As you will discover in this book, love is in the cards for everyone- we are love, and love is everywhere and in everything. When we begin to not only understand this but to feel it and live it, we start to see our lives rearrange itself in remarkable ways.

Knowing that this is a possibility is a huge change in his step forward to how you previously thought about love. Knowing that you represent the essence of love as a whole, will break the chain towards loving yourself, loving others, and opening yourself to being loved by others.

Love is the highest vibration and therefore the highest truth. Vibration is something that the atmosphere sends back to you when being filtered with good deeds and honesty. It is the measure in which we understand truth and the vitality of something. It is also the scale on which we judge the caliber of our meditation in our higher state of consciousness.

When we tap into this frequency there are infinite possibilities available to us. It is the vibration that literally creates everything.

It created:

- You.
- Me.
- The Universe you, me, and the universe.
    - More simply put, it is the universe.
    - Oddly enough, it is also what we are spinning around in circles looking for.

To the intellect, this may sound like a bunch of “spiritual mumbo-jumbo”. But these concepts are beyond the intellect anyway. We are attempting to go past the mind, which has held us hostage for long enough with limiting belief, to create what might be hard for us to picture now.
Some of the greatest ways your mind can hold you hostage are:

- Not allowing you to open up to greater thinking.
- Giving you trouble with focusing on something wholly rather than bouncing around too many linear subjects.
- By not shutting down an allowing you to listen to that still small voice.
- And in so many other ways.

Any great spiritual teacher would tell you to try it out and see for yourself, to put these ideas to the test. This is how I and so many others started out, by putting aside what we think we know about the nature of reality to go out on a limb. It is not magic. You do not need to do anything special or secret to find the love you are looking for when you understand your true nature. And once this true nature is understood, the methods and teachings presented in this book will help you to yield all of your desired results.
It is simply a matter of taking the steps needed to reach your goal and applying them to your life. Continuing on with the views of your mind and heart and applying that to what you have already accomplished will help accelerate your true purpose and help you find the love that you deserve. Keep in mind that love comes in so many different forms.
Whether you are looking for a soulmate or wondering if your twin flame is out there, or you have a crush on somebody at work, want an ex-back, or just want to feel and experience love in your life- this book has something for you in it.

Love

What is love? Is it having someone we care for and can count on? A person who we enjoy spending time with and hopefully are attracted to? These are certainly the things that love makes us think and feel, but they are not the thing itself.

Just as looking at a picture of a sofa is a sofa but is not the thing itself. You may not be able to sit on a picture of a sofa, you may not be able to decorate it, you may not be able to lay on it, but it is what it is until it isn't! Knowing reality versus what you feel is reality is very important when learning how to manifest your destiny in the love department.

Love is mystical. It is one of those things that when someone mentions the word, we typically know what they are talking about. But if we are truthful about it, it is not the easiest to describe. Often, people report the way that love made them feel or how it made them view life...

- The grass was greener.
    - In truth the grass is always the same shade of green as it was before.
    - It's honestly the weather and seasons that change the shade, not love.
- The air was crisper.
    - The air itself changes much like the shade of grass. Love itself cannot change the air.
    - The air also changes its crispness as it gets cooler outside. Love has nothing to do with the temperature drop or it is feeling crisp outside.
- The sun was brighter.
    - The sun holds the same brightness regardless of emotion.
    - It is possible that up until the point of love, you may not have noticed the brightness of the sun, but it has always been that way. Love did not change it; it may have awoken your senses a little better.
- And everything was happy and joyous.
    - Happiness and joyfulness have always been there, it just changed how you viewed those things.

When conducting an experiment on younger people, considering how they felt while being in love, it always differed according to age, gender, in location.

When in love, they felt free, and they felt young. These are the chemical reactions produced by love, and again, not love itself.

Then again, it's all about knowing. Knowing where love can be found and where the best place to look for it is.

Love is beyond the intellect and words alone. Sure, it can be felt, and many have done such a wonderful job of describing the feeling- namely poets, musicians, and artists. Love is not a concept that lives upstairs in our heads, it is down here in our hearts. We can ponder love all day, but this does us little good in finding it. The only way to really get in there to discover it is with our Being, and that is exactly what the Law of Attraction teaches us to do.

Why Love is so Elusive

When something is Elusive, it means that it is difficult to find, catch, or achieve. Meaning that love can seem to be all those things all wrapped up into one, when in fact it just simply does not have to be that hard in the first place.

We are all looking for love in one way or another, whether we are aware of it or not. It makes it even more difficult that love is not something that we can simply point to and say, "look, there is love over there and this is how you go about getting it".

This has been the problem of man for many years period this isn't anything new, however through the law of attraction, it can be assimilated into something new. However, this generation has a hard time accepting that.

Instead, our cultures have done terrible jobs at instructing us on how to go about finding it. And by it we mean love. We are left with poor directions by well-meaning but unhappy people who tell us to:

- You must get the job.
  - While it is important for everyone to work, have a job, some sort of career, and no what's important for the future, it isn't important to strive for the best especially when you're not qualified for such.
  - While climbing the latter success without knowing what you're doing, will only give you a wobbly ladder at the top.
  - Getting a job within the skill set you have is important and should pay off in a lucrative way in the end.
  - Remember it isn't what you do that impresses people and gets their attention, it is who you are and how you carry yourself.
- You need the material possessions.
  - A huge common misconception is that it takes material possessions to find the love of your life.
  - You can't find love in romance without the best house, car, possessions, but that simply isn't true.
- You should buy all of the things you want.
  - Within reason, buying things that you want versus buying things that you want when you can't afford it, are two different things.
  - Remembering the necessities come first for you, your spouse, your family members, and then whatever is left is deemed available for extra spinach is the best chance you have at becoming successful and having a lot of what you want.
  - Remembering that it doesn't take this to find love is also important.
- You need to impress the right people.
  - Feeling like you need to know influential people in order to get the attention of the right kind of people or the people you desire is a common conception, but the misconception is that this is I required action before finding the right person.
  - Remembering that it doesn't take people to get people to notice you is important.

In the end if you have accomplished all those things then you have succeeded and then we will be worthy of love. but that's not how it works either.

I think that at this point that it is safe to say people no longer buy into this lie. They never really did. And in all honesty, it was a lie that made us feel like people did buy into it in the first place. Even when they weren't buying into the process, we were led to believe they were which in turn has always been a lie. We have watched the older people around us who have taught us these lessons grow unhappy and unable to love. More importantly, we have tried it out ourselves, all our lives, and it has not yet worked. Remembering that with new generations and all, knew lessons and knew tradition should be brought forth teaching future generations that we can all go out with a bang, love and happiness for all.

There are many reasons why love can be so elusive though, but it all comes back to our ability to connect with it internally. Because we have a hard time remembering our true nature, which is love itself, so of course it becomes obscured because who we really are is obscured.

Some things that create human obscurity is:

- The supermodel syndrome.
    - The misconception that supermodels have to be a size 2.
    - The misconception that supermodels are one gender.
    - The misconception that a plus size supermodel starts at the size 14 rather than the size 20.
    - The misconception or obscurity that a supermodel must be a certain age.
    - The misconception that supermodels are that beauty always rather than being touched up digitally.
- Hotter by the millions.
    - This is the obscure misconception that it takes money to be beautiful.
    - You must have this procedure, or that procedure in order to look the best way you're supposed to look.
- It takes two.
    - You need a best friend to be happy.
        - While it is important to have friends and having best friends helps increase endorphins and make your life more fun, it isn't a necessity for survival.
    - You must have a spouse, a boyfriend, girlfriend, significant other.
- Friends with benefits.
    - It's OK to stay friends with someone that you're attracted to and have benefits on the side.
    - Having friends with benefits helps to hold your cravings over in the love department until somebody more suited comes along.
- The friend zone.
    - Keeping someone in the friendzone makes them happy that you are their friend, even when they want to be more.
    - Keeping someone in the friendzone means that they're there should you decide you want more.
    - The misconception that the friendzone is a good place to be.
- The five-year plan.
    - Including relationships in your five-year plan.
    - Including milestones for love in your five-year plan.

            - Having milestones and plans for your future is important, stressing yourself out to make sure that your plans happen in the order you hope they do or have written them down to do is absurd.
- Bucket lists.
    - Deciding you will go someplace before you die.
    - Deciding you will meet someone before you die.
    - Deciding you will achieve something before you die.
        - Just like having a five-year plan, this is important, a fun part of your life, but not necessary. Keeping to the plan so straightforward sometimes becomes stressful to the point that you miss out on love because you're not looking in the right places or allowing yourself to open up.

Understanding that even if things are obscure, it doesn't make them false or a lie. It is just up to the beholder as how obscure those things are. Bringing it into the light, makes it a little more relatable and easier to see by the people who are looking on. Remembering that while the greater portion of these is deemed necessary towards hopes and dreams for the future, they are great misconceptions as well. To make matters worse, in western society we are taught a materialistic worldview that says all we can see is all that there is. Or, if we are taught anything spiritual it has to do with an outside God who is separate from us who might reward us with something if we are good. This has left many of you thinking that you are not "good", and it is a lie.

The ones who have been the most successful with the Law of Attraction came to the point where they started to question this handed-down worldview. They had a strong intuitive feeling that there was something more than what meets the eyes, that there was something bigger than us and who we think we are.

Hanging on to the elusive side of love can sometimes drive people crazy. Remembering that there is a whole other side to it is important in making sure that you end up with or without who you are meant to be with. Sometimes we miss opportunities because our eyes are closed or were blinded too solid evidence that surrounds us.

Exclusivity can sometimes be our greatest downfall.

We are Love

Yes, it is true, we are love and love is love. It's hard to think about the fact that you yourself is love. Not the word love, but the feeling, emotion, and action of love.

Fewer have realized themselves to be love, that love is not something they earn or find outside in the world, but rather something they generate from within themselves.

Some examples of this would be:

- kindness.
    - When someone is kind, we only assumed that the kindness has been taught to them or that it has been bestowed upon them and has rubbed off, but we all hold the capacity to be kind.
- Well-being.
    - Showing concern for the well-being of others and the well-being of yourself is a huge step towards realizing that you yourself have the capacity inside you to generate interest for the well-being of others.
- Positivity.

- We all have the capacity for positivity though several people hide that or lose it at a young age.
- Fondness.
    - You are fondness. You are the Fonda feelings you feel in someone else and yourself. You yourself generate that emotion therefore creating fondness comes from you.
- Light intimacy.
    - This is not necessarily intimacy in the way you might think, it is intimacy as in showing affection through hugging, kissing, cuddling, or anything in between.
    - This does not have to be someone you are romantically involved with period it can be a family member, friend, or distant loved one.

It's not easy to realize that you have this capacity, but when you do it makes things so much easier. These people quite often have an easy time attracting love, since they always seem to be in love with something. They love themselves because they can recognize love's source which lies within. And is there anything more attractive than a person who genuinely loves themselves without putting on an act? This is true confidence.

Even more rare are the individuals who have concluded that "all is love." that love is the very thread that holds together the entire universe- present in everyone and everything and only obscured by our thinking. This used to be reserved for saints, sages, and mystics. Now, as more and more people awaken, it subsequently becomes easier for others too, and the realization that "all is love" is more common amongst even average folks.

But if this is so, if love is so easily accessible, then why has it become so difficult to find currently? Or how come the one we love does not love us back if they are made of the same love we are and connected to us?

This was somewhat discussed in the chapter above. The introduction chapters. It's more Simply put that those who are given the capacity of love, which is everyone, the divides how they take care of that capacity or bestow that capacity which makes it's even harder to decide who does what with their love. Breaking it down even further, you might consider even after bestowing love on someone or getting love bestowed on you, how that could even further be broken down. So, in the reference of the women getting the crystal Roseanne the men getting the diamond plated Babe Ruth baseball card and calling that the essence of love, you might also consider these as further rankings of how people view love and what they do while trying to find it.

- Casual dating.
    - This is the group of people that date casually, often resulting in multiple dates with multiple partners.
    - This is the person who is either looking for the one and sampling as they go, or for those who require the companionship but do not want the commitment.
- One night stand.
    - These are the people that require some sort of companionship most likely in an intimate way, usually for one night.
    - This could be a sexual act of love or lust for one or multiple nights as needed.
- Long term commitment.
    - This is the relationship that is singular and is planned to last a long time.
    - In this case there are not multiple partners nor the concept of dating around.
    - By now you are not dating as much as existing together.

- By now the word love has most likely been used and reciprocated.
- Dating around.
  - Similar to casual dating or one-night stands, this is the group of people who date multiple individuals.
  - This could also mean that one individual date several individuals at once trying to find who they want that long term relationship with if any.
- Friends with benefits continues.
  - As talked about before in the friends with benefits category, it's not always a good thing but can be depending on the friends and the level of love that that person has.
  - This is the relationship that is on again off again and has no strings attached though can become emotional should the friendship become rocky or develop into something more.
- Dating oneself.
  - This isn't necessarily how one might think it is. Dating oneself is basically taking yourself out, showing self-care, showing self-love, and not involving a second or third party.
- Not dating.
  - This is simply the individual or individuals that refuse to date due to commitment issues, being too busy, or the fear of striking out.
  - Sometimes this could be because they have never had a relationship before, and it scares them.
  - Other times this could be due to the fact that a previous relationship went wrong. Either it had been long term and was broke off for some reason or no long-term relationship had stuck and made the person feel less desirable.
- Not committing.
  - This is the relationship that has a loving companion but does not want to commit to a lasting relationship or even marriage.
  - Just because this relationship is not a committing one does not mean that it won't turn into that.
  - It is important that this is reciprocated an understood by both parties that they are not willing to commit at this time so that no one is led on.
- Proposal.
  - This is a marriage proposal, arrangement proposal, or proposal to add another aspect into the relationship such as a child, family, home, or living arrangements.
  - This is the next step in the relationship as discussed between both parties and executed to create a new beginning for the relationship.
- A promise.
  - This is a promise to continue on with the relationship to make it long term period it also includes promises to abstain from sexual activity, a promise to be faithful, a promise to continue until a proposal can be made.
  - This means that this relationship is not in a rush to create a proposal but is also beyond a simple long-term relationship.
- Marriage.

    - This is the activity after a proposal of marriage. It is often binding in a relationship unless an old or divorce happens later on down the road.
    - It is vital that one goes into this type of relationship without thoughts of divorce, or annulment.
- A long-term marriage.
    - This is a successful marriage that has lasted multiple years. In today's society, it is difficult for young people's marriage to last longer than six years, once you are past the 10-year mark, it is definitely considered a long-term marriage.
- After death.
    - This does not mean that you will be in a relationship after death, it means that if your spouse or someone you loved dies, you will abstain from continuing a relationship or having a relationship with anyone until you are emotionally ready.
    - Saying goodbye to someone that you love is hard enough without rushing into another relationship shortly after. It looks bad on you sometimes depending on the person and it feels bad as well.
    - There is one important thing to remember though, just because that person passed away and that you love them does not mean that you were cheating on them should you decide to move on. They love you and would want this to happen.

And in the long run although I know this seems a little difficult, finding which category you belong and how it applies to you is important period knowing what you want ahead of time and being in communication with any person or persons that a relationship might arise with is a turning point that will make any relationship or aspect of love blossom. Some people find it entirely too difficult to continue dating around or looking for a relationship, they sit back and hope it comes to them instead.

I agree that it should not be so difficult. Unfortunately, we have been programmed to think that it is, that love is always out of reach for some reason. What we do with the Law of Attraction, and what we will do throughout this book, is reprogram ourselves to accept this love. We will knock down the blockages that have kept the flow of love damned up, as we sit back and watch it rush in like it is naturally supposed to do.

What are some of these blockages? Well, let us find out right now.

The typical person who is reading this book will have certain negative thoughts and energetic blockages within their bodies when they think about love. What are these thoughts that hold you back from experiencing love within? Those are your limiting beliefs or just beliefs in general. It is literally what is creating your experience right now.

Once we can pinpoint these beliefs, why do we even attempt to question them? Ultimately, if we examine them, we are doing so with the same mind that believes these things. It turns into a mental wrestling match that is tough to win. Instead, I recommend throwing them out altogether. Sure, they will pop up in your thoughts, but let us attempt to pay them no mind. Let us go right to the source, right to our true nature, right to love.

Then there is the concept that we ourselves is the epitome of love. Considering that love is love and love is also an all-encompassing concept, it becomes a tad more difficult to learn more about how you should further love yourself and use that to guide your future relationships and less how bad we feel that love hasn't found us yet.

Instead of knowing ourselves as pure love, we are taught that we are what we think we are, and worse yet, what others think we are. Mental constructs such as:

- I am too skinny.
  - Think first about what defines body weight and type and what skinny means.
  - Are you skinny and healthy, are you skinny and unhealthy?
  - Do you think you're too skinny because of your own mind and thoughts or do you think you are too skinny because that's what society tells you?
- I am too fat.
  - The same thing happens with the concept of being too fat. Are you overweight to the point you are unhealthy or are you healthy and just fluffy?
  - Who told you your fat?
  - Did that person mean it in a mean way or were they being polite and concerned?
  - Then again, do you call those who are bigger than you, fat? Doesn't it hurt them the same?
- I am beautiful.
  - It's a lovely concept to think that you are beautiful and feel you are as well. Although it is a horrifying concept to know that certain people feel that their beauty is the only thing that measures their worth.
  - Telling a young child, they are beautiful so that they don't depend on someone else to do it when they're older is a good thing.
  - Telling a young child or even adult that they don't amount to anything because they're not beautiful or they need to add this certain amount of topcoat to be beautiful is detrimental. Detrimental to their self-worth and the love that is them.
- I am ugly.
  - There again, who told you that? Have you always felt this way?
  - What makes you ugly? Who defines ugly?
  - If beauty is in the eye of the beholder, perhaps the word ugly would only apply to those who are ugly on the inside rather on the out.
  - Is that you? Do you think an internal remodel would help you? Otherwise just don't listen to them you're beautiful!
- I am too short.
  - What's too short?
  - Does not being able to reach the top shelf make you too short? Does not being as tall as your friends make you too short?
  - At what point are you detrimentally short? Is that even a thing?
  - There are people all over the world that have height issues, but they aren't defined by being too short, they are defined by who they are.
- I am too tall.
  - Then what is too tall? Who told you that?
  - When did you decide to think that you are too tall?
  - Is it becoming a health risk to be the height you are? If not, like I suspect, you are beautiful just the way you are.
  - And for you Amazon women, embrace that! Sure, people may be mean and rude, but you show them the bombshell that you are!

- I am too wealthy.
  - OK, so you might sit back and wonder how this is even possible. To be too wealthy, is that a problem? Well, it can be!
  - If you have too much money to know what to do with it, and you don't donate, you don't share your wealth, you don't respect the things you have, then perhaps you have a problem, but otherwise if you have earned it, there is no such thing as too wealthy.
- I am too poor.
  - This is perhaps the most accurate statement. Someone could be too poor, but there are always resources to help boost financial situations and assist in programming that allows help you out of this situation.
  - Now, in knowing that, this category is mostly aimed at middle income teenagers that get bullied at school for not having the things that others do. They are being taken care of, they have what they need, and most everything they want, but because they don't have the new edition of whatever is popular, they are too poor.

But remember, just as you are love, you yourself are your qualities. Take for instance, a girl who wears hearing aids, she is amazing, brilliant, and has a bright future ahead of her period the fact that she wears the aids does not make her who she is. She is deaf, she has hearing deficit, but she is not just deaf. She is worth love, she is worth effort and time, she is worth relationships and friendships, she is love. Yes, she may be deaf, but she is love.

These constructs can never point to what we are, in fact, they do the opposite. By piling on construct after construct, we obscure the Light and the Love which we are. Therefore, it is a losing game to use the Law of Attraction to manifest love, or anything else for that matter, from these false ego identities. Some false identity egos are:

- Anger: is an emotion characterized by antagonism towards someone or something you feel has deliberately done you wrong.
  - Anger can be a good thing it can give you a way to express negative feelings, for example to motivate you to find solutions to problems
- Jealousy: the state or feeling of being jealous.
- Greed: is the intense and selfish desire for something especially wealth, power, or food.
- Resentment: is a negative emotional reaction to being mistreated a person.
  - Experiencing resentment will often feel like a complex variety of emotions that include:
    - Anger: as stated above.
    - Disappointment: is sadness or displeasure caused by the non-fulfillment of one's hopes or expectations.
    - Bitterness: is a complex multilayered emotion that has been described as a mixture of disappointment, disgust, anger, and fear. This is also known as being bitter.
    - Hard feelings: is feelings of dislike or anger towards someone that you think has mistreated you.
    - Hate: is to feel intense or passionate dislike for someone or something.
    - Grief: is deep sorrow especially that has been caused by someone's death.
- Lies: is to make an untrue statement with intent to deceive.
  - "She was lying when she said she didn't break the vase."

    - To bring about by telling lies.
    - "He lied his way out of trouble."
- Inferiority: is the quality of being worse than other things or people.
- Ego: is a person's sense of self-esteem or self-importance.

What you will learn in the proceeding chapters is how to create from a place of love. It is the highest vibration and presents us with endless possibilities. It is what we are left with when we put ego aside, and we have been looking for love and creating our lives from an ego position for long enough. Let us try something new.

These are the good things once all the bad are out of the way:

- Joy: is a feeling of great pleasure and happiness.
- Peace: is freedom from disturbance tranquility.
- Love: is an intense feeling of deep affection.
- Hope: is a feeling of expectation and desire for a certain thing to happen.
- Humanity: is the compassionate, sympathetic, or generous behavior or disposition the quality or state of being.
    - "Humane bespeaking humanity for the enemy in the midst of a bloody struggle," CG Bowers.
    - The quality or state of being human joined together by their common humanity.
- Kindness: is the quality of being friendly generous and considerate.
- Empathy: is the ability to understand and share the feelings of another.
- Truth: is the property of being in accord with fact or reality.

At what point does the same old song and dance get too old?

Is it possible that you have been bullying yourself by not allowing love in your life? When a world such as we live has adapted to bullying, condemning, and down trotting, then at what point are we to stand up for who we are and who the bullies are? Because yes, even those who down trot us have the capacity to love. They have the capacity to be love as well.

And so do you!

Law of Attraction

Everything in our world is energy and all energy vibrates at a certain frequency. Even our thoughts have their own frequency as well when you're thought goes from one side of your brain to the other. That is energy in and of itself and whatever energy that thought was thinking has its own frequency as well as bad thoughts which vibrate at a lower frequency.

Then it would stand to reason that all good thoughts vibrate at a higher frequency!

So, through the law of attraction energies that vibrate at the same frequency tend to attract to each other.

LIKE attracts LIKE. Because of that, it would make sense to why negative people like to be around negative people and positive people like to be around positive people. It's because they're vibrating at similar frequencies so whatever frequency your thoughts and your beliefs about yourself are, is what you are going to attract back into your life. You need to start thinking thoughts of a higher frequency if you want to attract good things.

What is the Law of Attraction? Is it as simple as "like attracting like"? Is it implying that we always get what we think about? Or is there more to it than that? Truth be told, it is a bit of all of the above.

To boil it down, the Law of Attraction is the creation of external effects through internal means. Or, causing an effect instead of being affected by our present circumstances and surroundings. Those who follow and use the Law will tell you that it does not matter what shows up on the screen of life because it is only an illusion being broadcasted to us, and we have somehow created it whether knowingly or unknowingly. To us, comparing a movie theater screen that has its images projected onto it to how we experience reality is not just a metaphor, it is literal. Reacting to this screen is pointless, it is just a screen after all. To change the screen of our lives, we have to go straight to the projector.

Without knowing how to use the law of attraction, it could completely corrupt a ruin your life. That's why it's so important to learn it the correct way and executed that correct way. If you don't know what you're doing read and learn so that you can know.

So many people these days are trying to extract a house or money or a relationship into their life, but they're just endlessly stuck in this rut of manifesting incorrectly...

And here's why.

- We attract what we are and not what we want.
    - A lot of people think about the things they want or need.
        - The house.
        - The money.
        - The relationship.
        - The job.

Because of the negative connotations involved with not knowing what you are doing beforehand, that will bring only a fractional kind of fulfillment. This is because in your here and now, you feel a lack of what's needed and more on why.

And so, for an example, you really want that house or that relationship or that job because you're not happy with your current living situation.

- Your relationship status.
- Your current job.
- The here and now.

So then, what you/we are doing is broadcasting a signal of lack and suffering which when the universe here's goes "oh they're trying to attract more lack and suffering," and therefore that is what you get in return.

It's like the universe calls out "table #43 wants more lack and suffering," and due to that, you get served more lack and suffering, instead of the *house *relationship *new job.

So, to manifest correctly you want to feel fulfilled and happy and successful and having a life of abundance. Well, right now in this moment that's kind of tricky for some, especially in the current state of the world.

It's understandable that you might feel defeated at this point, but you don't have too any longer. Here are the steps of how to get started.

- Keep a journal.
- Analyze your life.
- Write down 5 to 10 things you're grateful to have in your life.
- Write down 10 reasons why you're gifted and blessed.

A lot of people don't have that stuff figured out, but when they do, when you do, when we all do, we must look at what we have now then what we want when we establish out manifestation using the law of attraction. Our gratitude for all the abundance we have starts broadcasting like a signal to the universe. Then, the universe hears that message, and they go out and bring back what is needed the most. They are attracting what is needed in order to give you more abundance, and that abundance comes in the form of what you have needed all along.

- Every single day you read and execute the above list of the things that you're grateful for in the morning and then again in the evening you're establishing gratitude in your life.
- Then, you need to find three new things to be grateful for each day.
    - In less than a week's time you're going to notice a really big shift in your perspective of life.
    - And, after that we create a new list down and describe your:
        - Dream life:
        - How you feel physically:
        - How you feel emotionally:
        - How you feel spiritually:
        - How you feel mentally.
- And then you describe your success.
    - Your new work.
    - Your new house.
    - Your lifestyle.
    - Your family.
    - Your wealth.
- Has it all listed out then read it?
- Then, add to the list over every morning and every night.
- Visualize living that life.
- Have gratitude for having that life as if you are already living it.

In breaking it down and creating a system for reliving your mantra each day, will help you better keep track of what things have come true through the law of attraction and what things have not. It will also help you understand why certain things haven't happened and why certain things have.
Breaking it down even further, the Law of Attraction states that the reality we project is being caused by the states of consciousness or mental states that we possess. These states are composed of our thoughts, feelings, and actions- or in other words, what we truly believe and not merely what we wish for or are trying to convince ourselves of. This can also be called our subconscious mind; it is the programming that we run on and the less mindful among us are completely unaware of what is going on much less the projecting that it is doing.
They are not to blame though. We are raised with a worldview that tells us that if we do not like what we see in our lives that we should react to it until it changes or goes away. However, this reactivity only keeps what we do not like going. It feeds it energy and affirms to the universe that this is our reality, and therefore we are stuck creating more of it.
Five law of attractions hacks or habits you can get into that keep you on track are.

1. A vision board:
    a. When practicing visualization in general the brain doesn't know the difference between visualizing and reality.

    b. Your body secretes the same feelings of being where you want to be and that will change your life.
2. Journaling:
    a. Use a 3 6 9 technique.
    b. For example: "I am so happy and grateful for my complete freedom and abundance." Write two more affirmations and then speak each one three times for it to come true.
3. Speaking to your element:
    a. Speaking to your element allows you to see, hear, and feel things that you otherwise couldn't.
    b. For example: If you are a water element, put a citrine crystal at the bottom of a glass of water. Speak your manifestation to the water and it enhances your manifestations.
    c. Water and other elements hold memory so by speaking all your affirmations into your element every single time you get the chance, which increases your all over chances.
4. Change your diet:
    a. When you start changing your diet for the better you can start vibrating at higher frequencies.
5. Just become:
    a. Become that version of yourself or you never will attract what you want.
    b. You always attract what you are, so you have to become that version of yourself in order to get what you need or want.

If you don't put the effort forward, you will get little return. Following even the simplest steps can help you achieve the goals you have. Imagine putting a lot of effort into something, but not doing this studying beforehand needed to complete the work. Could you get a good grade on an assignment that you didn't study for first? Not likely!

If you are tuned into the food channel on your TV but are upset that they are showing food-related shows instead of a history one, it would be pointless, insane even, to get the show you want by messing around with the TV's screen. Most likely you would sit back, relax, pick up your remote and change the channel.

Have you ever had a bad hair day? You might have found out about it by going to the bathroom and looking in the mirror. To fix your hair, you would not grab a comb and start brushing the mirror, would you?

Some readers may already comprehend this but are still stuck on the same channel or frequency. It is important to understand that we can only experience and interact with life on the consciousness level that we are at. If I honestly believe myself to be unwanted, then this is the only way that I will be able to interact with life. I am not going to experience love, no matter how much I attempt to think about it or fake it if I still have a scarcity consciousness, or if I am filled with resentment and jealousy. In other words, I can only make changes to the outside world from that level where I am. This would be my "playing field", and each playing field only allows us so many options.

How many people are trying to overcome something so they amp themselves up by watching motivational videos, only to go out and tackle life through the consciousness that has created their problems in the first place? It is a losing battle that will only tire you out. The only way to lasting permanent change is to toss out that consciousness altogether. This is the metaphorical death that spiritual teachers talk about.

Attraction Vs Vibration, and why you need to know the difference.

Attraction is only secondary to the primary of vibration. Vibration is everything. Think of it this way. Everything in the room or space you are in is moving... nothing rests. For instance, the table in the room (should there be one) the table is moving. It just appears to be still. The long vibration decrease leaving behind the fact that everything moves... nothing rest.
When you think about it... you put you under a frequency. Then you can only attract what's on that frequency. You think about as your personal life... Just concentrated like that, then consider a second persons personal life and we go bump into them on the street... if you are thinking about it, that's when the law of attraction takes over.
You have now attracted to you what you're in harmony with. That person you ran into on the street... or when you set goals you got to see yourself already there in order to feel as though those goals will work.
That's called a mindset. Understand what it is you set your mind to and by knowing that said mindset is a frequency that you are on, is equal to being able to attract what you now have to attract because of your frequency.
That may seem confusing but think of it like a radio. If you are a truck driver and you know that a certain group of people will be turning into a certain channel, you will not be able to receive their frequency should you not also be tuned into that Channel.
A really great way to test your vibrations against attraction is to use the timeout method. This time at method is a twostep process that is super easy as long as you can achieve meditation.

- Find higher thought through meditation and complete control over your mindset.
- Have a timer or stopwatch on hand.

It may seem silly that those are the only two steps you need in order to create the vibrations needed to manifest your destiny through law of attraction, but it is a great step forward towards discovering what you need to do in the long run.
The steps are:

- Achieving meditation.
    - Make sure by achieving meditation you were doing it in a comfortable and safe environment.
    - Make sure that you have a deep understanding of meditation is an what it requires of your mind and your body.
- Continuing to a heightened level of meditation.
    - Once you have achieved meditation, reaching that heightened level is important for continuing on.
    - Making sure there is little to no outside distraction while meditating is key.
- Think positively.
    - Thinking positively while in the state of meditation is important so that you do not drop that positive meditative state.
    - While also thinking positively, it is hard to have a negative connotation.
    - Negativity has no place in meditation or attraction and vibration.
- Create realization as to what you are desiring.
    - Knowing what you want is important.
    - Knowing if it's achievable through this process is also important.

    - Anything is possible through manifestation, especially where love and attraction are involved, but knowing if you are worthy or if your mindset is complete enough to achieve it is what is important.
- Set a 17 second alarm or 21 second alarm.
    - By setting an alarm, you are giving yourself a small amount of time in order to assimilate yourself into a certain situation inside your brain that would simulate your desired outcome.
- While the timer is ticking down, project your thoughts and energy into one focus.
    - After pushing play on the timer, you were going to project one positive thought as if you were living that life even for a small amount of time.
    - If you have lived that life and enough small moments, it becomes harder to feel like it isn't obtainable.
- Come out on the other side and repeat up to three times.
    - When you have come out on the other side, your vibrations are stronger, and you feel like the wall of attraction can be better suited for something that you desire.
    - This is also important so that you know if this is something you really want or if this is just something you have thought you have wanted all along.

If the Law of Attraction Works, why is it not Widely Accepted?

It seems to me that people misunderstand the Law of Attraction because of how it has been portrayed in popular culture. People were led to believe that if they thought about a Lamborghini that one would just show up magically in their driveway one day, and even sooner if they made a vision board for it. To add insult to injury, there are no shortages of Law of Attraction "teachers" who are only looking to get rich quick and so they sell you a line. Thankfully, the Law has a bit more spiritual depth to it than how it has been sold.

You also have many people who have picked the Law up, given it a half-hearted go, then claim that it does not work, and proceed to go out of their way to discourage others from using it. But see, with the Law of attraction, you cannot be half in, it is an all or nothing game. And those who have gone all-in will tell you that they have been completely transformed and witnessing miracles is their new normal.

So, why are some interested in the Law of Attraction while others not?

Well, think of it this way, people are on different playing fields. Not one field is "better" than the other, yet at the same time, consciousness does have higher and lower levels. Kindness, compassion, and gratitude, for example, are higher than selfishness, greed, and vanity. The spirit is always higher than the ego, and people who see the world through a spiritual lens – knowing that there is more to life than what meets the eye -- tend to possess a higher consciousness than those who see the world through a strictly materialistic viewpoint. These people that all we see is all there is and therefore can only rely on our body and mind.

Some of us sought out spirituality (or maybe it sought out you?) and had varying degrees of awakening, even if only something you or heard or read resonated with you deep down. For us, these moments have changed us and now the old ways seem to not work as well. You know, the power-through and muscle-it type approach that we have been taught all our lives, and even the old strategic and calculated ways do not yield results, even producing the opposite effect than what we had intended. These dated paradigms still work great for some, not so good for us.

I tell "us" because something brought you here to this book. It is doubtful that you would be reading this if you were stuck in the old paradigm. But it can be difficult, as we look on at others who use old tactics as a way to succeed and get by in life, even more frustrating when we see them get the girl or the guy every time. It can seem like they have all the love in the world.

OK, so it works for them. But look at it this, we have it the easiest. Our path produces real success, real love, and real happiness. This way feels good, as opposed to going against the grain and stressing out. Our way is much closer to our hearts and true spirit, it is a way the benefits us and in return benefits the entire universe in its expansion.

Three reasons why the law of attraction hasn't worked for you or might not be working for you.

1. It's not your divine timing:
    a. Everybody has a divine timing and it's basically a chapter in your life that needs to open up. If it's:
        i. A child.
        ii. That job.
        iii. The spouse.
        iv. The home.
        v. The relationship.
    b. Whatever it is, maybe it's not your divine timing yet.
2. Your energy is blocked:
    a. Energetic blockages are energies that are often associated with emotions, conscious, and subconscious thoughts, spiritual awareness, etc.
3. You have contradicting energy:
    a. It's like wanting money but then feeling guilty when you get money.
    b. It's like wanting love but also being equally afraid of love.
    c. It's like loving yourself and hating yourself at the same time.

Is There Scientific Basis for What you are Saying?

Is the wall of attraction actually real? Yes, it is, if you don't know what the law of attraction is, it pretty much means that we have the ability to attract the things and people into our lives that we want by focusing on them. Now, it goes much deeper than that but I'm going to share some science behind it.

This is not to mean that science is the only thing to explain vibrations and the law of attraction, sometimes it's best not to explain away these wonderful phenomena.

So, there's a part of our brain called the reticular activating system or the RAS and what the RAS does is, it blocks out 99% of the stimuli going on around us and it focuses on only a few things at once. if we didn't have the RAS, we would literally go insane because there's so much happening around us at all times. So, the few things that you're thinking about your brain will look for...

An example of that is: Most people can relate to... You want to get a new car, and it's a red Mustang... nothing is wrong with a mustang to the fact you want it, but since getting it, what do you start to see everywhere?

Red Mustangs!

Your brain is focusing on red Mustangs you're seeing them everywhere and it's the same thing with anything you're trying to attract into your life if you focus on those things regularly you will start to see all the opportunities that are out there for it that you were missing before because your RAS was not focused on them.

Science that proves the law of attraction really works. Getting into it, the law as stated before basically states that whatever you focus on creates an elevated emotion which defines our reality. However, what's happening in the brain? We have this region called the reticular activating system as mentioned above, or RAS, and it's basically an interface for our external world and here's how it works... We have stimuli in our world, and it hits our brain in the reticular activating system and acts as a filter which gives us little tidbits of information into our awareness, and this is based on what we feel most strongly about at the time being. If we feel strongly about blue cars, just like the red mustangs, you will probably see a lot of those cars on the road for a while to come.

Then, if we feel like the world is against us, well then, we'll probably have a tough life, or so we plan, so we want to train our brain to see what makes us feel good. We can get more of what makes us feel good in our lives by practicing for 40 days right before you go to bed on imagining how it feels to achieve your goal.

- If you want love how it feels to feel the lover's embrace.
- And, if you want money, how it feels to receive that paycheck.

Then that brings on the scientific thought of quantum mechanics and quantum physics. Those are the scientific language behind the spiritual ideals that we become what we think about, or that we can manifest or use law of attraction. Through that, thoughts become things and those things work by what you can imagine and visualize.

Yes, you get to choose a potential feature or outcome, and you can observe it, and that observation with intention is what will call that forth. That will collapse possible outcomes and possible waves down into that physical experience in the future and that works because we are spiritual nonphysical beings first, we have an intellect which we can work with in the end. We exert energy with our mind and then we bring it forth into physical law of nature and attraction, bringing things away from a non-nonphysical spiritual reality, into a physical form.

I think many of us who come to spiritual practice and the Law of Attraction know that reality is something a bit different from what we are being fed, and we have listened to the experts for long enough. But still, science can point us towards interesting theories that give credit to the Law of Attraction, though nothing is definite.

This book is less about the scientific merits of the Law or even a debate on whether it is real. Rather, this is a straightforward and practical guide to using what we already know to work from experience. And besides, not all of the readers here will be the types to geek out on its scientific aspects. So, let us just briefly go over some theories in the realm of Quantum Mechanics that can back of the Law of Attraction's claims.

Most importantly, in Quantum we have a unified field of consciousness theory. This has many implications, such as objects do not need to be physically interacting to influence one another. But probably the most convincing argument science has to offer us comes from the holographic universe theory. This theory states that the universe is a connected field that holographs appear on and that the human mind is a holograph itself- a possible projector. This theory is closely related to the simulated universe, which theorizes that we are all in a simulation. But if that is so, who is animating it?

Who knew that there was so much study on the law of attraction? But if you put some thought into it, most everything has to be proved or disproved by science, but what about spirituality? Does that even come into play here? Can we even count this as being part of one's spiritual self?

And then what about science? What makes it a scientific observation? Knowing that something has or hasn't been disproved seems to be of an importance to the recent generations. Now, we like to know for sure if something is going to work for us, but in knowing that, or at least waiting for us to know that we are pushing belief, faith, and the knowledge of miracles back into the shadows.

There hasn't been much that has happened in history that didn't have to do with those things. And I'm not talking biblically here, this isn't necessarily the spiritual aspect I am Speaking of, for many beliefs and many deities support the practice of meditation, manifestation, and the law of attraction.

So, before you go wanting your scientific proof, think for just a second who has had their hand in the cookie jar. In saying that, do you think only people interested in the outcome of the wall of attraction or manifesting your love or destiny have study this?

The CIA has recently released a document on their website detailing experiments done back in the 1970s where they studied manifestation. The basis of the experiments was that our reality is a hologram and that we can imprint physical things onto the screen of life using our consciousness. If you are already a believer of the Law of Attraction, then what they concluded may not come as a surprise to you at all. The CIA scientist had success with this study.

In essence, this breaks down like:

- Manifestation: is the public display of emotion or feeling or something theoretical made real. Manifestation's origins are in religion and spirituality because if something spiritual becomes real it is said to be a manifestation.
    - Furthermore, manifestation is the pushing out of one's desires or thoughts into the universe knowing that it will come back to them.
    - The only key thing to remember during manifestation is to not allow negativity in and to follow the correct steps or else you may not get the outcome you want or an outcome at all.
    - Another thing to remember is that manifestation takes time sometimes, so if you haven't gotten your gift from the universe yet it does not mean you will not get it at all.
- Mental projection: is a supposit or experienced form of consciousness, spirit, intelligence, or projection from the emotional astral plane to the mental plane.
    - This is pushing your thoughts and feelings outward hoping to obtain a different placement in order to interact spiritually or emotionally within that placement.
    - A good practice is to lay down, mentally focus on a certain activity or area, even person that you would like to see again, and project that you are there with them or doing the activity, therefore you are there doing that activity
    - It has been proven that by using mental protection, people have been able to interact with loved ones that are at a far distance, causing the loved one to give full details of the experience even though you were not physically with them.
- Law of Attraction is a new thought philosophy the law of attraction is a pseudoscience based on the belief that positive or negative thoughts bring positive or negative experiences into a person's life.
    - This should be an easy concept to get behind, considering this is the main objective of this reading. Remembering that the law of attraction is viewed differently by several entities is important.
    - Remembering to study and learn and gain your own knowledge means that you are taking what others have told you or what you might have already heard and making an assumption of your own.

- The law of attraction is less spiritual as previously thought and more physical and emotional.

- Consciousness: is the awareness or perception of an inward psychological or spiritual fact intuitively perceived knowledge of something in one's inner self.
  - During consciousness this is like a Daydream that you are 100% aware that you are having. You are in control of this conscious state.
  - By using consciousness, you can practice projection, manifestation, various laws, and break boundaries that have been set for a long time.
- Reality is a hologram is part of the holographic principle which states that the entropy of ordinary mass is also proportional to surface area. It also says that this does not include volume, because volume itself is illusory and the universe is really a hologram which is isomorphic to the information inscribed on the surface of its boundary.
  - Saying that reality is a hologram and is an illusion does not mean it is fake. Sometimes we think that if something is a hologram it really isn't there, that isn't what this is meaning.
  - It's meaning primarily that to look at reality you are seeing various activities intertwining with other activities creating what looks like a solid reality but in "reality" you are just seeing everyone's variables creating a solid mass that is what you now consider reality.
- Imprinting the physical: is to impress or stamp a mark or outline on a physical surface or body or to imprint your thoughts onto reality or the screen of life.
  - Oddly enough, when you think of imprinting, a lot of people automatically go to the concept of mythological or made-up entities placing an imprint on someone who they then are meant to protect our love. This is a common misconception in the fact that we as humans can imprint or be imprinted on just in a slightly different way than what we're made to believe.
  - Just like someone would put an image on a T shirt, they imprint that image there and it is permanent or mostly permanent until the T shirt meets its demise. That is the same case here, in the fact that what we project, feel, see, share, and ultimately manifest, is an imprint of our lives and who we are.
  - A great example of this would be taking the T shirt for example. If a grandmother, had it made for her granddaughter, and the granddaughter wore the T shirt until she outgrew it, that granddaughter might have passed it on to someone else to wear which might pass it on to someone else to wear which might turn it into a pillow. Now, that doesn't mean that the image or imprint isn't still there it means it has been altered a little bit throughout the years. Remembering that, that imprint is still there, until it is destroyed or has given up its imagery, means that imprints that you have laid on society and reality at this point will live on for many, many years.
- The screen of life is the concept of projecting reality into our present as well as creating spiritual and scientific realities that we interject into what is considered the screen of our life.
  - This is perhaps the hardest concept in the fact that a lot of people assimilate screens with being televisions, computers, phones, gaming systems, anything that would devote

your time solely to one activity involving a screen, but that simply isn't what we're referring to here.
  - Imagine your life a television show, and the plain out in front of you is the screen in which your life is projected on. Now, think about the producers of that television show, the actors, the writers, the creators, it takes all of them to make that show a reality.
  - Now take that in the essence of your life. Yes, it is your show about you, but there are so many other factors that have played into your life or will play into your life that then become the reality before you set into your screen of life.
  - This is simply what other people view you as or your life as it is also what you view your wife and yourself as. Each person has their own screen of life they just intertwined with others quite frequently.

Studies for years have shown how true these factors can be. It doesn't take the CIA to prove or disprove these theories. It just simply takes the practice by a human to prove that it has worked for them. Remember that just because it worked for one person a certain way, does not mean it will work for all people That way. However, studies have proven that as we all have a different learning curve, different beliefs, different ways of doing things, it will work for everyone differently.
But then what about definitive proof of all of that?
There are many of these studies and theories emerging all of the time, but what we are left with is not definitive proof that the Law of Attraction works, but only more questions. The only thing we can be sure of is that nothing seems to make sense, and no one knows what is going on here. If that is the case, that nobody knows, that means that everyone who has taught you is wrong too. If we accept the Law of Attraction and live it and breathe it, and we find out it works, then we are just as right as anyone else anyway.

The Law has Been Around Forever
Now, when you are thinking on timing, we automatically go to how long will it take for these things to work for us, but have you really thought about how long this practice has been around? When was the first time you had heard about law of attraction? Why was it then and not earlier? Has it been around long enough for us to have heard about it earlier?
There is no exact time on how long it will take for the law of attraction to manifest your desires for you. In essence, it depends on three main factors.

- Your belief: that you can have what you want.
- Your ability to manifest what you want.
- Your alignment: with your desire and your ability to let go and trust in the outcome.

The law of attraction has been popularized in the early 21st century by books and films such as “The Secret” however it has been around since the late 1800s early 1900s. But then again, is that right? Perhaps not!
Perhaps that is the earliest the term has been pinned, but if you think about it, this concept has been a reality for thousands beyond thousands of years.
Going back to our earliest scriptures from our world’s religions and spiritual traditions, we see many passages alluding to the Law of Attraction without outright saying it. That is basically because the term didn't exist yet although the actions did. The ancients accepted that realized human beings could perform miracles, at the very least, people knew that God (or their god or deity) could perform miracles for them on their behalf.

For those that believe or don't believe in the Bible, it states that many miracles happened, and they were reverenced as being the greatest happenings since the start of time, but were those conceived from the above steps or was it just one God that made it all happen not allowing any explanation for it all? And then again if that is the case, then how do we explain things today that are similar to back then? Yes, miracles are a thing, they are a wonderful thing, but are the miracles done the way that we have always thought they were or are they due to spiritual practices from manifestation like prayer, meditation, or even the simple act of lighting a candle?

When considering that, almost nearly every religion or belief system allows the practice of one if not all of those three actions. If that's the case, then is it possible that we have aided the manifestation of those miracles? Sure, somebody has to be thanked for them, and they do come from somewhere, but to what level do we have involvement?

In western society, this how the Law of Attraction was introduced- that with faith, the average person could create wealth, health, and find love through God. These ideas first rose to prominence with Mary Baker Eddy's Christian Science in 1875, which took a biblical approach, but was more metaphysical than traditional Christianity.

This gave rise to a handful of authors in the early 1900s, most notably Florence Scovel Shinn and Neville Goddard, both of whose philosophies are practiced today. Of course, in that day and age, such teachings were considered blasphemous. And it was in 1906 when the term "Law of Attraction" was first used by author William Walker Atkinson in his book, "Thought Vibration or the Law of Attraction in the Thought World".

Shortly after this is when we really saw an explosion with this type of thought. Ernest Holmes wrote his book "Science of Mind" in 1926 and a religion of the same name was created. Science of Mind worked on the basis that our thoughts were creating our reality and offered up prayers to harness our God power to manifest our desired lives.

This was all part of a broader movement called, "New Thought", which has become a blanket term for alternative spirituality and metaphysics in the United States, all of which claimed that we created our reality.

This is important to highlight to point out that the Law of Attraction is not new, nor is it a trend. These same turns of the 20th-century books are still considered some of the best available today. Take, for example, Napoleon Hill's "Think and Grow Rich". It was written in 1937 and still considered the gold standard for prosperity consciousness literature even today. Not to mention that each of these authors has spawned generations of new teachers that go on to preach the same philosophies, but with a modern twist.

In this book, we will break down some of the above teachings as they have evolved today. There are a few different approaches and philosophies that we will learn how to blend to attract the love that you are looking for. You will learn how to shift your life permanently to a more loving state, how to attract that special person who you did not even know existed, and how to manifest a specific person who you already, including an ex or a past lover. If it is your soulmate or twin flame that you desire, this book and the principles in it will show you how manifest that type of love as well.

The only thing that I ask in return is that you keep an open mind to just one possibility- that there are infinite possibilities.

The word infinite means being truly infinite in nature, that there are no restrictions of space, ability, or power. To be infinite is to be everywhere and be everything all at once. There are no edges or limits to the infinite nor are there pockets where the possibility is absent.

Soul Connections Ex-Lovers, and Specific Person

While the Law of Attraction has been successfully utilized for just about anything and everything, love is by far the most popular reason for people to use it. This is because love, something so natural, has become a problem for us.

We either:

- Feel that we lack love.
    - This commonly happens when we are in a relationship which isn't reciprocal.
    - We feel like we give love, but we are not getting it back.
    - Or in some cases we are getting love but are not giving it back.
    - For whatever reason this lack of love either being given out or given two is traumatizing in the fact that we feel like we are incapable of either receiving or giving love. That just simply isn't true, but in this reading, you will learn how some of these things can be overcome.
- See that it's absent in our lives.
    - You can be happy in your life about absolutely everything. You may feel like you have the best job, house, vehicle, friends, even family, but if love isn't present in any of that, then it's meaningless.
    - If you love your friends due to the fact that they are just friends that fill the void of not having any, then that isn't love at all and in fact you are living a life absent of love.
    - The same thing stands for family. We could have a mother and a father and siblings, which would be the quintessential family group, but if we are not giving or feeling love from them in any way shape or form, then we are living a life absent from love.
    - This could be because somebody doesn't know how to reciprocate or even love in the first place, or it could be because of a misconception that someone isn't worth love or that someone hasn't been taught how to properly love.
- We are looking for it in all the wrong places.
    - I'm going to be very broad here, because I don't like to say looking on the Internet is the wrong place to look for love, looking at a bar is the wrong place to look for love, and all honesty looking at work, in a church, or in a coffee house could all be the wrong place to look for love.
    - So instead of saying the wrong place in general as in labeling a certain place as being ultimately a bad place to find love, this is talking about the wrong place for you.
    - Your best friend Susie may have found her husband at a restaurant off the beaten path that you both frequent. This could give you the misconception that you might as well find your love there, but this could be the wrong place for you.
    - Someone else might swear off dating someone you find on the Internet, though that might be the right place for you to look.
    - Knowing your true feelings about something and sticking to it is important for searching out that perfect place for that perfect person.

- Also, assuming that because you were looking in a decent spot, such as church, work functions, or even a town meeting, does not mean that person is a good one.

- Have chosen the wrong love.
  - Even at the beginning when we think someone is good for us, and even if they have been good for us for a really long time, which doesn't mean they will always be the right person for us.
  - I say person, because this could extend to certain family members that are toxic that we keep around, even friends that have been our friend for a long time but when the time comes for us to let them go, it's important to because of toxicity.
  - This can also be because we grow as we got older, and we may have grown out of a certain relationship where they haven't grown at all.
  - This could also be someone who is the opposite gender as you and you have cared for them greatly but then realized that you are attracted to the same gender, have decided to change genders, have decided to take a different path for your life.
- Haven't committed to love at all.
  - Sometimes as humans we have trouble committing to love. Sometimes we wait the maximum amount of time to say the word love or the words I love you to someone. This isn't necessarily a bad thing it's human nature to be that way especially when you've been hurt before.
  - Then again for commitment it could be the opposite. Perhaps we have been sitting here waiting for somebody to commit to us.
  - One of the biggest things I think about here and it's affecting younger people more is that we are sitting around waiting for one specific person or one specific type of persons that we allow our true soulmates, twin flame, love for the moment to pass because we're not even looking in their direction.
- We want to commit but our significant other does not.
  - This is kind of a sad situation in the fact that we are ready to commit either to moving in with someone, dating exclusively, or even promising our futures together. This includes marriage, abstinence, or anything in between.
  - It's difficult when we feel that we are ready for that, but our spouse or significant other is not. For whatever reason they may not be ready for this. That doesn't mean the love isn't true or that you aren't meant to be together in the long run it means that you have to decide whether you want to pass on to someone else or something else to try to find that commitment or if you are going to be patient.
  - Now, in being patient, you need to express to the person that you need an update every now and again, that you would like an answer in an extended amount of time, or that you would just like to converse back and forth about desires and once for the future. If someone doesn't seem like their agreeing on this conversation or at least a small timeline, then they most likely are not meant for you.
  - If you have been waiting for that proposal for years without them saying I just need another six months to think about this, I just want to be in a better place when I think about this, I just would like a raise before I think about this, then there are other issues to consider.

    - Lastly in this area, you need to consider issues that need committing to like sobriety, rehabilitation, a commitment to family, or agreeing to not be physical either sexually or abusively. If you don't have those kinds of commitments, and it doesn't look like it's on the horizon, then it might be time to reconsider your relationship.
- We don't understand love at all.
    - Sometimes it's just a matter of not understanding love at all. In those cases, a lot of the times people didn't experience the correct type of love or love at all as a child. Either by a parent that didn't understand love themselves or couldn't love for some reason.
    - This could also mean that you did have love, but you didn't understand why you got it. A great example of this is someone who was not exactly the best person growing up, yet they received unconditional love by those around them. They got the support they needed, but it wasn't easily understandable in the fact they knew they didn't deserve it.
    - Love is a fickle thing and unless you fully understand it or are willing to learn along as you experience it, it's difficult to get into the correct mindset that love is for you.
- We are literally petrified when thinking about love.
    - Sometimes love just simply scares people.
    - Either you've been in a past bad relationship, or you've seen relationships go bad, or you are afraid to commit because of previous commitment issues, either way it's an easy thing to weird people out or scare them.
    - When someone's had trouble committing to simple things like clubs and activities growing up, a religion, a belief system, or even committing to their own family, sometimes love can be a scary thing especially when you're starting to experience it truly for the first time.
    - Love with commitment can also be scary period when you're finally feeling like you're ready to commit but you're worried about how the outcome of your future would be or if the other person feels the same way, there is a certain percentage of fear in that category as well.
    - It's safe to say that when you fear love or commitment or any variant of that, that the best thing to do is to be in communication with your loved one or someone that you respect and trust that has had these experiences before that can guide you in the right direction.
    - Love can be Ant is a very scary thing it isn't a bad thing to be afraid, it's just bad if you live there and don't allow yourself to come out on the other side.
- We simply haven't decided in which way we want to love.
    - This is a huge thing period this was not necessarily in existence in a lot of people's minds 30 years ago. We didn't really consider in what way we wanted to love or who we wanted to love, it was more like a man and a woman only and if you felt the opposite way or you loved in a different way it was done behind closed doors.
    - Now with pride, LGBTQ plus, and every variant in between becoming legal, becoming common in the public eye, becoming accepted which is a good thing, considering how you want to love and who you want to love is important.
    - Also considering that if you have loved a certain way before that does not mean that is the way you will always love is a really neat concept.

- People have been married to the opposite gender for years, but that relationship has either fallen to the wayside or been separated by death or circumstances, and upon reevaluation perhaps even in the middle of your marriage, you might decide that this unity or this union is not what you have always wanted or expected.
- And, if you have trouble with this concept, that doesn't make you a wrong person or a linear thinker, it just means that you have not explored the options of this being appropriate at this time. Either way we need to consider that either side is worthy of love and that those who believe either way is not to be harassed or bullied because of the other belief.
- Equality for all!

But then you have the whole other factor that sometimes people get together when they're young and they stay together for years. The problem with today's generation is a lot of the times either marriage or relationship is committed to, and it doesn't last very long therefore you hop from one person to another, this can take a chip off of your essence or capability to love causing some turmoil.

However, a lot of us already know our soulmate or twin flame. Perhaps it is in an ex-lover or a person who we know but have never been romantically involved with. Whatever your specific case may be, the Law of Attraction has proven to us that finding love with a specific person is possible. In fact, there are entire social media groups dedicated to such a thing with story after story of success. The Mid-1900's metaphysics teacher, Neville Goddard proved to us it was possible when he manifested a specific person as a wife, and he turned around and taught the world how to do it.

The bottom line that we must hold onto is that when we understand that we are the creators of our realities, that you and you alone are solely responsible for it, manifesting a relationship with anyone is possible.

A great relationship example of this would be having your eye on someone for a really long time, most likely because of personality and the way they make you feel rather than the way you think they look, can weed too the capability to manifest that relationship into existence. By using the law of attraction and manifesting your destiny into love and relationship, you can very well end up with the person you have always wanted to just because you believe it, have faith in it, feel that it is true, and are true to your own self.

Remembering negativity and nonbelief will be the only thing that cancels this possibility out. Just because you have been negative in your past life or in the recent past does not mean that that is how you will always be. You can change that but only you can.

Once you are in the right mindset and can meditate to manifest. You can follow these steps:

- Think about the person or type of person that you want to be with.
  - Even if you don't have a specific person in mind, you can think about the type of person that you would like to end up with a project that.
- Write it down and say it three times.
  - By writing it down and repeating it in a journal or affirmation cards you are able to see what reality you want and therefore it's easier to think and believe it.
- Gain a great consciousness and projection of this person or type of person.
  - If you think about the consciousness and the projection sending it out into the universe even before meditation, you can ready your reality even though it is linear too previous beliefs, you can ready it for future actions a future belief.
  - This is exactly what you would need to do to get away from negativity and bad thinking.

- Meditate, pray, light a candle.
    - Then, whichever way your belief system has you do it, you prepare yourself for projection and manifestation.
    - Once you are prepared you begin the action of obtaining that higher thinking.
    - Then you achieve your higher thinking.
- Project or manifest this person or type of person into reality.
    - Then project or manifest your thoughts for that person or persons. Even the type of person that you were wanting.
    - Send it out in the universe an if you have been positive, had no negativity in your life, or have followed the steps in order to get rid of the negativity, then you will receive your gift.
    - Remember that if you haven't received it right away does not mean you won't receive it at all. It's all in the universe is timing.
- Achieve your goal.
    - Then you get your gift, whether it be now or in the future. You will have that person or type of person that you desire, and your love can grow from there.

Soul Connections

The idea of the "soulmate" has been watered down and muddied to the point where it is completely misunderstood by about everyone. The tragic part of this confusion is that it has caused people great pain. The idea that there is only one person out there for us and if we blow it with them then that is it for us has been the culprit of people's depression and giving up on love and sometimes life altogether. It is a needless and avoidable route to go down. We all know that breakups are hard enough as it is without all the added guilt piled on.

The twin flame has been a misunderstood concept too. Largely because people like to proclaim that every relationship, they are in is with their twin flame. They either do not know of the concept or lack general awareness of themselves and their partner. More innocent is those who confuse their soulmate for their twin flame.

Understand how this mix-up could occur because both of these relationships are highly special; sacred. So, before we go on to manifest it is a clever idea to be clear on what it is that we are trying to manifest as well as clear up some of the confusion around soulmates and twin flames, so when you meet yours there will be no doubt in your mind about which is which

Soulmates Vs. Twin Flame

Your twin flame is not your soulmate and vice versa. These are two different things entirely and are all too commonly mistaken for one another. Your twin flame is the other half of your soul, the one who completes you. We all long for this type of connection deep down. We see other couples involved in this kind of relationship and cannot help but be a little bit envious. We have known our twin flame for many lifetimes and yearn for them always. Some lifetimes we fail to connect with them because this relationship can be rare. But maybe not so rare nowadays, thanks to our knowledge of the twin flame, the Law of Attraction, and knowing exactly what is necessary to do for us to do to meet ours right here in this lifetime.

Those who have already met their twin flame, whether they are currently with them or not, know that when you see this person you already know them inside and out without even speaking a word. This is because they are you. If you have passed them on the street and shared a brief moment, then you already understand how powerful this connection is.

Your soulmates, on the other hand, with whom there are many, are more common than you may think. A soulmate is anyone with who you have shared a deeper, natural connection. These relationships are easy, the two of you just seem to click beyond the surface level. Chances are you have dated people like this in the past or they are some of your best friends or even people who you admire from afar.

You may have shared intimate experiences with soulmates and then lost touch. It could have been a terrible falling out because these relationships are passionate and can be intense. A soulmate can cross your path again years later and it is like you are still best friends. This is because soulmate bonds do not just last a lifetime, they last many lifetimes, for as long as we are traveling the cosmos. Whether lovers, friends, or pets- they are your tribe who you have known and come across many times already.

Soulmates are like a soul family so to speak. Currently, we are witnessing more people meet their own soul families and spending more time with them while watching their old, unhealthy relationship fall to the wayside. Likely, these soulmate relationships are healthy. These people bring out the best in you, show you your blind spots, help you in need, and push you to be the best version of yourself. They see all of the good in you that sometimes you fail to see.

This is not the downplay the soulmate relationship at all. If it sounds to you like just another typical relationship, they are not. They are deeply profound. If you have found a lover who is also a soulmate, this is incredible and more special than 99 percent of the relationships people have found themselves in out there.

But the twin flame relationship is the deepest of them all. Your twin flame is always a romantic partner, never a friend, parent, or pet. A twin flame is what completes you. So, when someone refers to their partner as their "other half", this is what they mean, literally their other half.

Telling the Difference

OK, so now we know the difference between the soulmate and the twin flame on an intellectual level, but how can we differentiate the two on an experiential level? How do you know that the person who you feel this strong connection to, and love is your soulmate or a twin flame?

Soulmates can come and go, and at the end of the day, it is not so difficult to say goodbye and go your separate ways only to connect again later on. You miss them, sure, but they never consume you. The twin flame, however, is someone who possesses a strong magnetism, drawing you in and rendering you helpless. You will feel as though you want to be attached to this person's hip permanently.

When you meet a soulmate, you will not notice right off the bat that the two of you same many of the same interests, thoughts, and beliefs. This is usually only realized after spending some time with them and conversing. Even though you and your soulmates share many similarities you are different and unique in your own ways too. This is because you are each an individual.

You and your twin flame are also individuals, indeed, but the two of you are only half individuals alone, together you make up one complete and whole individual. It cannot be mistaken; you will realize this right off the bat when encountering your twin flame. Unlike your soulmate, you do not need to spend any time with your twin flame before knowing that the two of you are the same.

Meeting a soulmate is always great and when it is romantic it is exciting. Meeting a twin flame is beyond exhilaration though, you will not be able to stop thinking about them, it is like an obsession. If you are not around them, you will not even be able to function because they are consuming so much of you. You will know without a doubt that you must do whatever you have to do to be near them.

Soulmates are great coffee and lunch dates. When you meet them, you probably extend your stay with them and are late getting back to work or whatever it is you have going on next. This is because you have many of the same struggles and triumphs, ups and downs, even if you are not currently going through the things – whether good or bad --- that they are, you can still relate and know exactly what it is like. You can talk to them for hours and actually enjoying listening to them. You may be on different waves but recognize each other as the same ocean. You love and respect one another and recognize each other as being different people with unique expressions and life purposes.

Your connection with your twin flame differs in that the two of you have the same mission. You both are going through the same things at the same time and have a feeling that you are headed in the same direction to the same place. You finish each other's sentences in eerie ways that would frighten you if you did not know better. It feels like you have traveled to another dimension, and you have met yourself, only in a different body.

We initially separate from our twin flame so that we can become healed ourselves before we connect again. While the soulmate can pop into your life at any time, they are sympathetic and aid us in our healing.

Manifesting Your Soulmates

Everyone wants their soulmate and a lot of us have already been practicing with the Law of Attraction trying to manifest theirs without success. At this point, many helpless romantics throw their hands up and proclaim that the Law of Attraction is bogus and that they are different than everyone else – possibly cursed with bad luck -- and destined to a life of loneliness.

Some have even used the Law of Attraction in other areas of life, such as their career or health, but manifesting their soulmate just never seems to work no matter what they do. Well, they are not alone. They would be If only manifesting a soulmate were as easy as feeling good and visualizing it. Sure, that is a large part of it. But many of us are blocking the love we want to flow to us without even realizing it. Let us face it, we want our soulmate, and they want us too. But are we really being the "us" that they want? The true us that is connected to our source who knows our power and worth?

Finding a soulmate is relatively easy. So easy in fact that I genuinely believe that people are doing so already and not even noticing it because of their internal blockages. If we are open and on a frequency that vibrates closer to our truer selves, we automatically draw in people who are just like us, some of them soulmates, and some who would want a relationship with us if only we were allowing it.

Other soulmates can be best friends or even a stranger who you briefly encounter at a coffee shop. Your conversation could have lasted only minutes, but when it was through you said to yourself, "wow I really like that person". That was because you had a soul connection to them. Talking to them seemed so natural and you were right there in the moment with them. Some reading this have even been romantically involved with soulmates, again, whether they have realized it or not. These relationships often end on a good note with the two parties remaining friends. Either that or the breakup was terrible, due to the passionate and intense connection that soulmates often share. There is really not in-between with soulmates.

So let us cut right to the chase because with all of the variations of soulmates that exist out there, we know you are looking for just one of them- the romantic type. Just think of how easy it was to draw to you the soulmate friend, the complete stranger in line at the grocery store, and the past relationships you were in. That is how effortless it can be with any type of soulmate, even the lover kind.

Some believe in spiritual topics and also soulmates, so they take to the streets and charge through the crowd looking for theirs. That is one way to do it if you are even aware enough to recognize your soulmate as such when you meet them. A more practical way would be to draw them to you through the Law of Attraction. Because not only is it just easier to do, but it feels so magical. And being in alignment on that level, you will automatically recognize your soulmate every time.

For us to manifest our soulmates we must love ourselves first. The Law will not bring love to you unless it is felt within first. I know, this sounds like something cheesy your mother would say, but it holds true. We will touch on tapping into this frequency in the following chapters, but before that is even done, we have to love ourselves the same way we want our soulmate to. We must look at ourselves with love, forgiveness, compassion, and practice self-care. If we are unable to do this even for ourselves, how can we expect anyone else to do it for us?

Before our soulmate just pops up ready to go out on a date, we must heal some of our past wounds. To say we need to be completely 100 percent healed is a falsehood since healing goes on for as long as we are alive. But in order to attract a loving partner, we need to at least come to grips with some of our bigger issues, particularly the ones involving love, our worth, and relationships. This book is not meant to tell anyone how they should heal, since there as many ways to heal as there are people. But it will be more than helpful if you can take stock of some of the wounds you think may be holding you back from love and then dealing with them in the manner most suited for you.

When we start to do the inner work, we see just how easy it is to manifest. You are probably thinking, "Work? I thought this was a book about the Law of Attraction". Yes, it is. And maybe you can manifest a loving relationship without doing the inner work, although doubtful. If we are holding inner resistance of any kind, it will only be a struggle, which defeats the purpose and also opens the door for anger, frustration, pity, and all types of low vibrational feelings.

When we start to love ourselves, if even just a bit, we are ready to create room for our soulmate partner to show up. There are two ways of doing this- mentally and physically. We can start imagining a life with them, everything about it, just like painting a picture on a blank canvas of the mind. Physically, we can begin to act as if we already have the partner we desire. To do this one only need to ask themselves, "what would I be like if my soulmate partner were with me? How would I behave, hold myself, and what would my actions look like? How would I treat others?".

Manifesting Your Twin Flame

Twin Flames have become all of the rage recently. It is almost like people that claim to have found theirs like to rub it in everyone's face, attempting to make the rest of the world feel left out. That is not what a twin flame relationship is about, and it is highly doubtful that people who do this sort of thing could even be ready for a relationship of such magnitude and maturity. The twin flame is the most sacred relationship that there is, so it is better to remain humble about it. But it is also important to understand that no matter how rare it seems, or what kind of fuss everyone makes about it, your twin flame does exist and that union with him or her in this lifetime is possible if we can make ourselves ready for it.

You may wonder, "if I have a twin flame, then how come it is so difficult to meet them?". Well, first of all, we all have twin flames. No one is exempt from this, no matter how unlucky in love you feel. They are literally our other half. But it should not be so difficult, you are right- only special, sacred, and divine. The part that we find difficult is paving the foundation for them to come into our lives and for us to be in alignment with it. Because we do not find them, so to speak, they just happen to show up and it is unmistakable just who they are when they do.

Many people will say, "things would be better if only I could find the one", yet they stand in complete resistance to the love that they desire. This resistance comes in many forms- our actions, the way we hold ourselves, speak, eat, and live our entire lives. See, the twin flame relationship differs a bit from the soulmate ones in that if we have not prepared ourselves for it, the universe will not bring it to us.

But do not fret. A little bit of spiritual, subconscious mind, and Law of Attraction work, and our twin flame will be in our arms a lot sooner than we expect.

The original purpose of us being separated from our twin flame other half in the first place was so that we could do the work, to find the spring of love inside us, to know that we are empowered creators. If we do not understand these things about ourselves then how could our twin flame even recognize us, or us recognize them? How could we possibly spot our other half without first knowing ourselves?

Many grasp this yet continue to battle in the mind- trying to manipulate the ego and convince themselves that they are something that the subconscious knows they are not. Partially because what we are is beyond mental formation and words, but also trying to trick ourselves into thinking we are "awakened" is a fool's game -- spiritual bypassing -- and it does not work. So, to save you the frustration of standing in front of the mirror doing affirmation work for hours on end when our subconscious does not even feel that our affirmations are true, we will give you an easier, softer road to take- the path of self-acceptance.

Self-acceptance and self-love are imperative in meeting your twin flame. The chances that the universe will send you your twin flame without possessing at least some degree of them are slim. And even if we were to meet them, we would not like them very much, nor accept them, if we do not like or accept things about ourselves. Because they are us, both mirroring and shadowing everything there is to us.

Nobody is perfect, let us be clear. Not one of us is floating above anyone else because they have done all of the spiritual work there is to do. As long as we are alive there will be spiritual work for us. It is the entire reason for being in this dimension and on this planet at this time. When the spiritual work is done, we go home.

So, contrary to popular belief you do not need to be whole and complete before meeting your twin flame, because you are already those things anyway. All it takes is to recognize it within. This is when the magic happens, this is when you have created the room needed for your twin flame to manifest in your life. And the two of you will be doing the spiritual work together not just in this lifetime but for many more lifetimes, whether connected or separated.

For those looking to manifest their twin flame, the best thing we can do right now is to set the intention. We intend to reunite with our twin flame. We intend to accept and love ourselves and to do all that is required to prepare the road for her or him to show up in our lives once again.

Ex-Lovers and Specific Person

It can be extra devastating when we believe, or know, that the person who has broken up with us is either a soulmate or twin flame, or that the person who we know, and love does not reciprocate the same feelings. It crushes so many people to the point of hopelessness. But armed with the knowledge of soulmates and twin flames along with the Law of Attraction, we remain calm because we know just what to do.

Still, others will look upon and offer their spiritual judgment, saying that you are interfering with another's free will by trying to make them fall in love with you. For this reason, it is best to keep quiet about it unless the person you are talking to understands these concepts.

You are not interfering with anyone or their will by using the Law of Attraction. That is what is called black magic. What is being done here is manifesting love between two soulmates or a twin flame and there is nothing sinister about it. The key thing here, and I cannot stress this enough, is that you are wishing well on everyone involved.

Let us say you are trying to manifest your ex back. You know they are the one, but they broke up with you and now they are dating somebody else. We do not wish bad on the person they are dating, as this would only harm us. We wish them good as well, sending them positive thoughts and feelings while imagining good for them. The way that the universe works is wild. Your ex's new partner could have met someone else that was their soulmate, they could have won the lottery and moved across the country, any number of things.

It is not possible to trick anyone into doing anything through the Law of Attraction anyway, only through manipulation and this will backfire every time. See, when we put out a frequency into the world, or towards another, it comes back to us via the Law. If we wish to control or harm another, then we will be controlled or harmed ourselves. When we wish to love, appreciate, forgive, and help another- we will be loved, appreciated, forgiven, and helped ourselves.

That is the Law simplified. But what is it that makes it this way? See, our subconscious minds are all connected, as well as being connected to the Quantum Field (which we will touch on in a bit). This can also be thought of as God's subconscious mind. What we put out we create through the field, and we create along with others with who we share this field.

It cannot be stated enough that we live in a universe with infinite potentiality. And in this universe, there are infinite states of consciousness, infinite frequencies, infinite realities, and infinite timelines. Anything you can think of you bet there is a timeline for that. There are timeless for you being every type of person imaginable. And so, there is the timeline of you and your ex, or any person for that matter, being happily in love together. One only need to tap into the frequency.

What is that frequency? Imagine you and that person together. That feeling that you feel, that and the thoughts combined is that frequency.

Subconscious Mind

With the Law of Attraction, we always start with the basis that we are vibrational beings. Without this foundation, there is little to nothing we can consciously create. But do not get it twisted, we always create regardless.

So, what is doing the creating, and what is dictating our vibrational (or frequency, consciousness) state? The simplest answer is the subconscious mind.

Think of it as a computer. You can see it and touch it. If you take it apart you can get a good look at its insides, or hardware. The computer has a screen that shows images on it, but it is not the screen or even the hardware that is dictating what images pop up. The computer's software is what does this, or its programming.

Much like computers, we have programming too. Neuroscientists have discovered that 95 percent of our thoughts, feelings, actions, and behaviors are governed by this program. This leaves us with about 5 percent free will. This 5 percent free will is what we do the spiritual work with. It is how we operate on our computer, uninstalling the old self-defeating programs to run new programming that is rooted in love, unity, and empowerment.

5 percent does not seem like much, almost like the odds are unfairly stacked against us here. But it is not so bad, because that 5 percent can be pretty powerful. It is the 5 percent that allows us to be aware of our programming and step outside of it. With this awareness, we can observe our thoughts, feelings, and behaviors without adding any fuel to the fire by giving it the energy and karma that keeps it alive. We can let things go with ease and watch as our awareness grows and expands until we recognize that awareness as ourselves, or at least closer to the truth of who we really are.

This is important work to do and should not be overlooked, and besides, we owe it to ourselves anyway. It was not us who installed this programming after all. Although, we have been the ones responsible for keeping it going. The ancient Greek philosopher Aristotle famously quoted, "Give me a child until he is 7 and I will show you the man".

This is because Aristotle was aware. He knew well before scientists that the bulk of our programming was handed down to us before the age of 7. At that age, we were entirely too young to weigh out whether things were true or not. Instead, we soaked up everything like a little sponge and just accepted it. In terms of love, the chances that we have received a bad download are pretty high. Even if our parents loved each other, we still witnessed them having disagreements and this left us confused. The perceptive little child in us saw it all, and society's take on love is no healthier. What we were seeing in the world as we grew did not seem to correspond with the loving and innocent nature that we came into this world with. This is where most of us begin to cover up the hurt anyway we can, mostly with worldly things.

We were taught, though not directly, that we had to do certain things and behave a certain way to obtain love. We had to please our parents, the teachers at school, and other kids our age. This starts the process of being cut off from our true nature, our inner well of love, and the search for external love began. Such an endless and disappointing pursuit.

We are Programmed

As we drift off at night, it can almost seem like we were a blank slate. Our problems, triumphs, wants, needs, our thoughts, feelings, and even our bodies, all seem to slip away. The same could be said upon awakening, the moment just before our programming kicks in.

We like to kickstart the program any way we can, by remembering what we are mad or worried about especially. We, meaning our egos, feel the need to be somebody because just "being" alone is scary to the ego. So, to remind ourselves of who we are, we think all of the same thoughts that got us worked up yesterday. This is considered “normal”, but it is also problematic. These past thoughts keep us stuck in the past, naturally. To manifest the love of our life we must move forward in thought to a new future while remaining consciously present.

Remaining present is key because the subconscious mind only understands the present. When we recall memories, we feel certain emotions attached to them. When we ponder the future, we feel whatever is associated with what we believe about the event- worry, doubt, excitement, joy, etc.

It does not matter whether we are thinking of a memory or planning for the future- the thought, feeling, and belief are what is creating our reality. Without awareness, we get stuck in this feedback loop which essentially creates more of the same. And when we experience more of the same, we produce yet again similar thoughts and feelings. So, for many, it is easy to predict their future.

What have we been affirming exactly?

How do we Reprogram our Subconscious Mind?

Since most of our programming is not even ours, why would we want to hold on to it? Especially if it does not do us any good? Is it our truth, or not? Most likely it is not, since no one can give us our truth. It may seem like such a heavy task, to overhaul our entire conditioning, a lifetime’s worth of brainwashing. Lucky for us, neuroscience has taken larger steps in not only understanding how the mind works but also giving us tools to work with it, even though some of these tools predate science and go back to our earliest spiritual traditions.

Below we will take a look at some of the tools we can use to rewire the subconscious mind. At the end of this book, we will guide you through some of them using techniques tailored to your specific goal of manifesting a specific partner.

Meditation

No longer just for the spiritual seeker, people use meditation for all sorts of reasons nowadays. This ancient practice even pre-dates the Buddha and has been the mystics' preferred practice of choice of seeking enlightenment for as long as we know.

Using meditation for enlightenment is not greater than using it to gain spiritual powers, or to attract money or love, or anything else for that matter. People use meditation for a variety of reasons- to relax a bit in a stressful world or to visualize specific outcomes, such as with athletes, actors, and businesspeople. This is because the list of things that we can accomplish through meditation is endless and should not be judged or placed on a hierarchy.

Through meditation, we are going to a place of awareness so that we can get behind the operating system and view or conditioning objectively. As awareness, we can take stock of our conditioning without reacting to it, which only feeds it energy and keeps it alive. And as awareness, we can let go of the things that do not serve us, that are blocking the love we seek.

Hypnosis

Hypnosis is the second oldest tool that we have available to us, and its old age is not a bad thing either. It only speaks of its effectiveness, which is why we still use it today. You might be picturing a doctor dangling a pocket watch in front of a client as they lay on a couch, but hypnosis has come a long way. When in a hypnotic state, it can be as simple as drop clicking a new belief into our subconscious mind. Also, a lot like meditation, hypnosis puts our brain into a natural state so that we can and work with our subconscious minds without all the reactivity and struggle. It is truly like booting a computer into repair mode. A good hypnotist can guide you through the process of removing and installing certain "files" – or beliefs – that are in resistance to what we desire. This could be done on your own as well while listening to the right audio, like the guided meditations at the end of this book.

Close to the hypnotic state is the hypnagogic state. This is the state of consciousness that lies directly between sleep and awake. Some meditation and certain yoga's effortlessly put us into this state where we can bring healing and love naturally. This state is easier to access, and one can do it on their own.

Prayer

People think of prayer as just one thing, a conversation with God mostly. In traditional Buddhism, prayer is used to purify one's mind and energy and not pray to any outside thing. Hinduism does something similar with its mantras. In the same way that these spiritual traditions have their devotional mantras, you too can come up with your own regarding love and relationships. You can bring your mind back to this mantra throughout the day to keep the focus on it.

If you ask me, it does not make a difference who or what the prayer is directed towards, because a focused and heartfelt prayer works to program our subconscious mind without a doubt. Which, if you get into it, the subconscious mind is divine anyway. It is God since God resides in us, and our subconscious thoughts and feelings go out into the universe, the Quantum Field (which we will get into), aka God's mind.

Any regular prayer practice, no matter how you chose to do it, is a highly effective way to rework subconscious beliefs. Your prayer does not need to be done within a religious context either. You could even cut out the middleman and pray to your subconscious directly by starting your prayer by addressing your subconscious mind directly. Such as, "I am now writing in my subconscious mind...", or even a simple, "I am praying to my subconscious mind...".

Once we have the subconscious mind's attention, we can begin speaking truths to it. In this case, the truth of our soulmate or twin flame relationship as if it already exists, thanking our subconscious mind (or Source, God, the Universe). The important part is only that you keep coming back to the prayer throughout the day for it to be effective. Practice makes perfect.

Law of Attraction

By far the most impactful thing on the subconscious mind is the way we utilize the Law of Attraction. The Law of Attraction is always in play, but the techniques we use, accompanied by the knowledge of ourselves and our understanding of the way the universe works, have the quickest turnaround time for subconscious mind reprogramming. It is a combination of faking it until we make it, believing it real, feeling it real, positive thinking, acting as if, and other methods. It is hitting your subconscious mind on all fronts, while vibrationally creating an effect in the universe.

The Quantum Field and Quantum Theory

Chances are you did not pick up this book to read about science, or perhaps you are someone who prefers if science can back up the claims being made here. Either way, spirituality and science have typically been at odds with one another, especially throughout history. In the past, religious figures labeled scientists as heretics and burnt them at the stake. Nowadays, some religious people even outright reject science altogether while scientists poke fun at spirituality calling it "woo woo". But would not a much wiser approach be to ask what happens when science and spirituality meet and can actually agree on some things? Because they can and do with Quantum Physics.

The word "Quantum" refers to the lowest microscopic levels. Quantum Physics is the study of what lies at this level, the things that we cannot see yet seem to govern our physical and material universe. And what scientists in this field are finding is that the things we cannot see are what bears the most influence over our reality. The influence, or "laws", that they find are pretty "out-there" and seem to only confuse us, leading to more questions. This sounds remarkably similar to the spiritual experiences the layperson has and the experiences of anyone who has used the Law of Attraction itself.

The Quantum Field Theory, or Unified Field Theory, is a theory within Quantum Physics. It has been described by mystics and ancient spiritual traditions for centuries, and only recently has science began to touch on its discoveries. According to the spiritual person, it is everywhere all around us, connecting everything, simultaneously while being us. It is the empty space that looks, well, empty. It is where material objects appear from out of nowhere, and what we broadcast out into it directly affects what we see manifested in our reality. In simpler terms, it is the invisible and intelligent "backdrop" to our holographic universe.

I know, empty space can sound pretty unintelligent, it can seem like... nothing! But what is "nothing"? And what if "nothing" were intelligent? These are the questions and ideas that Quantum Physics has been putting forward. The Quantum Field which permeates nothing, as well as everything, is known to the sage as "the mind of God", while Quantum Scientists see it as "more work".

That is because the paradoxes and contradictions of their findings leave scientists scratching their heads and asking more questions. To the mystic, the findings say that anything is possible and nothing that we have been taught makes sense, that this is the field of infinite possibilities. One only needs to realize this when what they see right in front of them -- their holographic and illusory reality -- has them feeling trapped and hopeless. If love has got you down and your soulmate seems so far away, just remember that this field of infinite possibilities connects the two of you at all times.

Quantum Field and Quantum Physics

Scientists are not known to make wild claims, especially when they are about things that they cannot prove. This is why the idea of God is typically shunned by the scientific community. But serious practitioners of spirituality and mystics look at the findings of Quantum Physics and shout, "we are talking about the same thing!".

Much of this suspicion of spirituality comes from Newtonian Physics, which was our widely accepted worldview for many years, pre-Albert Einstein and his Theory of Relativity. The claim made by Isaac Newton and his successors was that the universe was full of dead, non-sentient material objects which seemed to be governed by set universal laws and that we now know how all of them work. The mistake they made was in thinking these laws were not changeable, and so they figured they had an almost complete worldview until Einstein blew it all of the water.

E=Mc2 changed the
world and opened the door for a new school of physicists who would make extraordinary findings throughout the 20th century in the new field of Quantum Mechanics. To simplify it, Quantum Mechanics studies atoms, particles, and energy at their lowest levels. The findings and are that what we have considered matter really is not physical at all. Instead, we find at the lowest levels quanta particles, also known as light particle wave packets -- or energy -- and it makes up everything in the universe.
This energy is what we call, and what scientists theorize, the Quantum Field.
These small particles and the energy field behave in ways that run absolutely counter to everything we have ever known before. Particles can be in two places at once and even have an impact on each other despite being great distances from one another. Our minds also affect these waves and particles. Scientists have observed them behaving in certain ways depending on what we were doing. For example, they even know when they are being observed.

The Quantum in Spirituality
The Dalai Lama is the most prominent spiritual leader to back science, especially being a proponent of Quantum Physics who appears at conferences and meets with top scientific leaders. He has always held the position that if science were to prove Tibetan Buddhist concepts wrong then the Buddhist concepts must change. But he has not had to do that (that I know of), because the findings of Quantum Physics seem to go hand and hand with Buddhist philosophies and verify what they have been teaching in Tibet for centuries. This does not seem to surprise the Tibetans at all. The only reaction you will get from them is a shoulder shrug, because these findings have been so obvious to them all the long.
The least surprising to the Dalai Lama were the findings that we are all connected, that everything in the universe is. This is a core teaching of Buddhism, called inter-connectedness. Also not surprising the least bit to the Tibetan spiritual leader were the Quantum findings that when we zoom in on an atom, we find that it is actually "empty" (another major Buddhist doctrine), meaning that they have no structure to them at all, they are not physical but made of invisible energy. This energy is the same vibrating, pulsating energy that we talk about in the Law of Attraction and similar spiritual philosophies.
It is the Quantum Field.

If this does not lend at least some credibility to the validity of the Law of Attraction, I do not know what does. If we are all the same, if I am you and you are me, and what I wish for you comes back to me and vice-versa- what we put out there must have a direct influence over everything else.
But just because spiritual leaders are now meeting with scientists does not make any of this new, or more or less credible for that matter. The most ancient spiritual scriptures on the face of the earth, the Vedas, have much to say about the Quantum Field, vibration, and other similar topics.
Vibrations are spoken about throughout the Veda's and a cornerstone belief of this ancient wisdom is that the sounds we make ripple out into the universe and cause an effect. This is why they use mantras above all else- not only to focus the mind but to create a vibration. One of their most powerful mantras is the "Ohm" mantra. Somehow the ancient Vedic's knew that this was the sound of the universe; the vacuum; the void. They believe that the "Ohm" vibration was the energy that created the universe.
But there is something even more powerful than "Ohm" that both science and the Veda's describe, which is the backdrop for which "Ohm" appears. This backdrop in Quantum Physics is what we have

been calling the Quantum Field. In spiritual terms, it is called the "Brahman, the state of stillness where nothing exists, not even us as we know ourselves to be. It is where time and space are non-existent. Yet this energy, this intelligent nothingness, is all that there is.

How We Can Have an Effect on the Quantum Field

We always affect the Quantum Field, whether we like it or not. This is because at the deepest levels, we are this field. It runs through us and the entire cosmos. In a vibrational and interconnected universe, how could we not have an impact on it? On each other? And on everything?

But more to the point, how can we affect the Quantum Field to produce a favorable outcome? How can the Quantum Field bring us our soulmate? Or our ex back? How can we get that person's attention who we know beyond the shadow of a doubt to be our twin flame?

Some will think that statements such as, "we are all the Quantum Field" are nonsensical; only feel-good, spiritual gibberish. But you do not need to believe me, nor anyone else. Why would you when you could go directly to the field yourself to experience it?

Meditation practice can take you there, directly to the Brahman, the place of stillness. Even when using a simple breathing meditation, you will eventually go deeper and naturally let go of everything. All of the things that block your knowledge of this connection to the field slip away and you become one with it. It is in the space that we emit the feeling of love and the vibration of the relationship we wish to create. In doing so we imprint it onto the Field, and by law, when we imprint directly onto the field it must manifest in the physical.

The more you can "just sit" and concentrate on your breath, the longer you will find yourself being able to do it for, and the deeper you will go within. This does not take years or even months of practice, rather just an intention and commitment to practice it daily, and these visits to the field will become commonplace before you even know it.

Heart-Mind-Field Connection

If we are honest, not everyone has the temperament for meditation. Although, it would benefit anyone who gave it a try. There are still other things we can do outside of meditation practice to consciously create through the field. For instance, did you know that the most powerful energy broadcaster that we have is not even our brain? Turns out it is the heart. Which, believe it or not, acts like a brain itself. Thanks to the Heart Math Institute and other scientists in the new field of neuroradiology, we now know this and more.

For instance, we know that the heart possesses over 40,000 neurites, which are brain-like cells. In terms of the heart being a powerful broadcaster, studies at the Heart Math Institute have shown that it emits an electromagnetic field 1,000 times stronger than the brain and radiates a magnetic field that can be seen for many feet outside of and around the body.

Studies also prove that there is a heart-brain connection, a term coined by Dr. Andrew Armour. Previously, these two organs were isolated and studied alone- another remnant of Newtonian Physics. The heart feels our thoughts and emotions. If we are stuck in lower vibrational states such as hate and fear, our heart and brain are out of alignment with each other. This brings about depression, physical sickness (especially dealing with the heart), and manifesting outcomes we do not desire. Conversely, when we think thoughts of love, gratitude, and compassion, the brain and heart are in what is called "coherence" or operating together to broadcast higher vibrations into the field.

One only needs to think of love and feel it in their heart to emit a powerful vibe out into the universe. This can be made easy if we just take a few breathes and relax. In a calm state, we then place our hands on our hearts and notice the awareness and energy around it. Now we begin to think loving, grateful thoughts. This is the language of the heart and activates the heart-brain connection which not only charges our manifestations but also aids in our healing. In this place, we can forgive and let go with ease knowing that it is safe. Working a bit with the heart-mind connection in this way can heal any wound there is, none so special to be excluded.

Higher Vibrations

The famous Serbian American inventor Nikola Tesla once said, "if you want to understand the universe, think in terms of energy, vibration, and frequency".

Love is the highest vibration that there is. Some would go as far as calling God love. Love creates. It has created me, you, and the world around us. It is us at our very core, our true nature. So, how do we rediscover what has always been there? One simple answer, by feeling good.

I know what you are thinking, "Easier said than done. If feeling good were only as easy as deciding to do it, we would all be feeling good all of the time", right?

But it might be that easy. The problem discovered by the Buddha and others is that we are constantly looking on the outside of ourselves for things to make us feel good, and when they are not there we suffer. We now know our physical reality to be an illusion, and that our feelings are generated from within and have nothing to do with the outside world, only how we react to it. But it is the sad story of the human condition which makes us believe the opposite, that it is the things on the outside that govern the way we feel. Not only is this false, but it is also a form of slavery. The person controlled by everything on the outside while having no discipline within is like a pawn. And so, they go throughout life getting banged around like a pinball.

But not you, or you do not have to be at least, because you already are committed. You are reading this book, so it goes without saying that you are committed to manifest your life partner- whether soulmate, twin flame, an ex-lover, or just a companion. And you are likely committed to the Law of Attraction if you have made it this far into it. But there is another big commitment that we must make, the commitment to feeling good and also taking the responsibility for our vibrational state.

It takes a bit of work to get to a place where we can be in the love state all of the time. Thankfully, this is not our aim with this book, the Law of Attraction, or with doing what is needed to manifest your lover. But we must feel love and recognize the source of it as being within. Sometimes this can be difficult to do when we find ourselves bogged down by the stress of the world and other various lower vibrational states. But one thing we can always do is to feel just a little bit better than we do when we are down. If we can get ourselves up to the next higher state, then this is the easiest way to go all the way up.

For example, if you are depressed, you may have to feel anger for a moment. Anger can also be used as a tool to help you take action if needed. But, please, do not stay there. Anger is still a low vibrational state. This is only an example of how you can move up.

From there you could even go to acceptance. From a place of acceptance, we can choose the higher vibrational states of forgiveness, compassion, peace, gratitude, and joy. In other words, there is always a better feeling vibration for us to choose.

But do not get complacent, because there is still a wolf at bay. Implementing a mindfulness practice or even just checking in with yourself throughout the day to see where your vibration is at will help to fend off the ego and old conditioning until we can let go of it completely. This is important because the ego is good, so good in fact you will likely find yourself being talked into going to a low vibration state by it time and time again. The ego will remind you of something you have to be mad about or convince you of why you should worry about a bill, upcoming event, or any number of things.

When we find ourselves slipping up in this way, we need not be hard on ourselves, as this brings about undesirable states and manifestations. We only need patience, compassion, and to understand that everything is already whole and complete and that these perceived "slip-ups" are perfect in their own way too.

If we practice what is recommended in this book, we loosen our grip on everything undesirable and find that we need not grasp for anything else, because love and the higher states that we seek will shine through on their own- naturally, because it is who we are.

Table of Contents

Introduction

Love for most people can feel like a losing game or a series of hits and misses. Yet, this beautiful feeling of belonging and being connected to another human being is what we crave the most. If you have tried everything and cannot seem to figure out your love life, there is still a way to create the healthy relationship and love life you want.

You may be hoping that your soulmate is still out there or waiting for that special someone to finally take notice of you but nothing seems to work. If you are tired of putting yourself out there and getting nowhere, it is time to look inward for the answer to your love life. Using the law of attraction, it is possible to manifest the person you want in your life by tapping into your sun conscious energy.

The law of attraction is a law of nature and just like every other law of the universe, it works perfectly every time. You do not question the laws of physics such as gravity because you witness them around you every day. Nature has a lot of laws, and some like the law of attraction are barely tapped and utilized because most people simply do not know how.

The principle of the law of attraction is not complicated. Just like a magnet creates a magnetic field that attracts other magnets, people radiate a certain internal energy or vibration from their subconscious mind. The nature of the energy you emit is what determines the kind of things you attract in your life.

This means it is not just bad luck that causes you to have a string of failed relationships. Rather, the universe reflects back the energy you put out so the things that manifest in your life are simply a reflection of your own internal energy. What can you do about it? Fortunately, there is a key that allows you to reset your subconscious energy and align it with your heart's desires. This key is meditation and it is one of the most effective techniques to raise your love vibration and attract the person you want in your life.

The meditations in this book are intended to help you attract the love of your life or your soulmate. We have detailed meditations that guide you step by step through the process of aligning your subconscious energy to attract the love you want. Whether you want to attract your twin flame, reunite with an ex, get your crush to notice you, or even heal a broken relationship, we have the meditations you need to do just that.

If you have been looking for a way to use the powerful law of attraction to manifest love and love in abundance, this book is meant for you. I invite you to join me in this journey and say goodbye to your relationship woes as you breathe new life into your love life.

Happy listening!

Chapter 1: Meditations to Get in Alignment with Your Desire (70 mins)

The laws of nature are not subjective. There is no right or wrong just cause and effect. Gravity works the same whether it's a pear falling from the tree or someone plunging from a cliff. The universe does not pick and choose when to apply its laws because that is not how nature works. In nature, every law follows its own path and the law of attraction is no different. Maybe you have tried to manifest the love of your life to no avail. Maybe all your relationships go off the rails and you keep wondering why you can't seem to get love right.

No matter where your love life is right now the most important thing is to understand that it is not up to fate, or cupid or someone else to get you the love you want. The ability to manifest the love you want is up to you and only you can attract the soulmate you want. Only you can attract the healthy relationships you want. Only you can end the cycle of heartbreak and toxic relationships. The law of attraction manifests what you put out into the universe and that for most people is the very thing that keeps them stuck in a broken loop of heartbreak and bad relationships.

The human mind is a powerful thing and the first step in attracting the things you want is understanding your subconscious mind. Your subconscious mind is the reservoir of all your fears, beliefs, expectations, memories and experiences. This part of your brain works in the background but it influences how you feel, think and act. It influences how you see others, how you see yourself and how you see the world around you. This means that the energy that you put out into the universe comes from your subconscious mind, not your conscious thoughts. That is why the law of attraction does not work if all you do is focus on positive thinking.

You have to go much deeper and tune in to your subconscious mind. What energy is your subconscious projecting? On the surface, you may be yearning for the love of your life. You may be ready to settle down. You may want to heal that broken relationship. But, is the energy that is coming from your subconscious mind in alignment with these desires? Do you want one thing on the surface and yet you are projecting something else entirely?

For the law of attraction to work, you have to be able to harness your subconscious energy and use it to fuel your desires. It is not enough to think positive thoughts, you must radiate positive energy that helps to attract the things you want. For instance, if all you ever think about is the kind of relationship that you do not want, then the universe only receives that negative energy from you. To truly manifest your desires, you have to start by devoting all your attention to what you want to attract not what you do not want to attract. Your thoughts should be centered around what you want to happen not what you want to avoid.

To help you get past your subconscious blocks, the meditations in this chapter are intended to help you align your subconscious energy with your desires. These meditations will help you create a powerful harmony between your desires and your subconscious.

Meditation to Remove Subconscious Blocks To Love – 30 minutes

In this meditation we shall be releasing all the fear, worry and anxiety you may be holding on to when it comes to love. I want you to immerse yourself in this experience and allow your subconscious to release all the negative blocks to love.

Let's get started.

Duration: 30 minutes

Sit in a comfortable chair with your feet planted firmly on the ground.

Sit in an upright but relaxed posture with your neck and head aligned. Release any tension in your shoulders and allow yourself to be in the moment.

Shut out the external noise, the busyness of life and the countless thoughts in your mind. Simply concentrate on being here in this moment.

Now, take a deep slow breath and as you inhale deeply, I want you to focus only on the air entering your body, the rise of your chest and the simple act of breathing.

Now exhale slowly and as you breathe out, I want you to release any errant thoughts. Let them wash over you and leave. Concentrate on your breathing.

Take another deep breath in and exhale slowly. As you continue with the deep breathing feel your body start to relax.

Any tension in your muscles is slowly getting released. You are sleeping deeper and deeper into a relaxed state.

Your mind is emptying of any doubts, fears and worries and with every breath, a feeling of calmness is taking over.

You can feel the ground beneath your feet, supporting you and holding you up.

With every breath, you are letting yourself go. You are relaxed and open and calm. Every inhale is a cleansing breath that brings it new vitality. Every exhale is easing the tension in your body.

You are sinking deeper and deeper into relaxation and every part of your body feels light and open.

Now in this state of deep relaxation, I want you to ask yourself this series of questions. Listen deeply for the answer. Without judgment or regret or worry. Let us uncover your blockages with an open mind and open heart.

Now ask yourself, "What outdated beliefs about love am I holding on to?" Listen quietly for the answer. It could be anything from waiting for someone to find you or believing that you are somehow not good enough or assuming that all your partners will be a certain way because that's just the way love is. Whatever it is, take time to listen to the answer.

Now ask yourself how this belief has served you. Are you happy with your love life? Is this belief helping or hurting your chances of being with the person you love? Is this belief holding you back from embracing the love that is around you?

Again, let the answer come to you without judgment or fear. This is your truth and the only way to get past it is to acknowledge it and release it.

Now, I want you to take a deep breath and then exhale slowly. Again, deep breath in then exhale slowly.

Ask yourself, "What past hurts or emotional baggage am I holding on to? What bad experiences keep me from having a healthy relationship?

Listen for the answer. Do you have a problem trusting people? Do you have a problem trusting yourself? Are you jealous and insecure? Are you always trying to live up to a certain ideal so you can be good enough?

Take your time to think about it. Explore your innermost thoughts and see how your past has shaped the way you see your relationships. To change your path, it is important to understand how you got here.
What old hurts are still taking up space in your heart? What memories keep you from opening up? What walls have you created to protect yourself?
As these answers keep coming to you. I want you to continue breathing in slowly and exhaling slowly. No matter how difficult it is to process, I want you to hear the answer acknowledge and release it.
Every inhale is healing energy and every exhale is taking away all the darkness within. You are letting go of the pain, the hurts, the negative beliefs.
You are making space in your heart for new and better experiences.
Now as you continue with the slow deep inhales and exhales, I want you to bring your right hand and place it over your chest.
Now repeat after me slowly,
My past is not my future. I am releasing myself from the negative emotions and past hurts.
Take a deep breath in and exhale slowly.
Repeat after me,
I am opening up myself to love. I will no longer carry the weight of the past in my heart. I am making room in my heart for new experiences.
As you finish this affirmation, I want you to picture a bright golden light. This light is now shining directly on you, bathing you in a warm radiant glow.
The golden light is spreading slowly from your forehead to the rest of your body. Take a deep breath and exhale slowly.
Feel the light as it travels down your face, living it aglow with radiant light. Your face is feeling a warm comforting glow that makes you want to smile. You feel lighter and calmer and at peace.
As the light travels down your body. Feel its warmth ease any tension in your shoulders. Feel any tightness leave your chest. You are radiating light and as this bright golden light bathes you feel it wash away any anxiety or fear in your heart.
It is ok, you can let go now. This golden light is surrounding you in a protective cocoon full of love and light.
As the light travels down to your legs, I want you to become aware of the ground beneath your feet. The golden light is now anchoring you to the present. You are grounded in the now and the past no longer has a hold on you.
You can let yourself be free because the ground beneath your feet is supporting you and the bright light all around you is surrounding you in its warm glow.
Now I want you to inhale deeply and as you do so, luxuriate in this moment of light and positivity that you are in. Exhale slowly and feel yourself become one with the bright golden light. The light is not just surrounding you but it has infused every part of you.
You are radiating this warm glow and everything you touch from now on will be lit up by your light. Everyone you reach out to from now on will feel your warmth because you have a ray of light within you and around you.
Take a moment to attach to this moment. Feel the lightness in your mind and body. Immerse yourself in it. You are open to love. To give it. To receive it and to be part of it.
Now I want you to slowly bring your awareness back to the present. Slowly start to focus on your breathing. Feel the air enter and leave your body as you breathe in and out.
When you are ready, open your eyes.
This meditation is now complete.

Unblock and Activate Your Heart Chakra – 15 minutes

Heartbreak is an inevitable part of love. The people you love the most are the ones with the potential to hurt you the most. That is why recovery from heartbreak is often difficult and painful. Even when you think you have healed from your past, sometimes negative experiences in love slowly start to close your heart chakra little by little. Every time someone breaks your heart, it gets a little harder to love the next time because there is a little part of your heart that is closed off because of past hurts.

This meditation will help you unblock and activate your heart chakra. It will guide you to opening up yourself to love and allow you to connect with others in a healthy way.

Let's get started.

Duration: 15 minutes

Sit in a comfortable position, on the floor or a chair. Get rid of any noise and distractions and allow yourself to immerse yourself fully in this meditation.

Start by closing your eyes.

Now let's do some deep breathing to help you relax and calm your mind.

Deep breath in. Exhale slowly. Deep breath in. Exhale slowly. Deep breath in. Exhale slowly.

Feel your body and mind start to relax. Allow your mind to clear and release any thoughts. Focus on being here in this moment.

Become aware of your body and let your awareness travel from the bottom of your feet to the top of your head.

Start by bringing your awareness to your feet. As you focus on each part of your body feel it relax and any tension in the muscles slowly dissipate.

Now slowly let your awareness start to travel up from your feet to your legs. Feel your knees your upper thighs and your waist. As your awareness continues to move upward, the relaxation and feeling of lightness is also traveling all the way up from your feet.

Your awareness is now on your torso, your chest, your shoulders. Your spine. All the tension is leaving your body and you feel relaxed and at ease.

Now let your awareness travel up your neck to your face. Your jaw is relaxed, you feel a calming energy feel your mind. Your entire body is now fully relaxed and open to receiving what the universe has to offer.

Now in this state of complete relaxation. I want you to look up as if you are looking at a point high up on the wall. Just lift your chin slightly so that your face is upturned but you are not straining your neck.

With your eyes still closed, you are now looking up and as you do so, a spot of light is shining on your forehead. As the light touches your forehead, feel it fill your mind, wash over your entire face and start to move slowly down your neck to your shoulders and your chest.

This light is not just on you, but it is also permeating your entire being. It is in you and you can feel it light up your heart.

You're inviting this light even deeper into your heart. You can feel its cleansing and healing energy start to vibrate gently in your chest.

It's vibrating at the highest rate, feeling you with healing energy. You can feel it lighting up all the corners of your heart. From your deepest and darkest desires to the old pains and hurts that have left craters in their wake.

This vibrating light is healing all wounds and mending all the broken places in your heart. You can feel its healing power. You can feel your heart connecting with its healing energy.

Feel this healing vibrating energy fill every part of your being. Radiating from your heart outwards. Its gentle and powerful vibration infusing everything with a powerful and healing consciousness.
Now I want you to repeat this affirmation after me as you continue to feel the vibration within your heart.
I love. I love. I love.
I open my heart and receive the energy of more and more love.
Now inhale deeply and as you do feel the healing energy get even stronger within your chest. Breath out slowly and feel the healing energy radiating outwards.
You are open to love. You are open to giving love. Your body is a reservoir of love that is vibrating and coursing through you.
Take a deep breath and then exhale slowly. As you breathe in feel the light in the middle of your heart and allow it to expand out around as you exhale.
Now your body into a bubble of pure loving energy, surrounding and encompassing your body.
Repeat this affirmation out loud.
I love. I love. I love.
I open and receive the energy of more and more love.
As you continue to feel the loving energy vibrating through you, attach to this moment firmly in your mind. Connect to this feeling of loving energy that is within you right now. Know that you can always return to this space of love at any time.
Now take a deep breath and exhale slowly. Another deep breath followed by a slow exhale. As you take this last breath, I want you to look back down by allowing your chin to return to its natural resting position.
When you are ready, gently open your eyes.
This meditation is now complete.

Fixing a Negative Love Vibrational Energy – 15 minutes

Meditation is one of the most powerful ways to harness your vibrational energy. The law of attraction acts in response to the energy that you are putting out into the universe. This means if you have positive vibrational energy, you will attract love and healthy relationships.
This meditation will help you clear any negative love vibrational energy that may be blocking your path to true love.
Let's get into it.
Duration: 15 minutes
Start by sitting in a comfortable position.
Now close your eyes and begin to allow yourself to relax.
Inhale deeply and as you exhale that breath, start to slowly release any tension both in your mind and body.
Continue with the deep breathing and with every exhale feel yourself release tension, anxiety and stress.
With every inhale your body is relaxing more and more. With every exhale you are offloading negative thoughts, negative emotions and negative energy.
Keep taking deep healing breaths and exhaling slowly. You are getting more and more relaxed as you release all the tension from your body.

Take in one more deep breath feel your body begin to let go noticing how good it feels to totally relax and then gently exhale once again.

In this state of relaxation allow your breathing to go back to its natural rhythm.

Now focus on the rhythm of your breathing. Feel your chest rise every time you inhale and gently relax as you exhale.

Now I want you to imagine that you are standing outside an elevator. Inside this elevator is a guide that will escort you on the journey you are about to take.

Now I want you to visualize yourself pressing the button to open the elevator doors.

As the doors open and you step into this elevator, feel the confidence of knowing that there is someone beside you. Guiding and supporting you on this journey.

Now envision the elevator doors closing and now your guide has pressed the button to the highest floor. Gradually you can feel the elevator begin to ascend. As it gradually makes its way to the top floor, on each floor your guide asks you to let go of one negative emotion. Every time you release a negative emotion, you get a little bit lighter and the elevator ascends to the next floor.

So, at this point think of all the negative emotions come to mind when you think of love. Fear? Insecurity? Jealousy? Worry? Past hurts? Betrayal?

Whatever negative emotions are plaguing you, offload them one by one.

At each level the elevator ascends to, you are one negative emotion lighter.

As the elevator keeps rising, you feel your heart become lighter and brighter. You are freeing yourself from negative emotions as you continue to ascend.

All the things that you are leaving behind are all the things you do not want to carry into your next relationship.

Insecurity, the need for control, selfishness, jealousy, lack of trust, past hurts, false comparisons and ideals, possessiveness, toxicity.

Let it all go. You do not need them. They have no room in the place you want to go.

Now as you gradually approach the top floor, realize that you are about to step into the person you want to be. The love you want to have. The relationship you want for yourself.

Before the door opens on the last elevator, visualize that on the other side of that door are all the things that you want to be and to have in your next relationship.

Visualize yourself as an open, giving warm and loving person. Visualize yourself as a partner in a healthy relationship where you receive and give love freely. See yourself stepping into a future full of love and acceptance and healthy attachments.

Now the elevator has reached the topmost floor and your guide opens the elevator doors. As you step out, you are stepping out of the past and into the future.

You have carried with you only the positive energy that you want to bring to your relationships. You are now anchored to the love you want and not the relationships that did not work out.

All of the negative energies that you had accumulated from the past are left behind as the elevator door closes and now all that is left is the positive frequency of healing love.

As you step out of the elevator, you step into a bright room. You can feel yourself luxuriating in a warm glow that feels you with hope and positivity.

Now take a moment to immerse yourself in this positivity. Feel the hope for new love. The gratitude that your love life is finally going to be everything you have ever wanted.

Feel the bright light of the future drawing you forward and urging you to open yourself up to all the love the universe has to offer.

Open your mind and your heart to new possibilities.

As you allow yourself to experience this moment, take this feeling with you. Hold on to it and make it your anchor to positive love energy.
Now, take a deep inhale and slowly breathe out as you start to bring your awareness back to the present.
Inhale deeply and exhale slowly. Repeat the deep breathing one more time.
Now allow your breathing to get back to normal. When you are ready, slowly open your eyes.
This mediation is now complete.

Affirmations to Clear the Path of Your Love Life – 10 minutes

For people who find their relationships playing out in similar dysfunctional patterns, it is time to step out of the cycle. When you want to free yourself from the past and anchor yourself to the things you want to attract, affirmations are the most effective way to do it.
Repeat these affirmations first thing in the morning or before you go to bed to clear the path of your love life. As you repeat the affirmations, make sure you connect with them deeply and let them set your intentions for yourself.
Let's get started.
Duration:10 minutes
You can choose to do these affirmations while seated comfortably or lying down with your eyes closed.
Now repeat these affirmations slowly and taking time to absorb and internalize the intention.
I am a powerful creator who can use my mind to attract perfect love
The universe is guiding me to a healthy loving and committed relationship
I am receiving the blessing of love right now
In this moment every cell in my body is in alignment with the feelings of intense love
I am manifesting my ideal partner I am sending love to my perfect partner
I attract loving people into my life
I am attracting the perfect partner to me
I enjoy loving others and being loved
I allow myself to have the perfect relationship
My mind and body come into perfect alignment with my desire for love
I am using my heart to radiate and attract love
I receive back in abundance all the love the universe has to offer
I am attracting love and happiness now
My body is filled with love and harmony
Each day my mind creates a bridge to my perfect partner
I am love I am grateful for the newfound love
I receive in my life I embody complete and pure love
I now manifest love in infinite ways
I manifest perfect love with ease
I am now giving myself permission to experience all of the ways in which love can show
itself in my life
I am enjoying my new healthy relationship
I am engaging in self-love each and every moment of each and every day as I focus on more love in my life
I send a strong signal of love into the universe

I am choosing thoughts that align with love
My mind and body come into perfect alignment with my desire for love
I am using my heart to radiate and attract love
I receive back in abundance all the love the universe has to offer
You can now open your eyes; this meditation is complete.

Chapter 2: Meditations For Building the Right Foundation For Your Relationship (90 mins)

Often, we expect others to love us when we have no idea how to love ourselves. A healthy relationship is one where two whole people come together. If you are not sure how to love yourself, you will constantly be looking for love because you do not know what that looks like. To help you have better and healthier attachments, the meditations in this chapter are geared to helping you find self-love and acceptance. Only when you truly love and accept yourself can you love and accept love from others.

If you want to create the foundation for healthy relationships, these meditations will help you get the confidence and faith in yourself you need to be in a positive relationship.

Meditation for Self-Love and Acceptance -25 minutes

If you struggle to find healthy relationships or love, you may find yourself questioning your self-worth and losing your self-confidence. These negative emotions interfere with your ability to attract love and realize your innermost desires because negative energy will never attract positive outcomes. It is therefore important to start your journey to finding your soulmate by making sure that your heart, emotions and subconscious mind are in the right place. That is why this self-acceptance meditation will play a key role in helping you develop the positive love vibrations you need to attract healthy relationships.

Let's get started

Duration:25 minutes

Start by sitting in a comfortable position with your feet planted firmly on the ground.

Relax your shoulders and align your neck and spine in a comfortable but upright posture.

Now close your eyes and become aware of the stillness around you.

Tune into the rhythms of your breath as you inhale and exhale. Bring all of your awareness to the soothing rhythm of air entering your body slowly and leaving.

Feel the rise and fall of your chest as you breathe in and out. If there are any thoughts in your mind, release them and continue focusing on your breathing.

As you sink deeper and deeper into relaxation, feel your entire body relaxing and becoming one with the stillness and calmness around you.

Lose yourself in this peaceful space where you can feel your mind and body letting go of tension and stress. Feel a healing energy and radiant warmth start to take root from the pit of your stomach.

Now slowly as you feel the radiant energy start to vibrate through you, start to feel the love, peace and positivity this energy brings. You are awash with it and it is permeating your every pore.

In this moment I want you to start feeling like you are in charge of this radiant energy and the love and positivity it brings.

I want you to realize that you are the creator of all of your feelings and that you are not a victim of them. You have the power to take charge of the radiant energy within you and use it to create positive feelings of love, acceptance and calmness.

Love is a feeling that you can create. It is not a commodity to be given or taken away from you. You have power over it because you can create it.

Now I want you to take a minute and think of the kind of love you want to create for yourself. Think of the kind of love that starts from within and radiates outwards.

The kind of love that does not depend on others but you because only you have the power to create your feelings.

Start to describe and see this kind of love in your mind. The kind of love that lets you be who you are. The kind of love that allows you to go after what you want because you know you deserve it. The kind of love that allows you to know what you want and stops you from settling for anything else.

Create this kind of love in your mind and make sure it includes all your innermost definitions of what real love looks like.

Visualize and feel this love. You want to create it in yourself because that is the only way you will recognize it in others.

All the things you want your soulmate to be for you and to feel for you, first find them in yourself.

Unconditional acceptance of yourself. Letting go of self-criticism and negative self-talk. Being kind to yourself. Being your own best friend. Cheering yourself on. Supporting yourself. Self-love.

Honoring your true spirit and being mindful of the essence of who you really are. Your emotions, your needs, your body, your desires. Let it all come to the surface.

As you continue to create the kind of love you want in your mind, allow yourself to connect with this version of love that you are creating. You deserve to feel that from yourself and others.

Recognize your role in creating the love you want. Understand that the energy and love vibration you are creating is exactly what the universe will give you back.

If you hold yourself in high esteem, the universe will give you back love that holds you in high esteem. If you create unconditional love and respect for yourself, the universe reflects it back to you.

In this moment, be mindful of the kind of love you have created. How does it feel? How will it feel if the universe amplifies that love and sends it back to you?

Whatever you want from the universe must first flow into and through you. So what kind of love are you creating for yourself?

If you want others to value you, you must first value yourself. If you want others to accept you, you must first accept yourself.

You have everything you need to create the kind of love you want for yourself. It is radiating through you right now in this moment. Only you can create the kind of love you want. You are in control.

Now I want you to take a deep breath in and as you inhale feel yourself get filled with this new love you have created for yourself. Let it come in and cleanse all the negative self-limiting beliefs.

As you exhale, release the self-doubt, self-criticism and negative beliefs about yourself.

From this moment on, you are going to be true to yourself. You accept yourself as you are and you will no longer allow your own beliefs to keep you from loving yourself.

You are anchoring yourself to this new kind of love that you have created and every time you start to lose self-esteem or your sense of worth you will come back to this love that is radiating within you in this moment.

You will treat yourself with compassion and love because you are in charge of your emotions. You are in charge of your energy and from now on you will only breathe hope and life to your desires.

You know what kind of love you want. You know how you want to feel and you are going to create that feeling from the inside out and radiate it to the universe.

Now I want you to take a deep breath then breathe out slowly.

Repeat this affirmation, stating it with intention and connecting deeply to the words.
I fully accept myself and who I am. I recognize my strengths. I accept my flaws. I will keep making progress towards who I want to be. I will value and treat myself with respect because I deserve it.
Sit with this intention for a moment then breathe in deeply and exhale slowly.
Repeat the affirmation,
I fully accept myself and who I am. I recognize my strengths. I accept my flaws. I will keep making progress towards who I want to be. I will value and treat myself with respect because I deserve it.
Again, let's take a deep slow breath and exhale slowly.
Repeat the affirmation,
I fully accept myself and who I am. I recognize my strengths. I accept my flaws. I will keep making progress towards who I want to be. I will value and treat myself with respect because I deserve it.
Sit with this intention in your mind for a moment and allow it to sink deep into your subconscious.
Now, I want you to slowly start to bring your awareness to the present by tuning in to the rhythm of your breathing.
Gradually allow yourself to become aware of your surroundings. When you are ready, you can gently open your eyes.
This meditation is now complete.

Guided Meditation for Rebuilding Your Self-esteem – 20 minutes

It is often said that people treat us the way we teach them to treat us. All this means is that unless you can truly learn to love yourself you will have a hard time attracting positive and healthy relationships. This meditation is a great way to rebuild your self-esteem. Whether you have lost your sense of self-esteem after a bad breakup or have gone through something that undermined your self-worth, this meditation will help you restore your faith and confidence in yourself.
Let's get into it.
Duration: 20 minutes
You can practice this meditation in bed before going to bed.
Lie down comfortably and close your eyes.
Place one hand on your stomach and bring your awareness to the rise and fall of your stomach as you inhale and exhale.
As your mind starts to relax and your body starts to release any tension in your muscles, I want you to imagine that you can hear the sound of a gentle stream soothing and washing over you in gentle calming waves.
As you immerse yourself in the soothing sound of the stream you can see yourself seated beside the stream on a beautiful patch of soft grass.
You can feel a gentle breeze softly caress your skin and as you inhale, fresh healing air fills your lungs with a vibrant clean energy.
Everything around you is calm, serene and beautiful. You feel safe and protected in this space and the longer you sit by the stream, the calmer and more at ease you feel.
Now as you embrace the tranquility and serenity of the gentle stream, I want you to repeat these affirmations. Take time to connect to each intention and feel it in your mind and heart.
I am peaceful. I value myself as a person.
I appreciate myself and I am grateful for my life.

I am happy with who and what I am.
I deserve to be healthy and happy.
I deserve my life to be wonderful
I will allow times of self-doubt to pass and wash over me like a passing cloud.
I will not attach to negative thoughts and emotions.
I will embrace myself as I am and live the life I know I deserve.
I am attracting a wonderful future and I know that I will have everything I have ever wanted.
I am manifesting self-love and abundance for myself.
I attract good things with ease.
I am enjoying life now.
I embrace my past self and I promise I will be good to myself from this moment on.
I accept myself for whom I am.
I care about myself. I am worthy of self-love.

At this moment, I want you to take a deep breathe followed by a slow exhale. Take another deep breath and exhale slowly.

Now I want you to visualize the person you have always known you could be. Your most confident self, your most beautiful self, your most accomplished self.

As you visualize this image, I want you to see this version of yourself in vivid detail. How are you feeling? How do you look? Who are you with? See all these details that make up the future you that you want to be.

As you see each detail, I want you to connect to that future version of yourself. Feel the confidence of being exactly who you want to be. The sense of security of knowing that you are where you want to be. Notice how it feels to be this person. Confident, unafraid and sure of your place in the world.

Take a moment to really connect with this version of you. Everything you see is right there waiting for you to claim it. Make up your mind to live as that version of yourself.

The version of yourself that is free from self-doubt, self-criticism and constant anxiety. From this moment you are living the past behind and you choose to attach to the future and leave the doubts and negativity in the past.

Allow yourself to feel yourself falling into this new persona. Let it infuse in every pore of your being like a ray of sunlight that lights you up from head to toe and leaves you glowing.

You are absorbing this positive self-image and you are becoming one with it. Let it soak into your inner being and cleanse you of every negative thought you have about yourself.

As you sit bathed in this positive energy, we are going to repeat the affirmations one more time.

I am peaceful. I value myself as a person.
I appreciate myself and I am grateful for my life.
I am happy with who and what I am.
I deserve to be healthy and happy.
I deserve my life to be wonderful
I will allow times of self-doubt to pass and wash over me like a passing cloud.
I will not attach to negative thoughts and emotions.
I will embrace myself as I am and live the life I know I deserve.
I am attracting a wonderful future and I know that I will have everything I have ever wanted.
I am manifesting self-love and abundance for myself.
I attract good things with ease.
I am enjoying life now.
I embrace my past self and I promise I will be good to myself from this moment on.

I accept myself for whom I am.
I care about myself. I am worthy of self-love.
Now, let us take a deep breath and release it slowly. Take another deep breath and exhale slowly.
You can now start to bring your awareness back to the present by focusing on the simple act of breathing in and out.
You can allow yourself to drift into sleep now: this meditation is now complete.

Meditation for healing your Inner Child and Overcoming Codependency -25 minutes

One of the biggest reasons we struggle with relationships is when become overly reliant on the other person to validate us and make us feel worthy. This kind of negative attachment stems from insecurities that we develop from an early age depending on our immediate environment. When your inner child is broken, you will struggle to attach to people positively without being codependent.
This meditation is intended to help you overcome codependent tendencies and restore your happy inner child.
Let's get started.
Duration: -25 minutes
Begin by sitting in a comfortable position on a chair or on the floor in the lotus position.
Now close your eyes and take a nice slow deep breath
Relax your body and allow your mind to empty of all thoughts as you bring all your focus to the breath entering your body as you breathe in and out.
Feel everything begin to slow down and a gentle tranquil energy start to settle over you like a soothing blanket.
As you sink deeper into relaxation start to think back to your past experiences. The ones that have shaped you into who you are.
Think back to past hurts and self doubts that you may be holding on to from childhood. Maybe a caregiver or teacher said something that dented your sense of self-worth and their words haunt you to this day.
Maybe a loved one said something that made you begin to question whether you were lovable.
Maybe your experiences have turned you into an enabler who allows people to walk all over you because you never learned how to set clear boundaries.
Maybe you think that the only way to be loved is by forgetting who you are to become the version that others want you to be.
Maybe you feel stuck in a cycle of toxicity because you do not know how to stop being dysfunctional.
Maybe you have no idea how to take control because all your life other people's needs came first.
You may have grown up longing for approval that never came so as an adult you are still carrying this need for approval and validation.
Maybe as a child, you did not get unconditional love so as an adult you do not dare to hope that you deserve that kind of love.
You feel like you always need to be making up for something to get approval and acceptance. You fight for toxic relationships even when you know that deep down inside they are only causing you pain.

You settle time and time again for less than you deserve because deep inside your experiences have programmed you to think you are unlovable, unworthy or unacceptable as you are.

Now as you let all these painful realizations come to you, allow yourself to acknowledge and release them.

With every breath you take, feel yourself letting go of this negative energy that stops you from growing into yourself.

Deep inside you are still a broken child looking up to others for approval and validation.

I want you to visualize your inner child as a real child that is standing in a dark corner, lost and afraid. See the worry in their face and the fear in their eyes. This child is lost in the dark and they are waiting for you to walk them towards the light.

The experiences of the past cannot be erased but you can release them and unburden yourself of all the baggage you have been carrying around.

As you visualize your inner child in your mind standing alone in the dark, I want you to walk towards them and reach out your hand and take theirs.

Feel the little palm in your hand and let your hand close over it with confidence and assurance. You will guide this child away from the dark and into the light.

You will unburden them of their fear that they are not good enough. You will unburden them of the constant need for approval and you will leave all the negative experiences in the dark and walk towards the light.

From now on, every time you are tempted to settle for less than you deserve or feel yourself becoming self-critical, you will remember that defenseless child who is holding your hand and counting on you to lead them to the light.

You will protect that child and nurture them to see all their desires come to pass. You will transform them from living in fear and self-doubt to embracing positivity and moving forward with confidence.

Now, as you continue to visualize yourself holding the hand of your inner child I want you to see yourself walking forward hand in hand. As you start to walk forward, with every step, you are walking towards a vibrant glowing light.

The closer you get to the light, the more confident and self-assured your step gets. You are leaving behind all the bad experiences and walking towards a positive future.

Your inner child is smiling in joy as they walk beside you towards the light. They are no longer trapped alone in a dark dingy place. With every step you take, your inner child grows more confident and hopeful.

As you get closer and closer to the light you can feel yourself losing the shackles of the past that have held you back for so long.

You are now standing in the light, bathed in its healing radiance. Your inner child is still beside you and as you stand there soaking in the light, a warm glow is spreading from the tips of your toes all the way to the top of your head.

You can feel positive energy coursing through you and in this moment, you know that you no longer have to be anchored to the past. You belong in the light. You belong here where the gentle warmth coursing through you and enveloping you comforts and soothes you.

Now I want you to take a moment to really feel this moment. Feel the positive energy that is coursing through you and your inner child as you both stand in the healing light. Open yourself fully to it and receive the healing power of the universe. Take it in. Take it all in.

In this moment you are liberating yourself and setting yourself free. You are in control of your emotions, your inner energy and you are ready to keep protecting your inner child. You have surrendered to the positive energy of the universe and all the dark that you have left behind no longer has a hold on you.

Luxuriate in this feeling of freedom and positivity, knowing that every time you feel desperate or afraid, you can come back to this safe space and bathe yourself in positivity.
Now take a deep breath and exhale. Breathe in again deeply and exhale. As you breathe in, let your mind slowly come back to the present.
Slowly become aware of where you are and your surroundings. When you are ready, you can gently open your eyes.
This meditation is now complete.

Guided Meditation for Self Confidence and Positive Self-image: 20 minutes

To attract positive happy people, you must radiate positivity and confidence. The law of attraction simply reflects back to you the energy that you are putting out into the universe. If you are constantly surrounded by negativity and self-doubt, you will always find yourself in dysfunctional and toxic relationships because your negative energy keeps attracting negative people.
This meditation will help you cultivate a positive self-image and boost your confidence. It will reset all those self-limiting beliefs that have kept you in a negative space where you are unable to manifest positive outcomes.
Let's get started.
Duration: 20 minutes
I invite you to get comfortable. Sit in a chair with your feet planted firmly on the ground.
Let your hands rest easily in your lap and gently close your eyes.
As you breathe in and out, I want you to allow your whole body to get limber and relaxed.
Begin to think of your facial muscles relaxing and as the muscles of the forehead relax you may notice a slight increase in tension around the eyebrows.
I want you to concentrate on the eyebrows and all around the eyes and slowly feel this tension fading away.
Feel the tiny muscles of your eyelids relax and feel that relaxation move deeply into your eyes.
As your whole face relaxes, feel this soothing calmness start to spread to the rest of your body. feel the tension in your neck and shoulders ease and let your whole body lean on the support of the ground beneath your feet.
You have released every pent-up stress and tension in your body and you are now open to receiving the universe's energy.
Now in just a moment, I will begin to countdown.
With every descending number, you will feel yourself drawing close and closer to a powerful source of positive energy.
Five
Take a step forward towards the light and start to feel safe and relaxed in a private sanctuary where nothing can harm you.
Four
Take another step forward and visualize yourself becoming carefree and confident as you get even closer to the light.
Three
Your mind is at ease and you feel yourself getting ready to absorb boundless positive energy from the light that is getting closer and closer.
Two

You are feeling lighter and as you drift even deeper into your subconscious mind you can feel it open up to receive from the universe.

One

You are now standing in the light and its golden rays are bathing you in a soothing energy that is seeping into you and becoming one with your being.

Now as you stand in this light, I want you to breathe in slowly and exhale slowly. Take another deep breath then allow your breathing to go back to your normal rhythm.

Your mind is now completely open and the light that is surrounding you is making you receptive to all the positivity the universe has to offer.

In this moment, I want you to remember a time when you felt truly good about yourself.

It doesn't matter how far back you need to go but go back to that time when you were truly happy and see it clearly in your mind.

Allow yourself to drift back to that time and notice what is going on around you at that time. Where are you? Who are you with? What are you doing?

Notice what's happening and become aware of some of the feelings and thoughts that you have about yourself at that point when you are truly happy.

Are you proud of yourself? Do you feel a sense of accomplishment? Are you content with who you are? Take time to really notice how you feel in that particular moment.

Now I want you to take that image and connect with it deeply. Internalize the feelings you are experiencing in that moment of happiness. Take those thoughts you have about yourself in that moment and hold on to them.

As you bond with these emotions and thoughts I want you to cement them in your mind. As you hold on to this positive self-image I want you to allow yourself to make it the image you go back to when you think about yourself.

Feel the positive image replacing all the negative thoughts and emotions that you may have about yourself. From now on, every time you think about who you are, the positive image is what will come to mind.

Repeat this affirmation,

I am beautiful. I am accomplished. I am confident. I am strong and each day I get better.

From this moment on, you can always access your inner beauty because you have bonded with the most positive and happy version of yourself.

Let us repeat this affirmation one more time,

I am beautiful. I am accomplished. I am confident. I am strong and each day I get better.

Sit with this intention and let it sink deep into your subconscious. Connect with it again by repeating the words allowing them to resound in your mind.

I am beautiful. I am accomplished. I am confident. I am strong and each day I get better.

Now in just a moment, I will invite you to return from your experience and as you return you'll bring back the positive self-image with you.

You feel both calm and refreshed and there is a positivity that is radiating all around you and inside you.

Here and now you are connected to your inner beauty and your self-esteem and confidence will keep growing each and every day.

As you hold on to this positivity let us slowly get back to the present.

Inhale deeply and as you exhale slowly bring your awareness back to your body. Feel the pressure of the ground beneath your feet and slowly start to focus on your surroundings.

When you are ready you can open your eyes.

This meditation is now complete.

Chapter 3: Guided Meditations to Attract Your Soulmate (65 mins)

Love can sometimes be complicated and you may sometimes feel like you keep attracting the wrong kind of people. When this happens over and over again it is simply because your desires and the vibrational energy you are putting into the universe are not aligned. When your energy is in conflict with what you want then you attract the wrong kind of person. You keep wondering why it so hard to attract the love of your life or the soulmate, yet all this time the resistance is coming from your subconscious.

Your subconscious mind acts as the blueprint that sets the tone of your vibrational energy. This means that unless you can get this energy to align with what your heart desires you will keep sending out mixed signals into the universe. The law of attraction works every time without fail but remember it will attract what your subconscious energy puts out. If you are constantly afraid and anxious that you will never find your soulmate or true love, this negative love vibration blocks your ability to attract your soulmate. This means that the most powerful way to manifest the person you want in your life is to reset your love vibration.

Think of it this way, magnets do not just attract anything. There are rules and exceptions to a magnetic field and what it is able to draw in. In principle, this is how the law of attraction works. You can only attract what you want by creating the right type of energy to get what you want.

The meditations in this section are to help you attract your soulmate. This can be a specific person that you already know or a soulmate that you may not have met but you know is out there for you. One common mistake that people make that keeps them from attracting the love they want is focusing too much on the other person. Attraction is not about getting the other person to notice you or fall in love with you. It is about fixing your energy from the inside and letting this energy draw the person to you. When you harness your subconscious energy to fuel your desire, you do not need to struggle to find love. Simply create the right energy internally and trust the universe to bring you the love of your life.

Guided Meditation to Attract a Specific Person – 25 minutes

If you know who you want to attract into your life but you simply do not know how to draw them to you, this meditation is meant to help you attract that person. This guided meditation is also for people who may not know who their soulmate is but want to attract them and bring them into your life. Whether your soulmate is known to you or still just someone you visualize in your mind, the law of attraction can help you manifest that person.

Lets us get started.

Duration: 25 minutes

Lie down in a comfortable position and close your eyes.

Now, let us start by turning inward and shutting out all the external noise and stimuli. We are going to calm your mind and relax your entire body by taking a series of deep breaths.

Take a deep slow breath and as you inhale count to six, hold for a moment then exhale slowly to a count of six.

Again, deep breath in and as you inhale count to six, hold for a moment and then exhale slowly to a count of six.
One last time, inhale deeply and count to six, hold for a moment, then exhale slowly to a count of six.
Now allow your breathing to go back to normal and allow yourself to relax completely, clearing your mind of all errant thoughts by simply focusing on your breathing.
As you sink deeper into relaxation, I want to now take your hand and lay it above your heart.
With your heart above your heart, open up your heart to the universe and set the intention to accept the love the universe has to offer.
Feel your entire body relaxing into a positive field of love. Imagine that this love vibration is a pink mist that is slowly surrounding and engulfing you in its vibrant energy.
Let it travel from your heart up to your head all the way to the base of your skull. Feel it spread to your neck, your shoulders and down to your arms.
Every inch of you is being covered by this loving energy and you can feel your body open up to it and embrace it.
Let it spread downwards to the rest of your body, warming you gently and relaxing any tension in your muscles.
You are now enveloped in a safe loving vibrant energy that is bathing you in its pink light and warmth.
Now, in this state I want you to start to call to mind all your past loves. The ones that did not work out. The ones that left you hurting. The ones that you walked away from. Call them to mind one by one.
As each one comes to mind, I want you to see them in detail and then slowly take a deep breath and then exhale. As you exhale you are releasing that old love and detaching from them.
One by one, call them to mind, see them and release them. The more you let go of this past loves the brighter the love force around you gets. You are now surrounded in a beautiful vivid pink energy and every time you let go, it gets even brighter.
As you get rid of all this past loves, open yourself up to the awareness that there is something better for you. You are releasing the past to make room for the future.
Now your love energy is untainted. It is pink and bright and beautiful just waiting for the right person.
In this moment you are opening yourself to the infinite love of the universe. You are no longer interested in what was or what could have been. Here and now, in this moment your heart is open to what's coming. Ready to receive love, ready to give love. Ready to enjoy love.
Now in this state of openness, I want you to call out to your soul mate. In your mind, in your heart and with every fiber of your being.
Reach out to your soulmate. The one who was created just for you and you for him or her.
If you know the person, see them clearly in your mind. The shape of their face, their eyes, their smile, the line of their jaw. See everything about them and as you hold this image in your mind feel yourself connecting with them.
Feel that connection from heart to heart and soul to soul. Feel yourself drawing this person in and inviting him or her into your life. Speak to them in your mind and tell them it is time for your life together to begin.
As you say those words I want you to imagine that this person is already in your life. How does it feel to know that you have them? Open yourself up completely to this feeling of having them.
Imagine the first time that you touch and the electricity that the two of you feel. Feel the thrill that courses through your body when they look at you, when they touch you, when you hear their voice.
Imagine what it feels like to have this person in your life. Laying on your couch, riding in your car, walking with you around your neighborhood. Feel these moments clearly in your mind. See that person next to you, being a part of your life every day. See it, feel it.

Now take a moment to feel the first kiss that you have with each other. The feel of his lips on yours, the sweetness of it.
Feel what it feels like to cuddle together as you watch a movie. Imagine this person kissing you all over your face, rubbing your back and holding you.
Visualize spending days together with your soulmate. Talking, sharing your life, sharing your feelings, feeling your way closer and closer together.
Visualize yourself learning each other's rhythms and connecting emotionally, physically and spiritually.
In this relationship, you can really be yourself. This person accepts you fully and completely. Take a moment to feel what that feels like; being loved completely and unconditionally. Let yourself absorb that feeling of complete acceptance.
You are sharing your whole life together and building a life together.
This relationship flows and feels better. You have trust, you have confidence in each other and you are bonded together.
There's no fear or anxiety in this relationship. You are safe and secure in your love.
Now I want you to take a minute to embrace this person wholeheartedly. Give them a tight hug and feel them next to you. Feel the warmth of their embrace and the comfort of their arms around you.
Now, Look them in their eyes and say, I commit to this. I want this.
As you say those words I want you to do it with intention and in your soul invite this person into your life. Know that this connection is real and allow yourself to feel yourself connecting with that person.
Feel the love that you two share permeating every part your being. To connect yourself to this moment I want you to repeat this affirmation.
I am love and love is abundant in my life. My soulmate is coming into my life easily and with great love.
Allow yourself to sit with this affirmation and feel it deeply.
When you feel ready, you can start to slowly bring yourself back by focusing your mind on your breathing. Bring your mind back to the present and take a moment to hold on to the love you have just experienced.
Gently open your eyes.
This meditation is now complete.

Defining & Attracting Your Ideal Partner & Soulmate – 25 minutes

Have you ever felt like you know who the perfect soulmate for you is even though you have never met them? Do you feel in your heart that there is someone out there who is the ideal soulmate for you? The law of attraction brings us what we think about, what we believe in, every single time. If you can align your desire with your subconscious energy, then you will manifest the person that you want in your life.
This guided meditation is intended to help you define and attract your ideal partner or soulmate. It will help you create a strong love vibrational energy to draw and attract into your life the soulmate or partner you have always wanted.
Let's get into it.
Duration: 25 minutes.
Start by sitting or lying down in a comfortable position.
Allow your mind and body to relax and let go of any stress or tension.
Gently close your eyelids and take a deep and slow breath in and, as you fully breathe out, feel how you release all the tension you may feel in your body.

Again, take a deep and slow breath in and, breathe out all the static and negative energy you may have stored in your body.
Feel how your body sinks into a deeper and deeper rest each time you take a conscious breath.
Take another deep and slow breath in and, breathe out all the distracting thoughts or emotions that you may be experiencing still in this present moment.
Release them all and let them float away into nothing.
Feel how your body sinks deeper and deeper into a gradual and complete bliss as you allow your mind and body to relax completely.
If your mind starts to wander, just bring your attention back to your breathing.
Relax.
Now, imagine a flower of your choice, a flower radiating petals that are closed.
Choose the color of your flower by asking yourself, What is the color of my flower, right now?
What color does my heart seek, right now?
Now place the flower with its closed petals in the center of the chest which is your heart center.
As you pay more and more attention to it, the flower slowly opens its petals and the color becomes more and more radiant.
Its radiating bright glow that is emanating from its center and its illumination is lighting up your heart and everything around it is also alight with this glow.
The radiant glow smoothly travels and spreads through your abdominal area, pelvis, the whole pelvic region, hips, upper legs, knees, lower legs, ankles, heels, soles, feet.
It goes through your shoulders, upper arms, elbows, lower arms, wrists, hands, palms, fingers.
The sides between the armpits and hips, lower, middle and upper back, the entire back, neck, head, forehead, ears, eyebrows, eyelids, eyes, nose, cheeks, lips, chin, jaws.
Your entire body is bathing in this radiant glow. Your body and mind are deeply relaxed.
This free-flowing and radiant energy of the universe's infinite love circulates throughout your entire being.
In this moment I want you to feel your heart radiating openness, love, warmth and gratitude.
The magical glow is now expanding beyond your body, it pervades the space close to you and goes further away to the space of all possibilities.
Your creative power is directed towards the attraction of your ideal partner and their manifestation into your life.
You are paving the path for manifestation right now.
Say to yourself out loud, I love and accept myself totally. I am ready to love and be loved. Each and every day I wholeheartedly commit myself to positive and high vibrational energy. I trust the universe to bring the right people, timing and circumstances into my life.
Now sit quietly for a moment and ask yourself, who do I want to share my heart with? Who do I want to grow with, laugh with and share life's experiences with?
Who is my loving, nurturing and supportive significant other?
What do I want to experience in the relationship?
Allow yourself to really look inward and answer these questions openly and without judgment.
Now, I want you to imagine the partner you want in a very specific way. Clearly state in your mind all the qualities, attributes, and physical appearance of your ideal partner.
What do they look like? What color of eyes and hair does your partner have? How does it feel to hear your partner's voice?
What are the specific physical features that you really like about your partner?

Ask yourself questions about the qualities that matter the most to you. Then take a few moments to create the mental image of the partner you have described.

Allow your imagination to be as vivid and as detailed as possible.

How do you see your partner as a person? Is their sense of humor important to you? If the answer is yes, then you can visualize yourself sharing beautiful and playful moments.

Whatever qualities you want most in your partner, see them playing out in your mind. Do you want someone you can count on? Someone compassionate? Someone who supports and cheers you on?

Visualize the specific ways you want your partner to be, as a person, as your soulmate and as a human being.

Feel it. See it. Connect with it.

Do you want a person who shares your vision for the future? Do they live in the same place you do or maybe, in another country?

Visualize the person how you think they are and what you imagine them doing right now.

Now, what about your interests, passion, hobbies. What kind of hobbies and interests does your partner have?

What interests and activities do you like to share with your partner? Visualize both of you spending some time together enjoying activities together, perhaps watching your favorite movie, playing sports, traveling together or hiking in nature.

Visualize it in as many details as you can and feel what that experience feels like to you and how much you enjoy it.

In the next few moments, think about other important traits of your ideal partner for a while.

Now I want you to imagine that you are holding a puzzle in your hand. Begin to take pieces of the puzzle and write down all the qualities and traits you want in your soulmate. Each quality you put down brings the puzzle closer and closer to completion.

As you put together your puzzle, visualize your partner displaying these qualities or sharing them with you. If it's a sense of humor see them cracking jokes and laughing with you. If it's kindness, visualize them reaching out to help others. Whatever quality you want, visualize it in vivid detail and bring it to life.

By adding each piece of the puzzle to this perfect circle, you are increasing your awareness of the partner that you want to attract.

The more aware you become of what your soulmate is really like, the stronger the signal and energy you are sending to the universe to bring this person into your life. You are creating the vibrational energy that will draw this person to you.

As you finish putting all the pieces of the puzzle together, feel this new and uplifting vibration circulating throughout your being and expanding further to the place where the connection between you and your partner becomes stronger.

See yourself and your partner standing a short distance apart with your backs turned to each other. Feel the presence of your partner.

Now, imagine that as you stand there close but apart, a ray of light is extending from the space in between your eyebrows to its parallel point at the back of your head.

The particles of light are slowly traveling, floating and spreading beyond the back of your head towards the back of your partner's head.

Feel this unifying ray of light connecting you with your partner. Feel its magnetic force drawing the two of you together to become one soul.

As you become completely connected, both of you are slowly turning your bodies to face each other.

As you come face to face, you and your partner are slowly lifting your arms towards each other.

Now, feel yourself holding each other's hands and smiling at each other. You can feel a warmth and loving energy passing from your body to them and from theirs to yours.
Focus on the feeling of touching and the sensation you feel in your hands as you hold your soulmate's hands.
In this moment you feel as light as a skillful dancer who is ready to surrender to their partner's movements.
You are dancing together and the shiny particles of light that are surrounding you are moving with you as you dance. You are bonded by this powerful radiant love energy.
Feel the elevation and the ultimate unity in this very moment. The bond between you and your partner is strong. The energy that you have created is real.
You can now leave it up to the universe, to manifest what you created. You are no longer anxious or afraid, you know that you have been connected and bonded to your soulmate, it is only a matter of time before they manifest in your life.
Now, slowly I want you to take in this feeling of confidence and security in knowing that the universe is bringing you your ideal partner. Soak in this feeling and carry it with you.
You are now ready to bring your attention back to the present. Focus on the rhythm of your breath and let it bring your awareness back to your surroundings.
When you are ready, you can open your eyes.
This meditation is now complete.

I AM Affirmations for Attracting Your Soulmate -15 minutes

Affirmations are a powerful way to align your subconscious energy with the desires you want to manifest. When you practice affirmations consistently for the things you want to attract, you create a strong positive energy that draws and attracts the things you want. These love affirmations will set your intentions to manifest your soulmate in your life.
You can practice these affirmations daily before you go to sleep to focus your subconscious energy on attracting your soulmate.
Let's get started.
Duration: 15 minutes
Start by lying down in a comfortable position.
Now relax, close your eyes, and begin to breathe slowly and deeply.
With each breath, let your body relax. Just focus on your breathing and feel yourself release all the thoughts in your mind and the tension in your body.
Continue to take deep slow breaths, letting each breath drive you further and further into peace and tranquility.
You are now completely relaxed and your mind is open and calm, ready to receive whatever the universe has in store for you.
Now I want you to repeat these affirmations quietly in your mind. As you say each one, take a moment to absorb and connect to the intention.
My soul mate is strongly attracted to me.
I am beautiful and worthy of love.
I release everything that stands in the way of finding my soul mate.
I attract only loving people into my life.

My soul mate is entering my life now.
Love is attracted to me.
I love myself, and I feel complete.
I am ready for true love.
I draw love and romance into my life.
I attract love easily.
I am magnetic and irresistible to my soul mate.
I feel happy now that I have met my soul mate.
My heart is open to receiving and giving love.
I have made room in my life for my soulmate.
I open my heart, and trust that true love will follow.
I attract the love that I desire.
I have now found the love of my life.
It is my destiny to be with the one I love.
I believe in my ability to attract my perfect partner.
I have more love than I ever thought possible.
I easily attract a perfect relationship into my life.
I trust my soul mate completely.
Love is all around me every day.
I am guided to my soul mate.
I let go of everything that is standing in the way of love.
I have the power to give and receive love endlessly.
I have found a special someone to love.
I accept perfect love into my life, right now.
I am deeply loved and cherished by my soul mate.
I attract love everywhere I go.
My soul mate and I are destined to be together.
I am in the perfect relationship.
I release any fears of being loved.
I am lovable and worthy of receiving love.
There is a magical connection between my soul mate and myself.
I am open to experiencing true love in my life.
My perfect partner and I will easily find each other.
I am the perfect life partner for my soul mate.
I am surrounded by love.
It is safe for me to give and receive love.
I am destined to be with my soul mate.
I attract love in all that I do.
I am a magnet to love, and attract my perfect partner now.
I am in a loving relationship with my soul mate.
Every day, I attract true love.
Love is my birthright, and I claim it now.
I am attracting my perfect loving partner.
Love is flowing to me, and through me, at all times.
I am so grateful that I have attracted my soul mate.
I enjoy all the love my soul mate showers upon me.

My life is filled with passion and romance.
I am safe and cherished in my loving relationship.
I attract my perfect life partner now.
I welcome true love into my life.
My heart is always open, and I radiate love.
I now attract my soul mate into my life.
My soul mate and I are being drawn together.
My heart is open to love.
I am very grateful for all the love in my life.
My partner is the perfect match for me.
I know that my soulmate and I will be together.
I am attracting my ideal partner with grace and ease.
My soulmate is strongly attracted to me.
I am loved for who I really am.
I spread love to everyone around me, and it returns in abundance.
I release the past, and let love flow into my life.
I am in the right place at the right time to meet my soul mate.
I allow myself to attract a perfect relationship into my life.
I am ready to love and be loved.
I accept perfect love into my life, right now.
I am deeply loved and cherished by my soul mate.
There is a magical connection between my soul mate and myself.
I am open to experiencing true love in my life.
I am a magnet to love, and attract my perfect partner now.
Love is my birthright, and I claim it now.
I am attracting my perfect loving partner.
Love is flowing to me, and through me, at all times.
I am so grateful that I have attracted my soulmate.
I have created space in my life for my soulmate.
I radiate pure, unconditional love towards my soul mate.
My life is filled with passion and romance.
I am safe and cherished in my loving relationship.
I attract my perfect life partner now.
I welcome true love into my life.
Now is the right time to meet my perfect partner.
I welcome love with open arms.
I attract positive and loving energy.
I release everything that stands in the way of finding my soul mate.
My soul mate is entering my life now.
I am ready for true love.
I draw love and romance into my life.
I attract love easily.
I am magnetic and irresistible to my soul mate.
I have made room in my life for my soulmate.
I have found a special someone to love.
I accept perfect love into my life, right now.

I am very grateful for all the love in my life.
I know that my soulmate and I will be together.
I am attracting my ideal partner with grace and ease.
I am in the right place at the right time to meet my soul mate.
I welcome love with open arms.
I radiate love and receive it back many times over.
I have created space in my life for my soulmate.
I draw love and romance into my life.
I attract love easily.
I am magnetic and irresistible to my soul mate.
My heart is open to receiving and giving love.
I am a magnet to love, and attract my perfect partner now.
Every day, I attract true love.
Love is my birthright, and I claim it now.
Love is flowing to me, and through me, at all times.
Now is the right time to meet my perfect partner.
I now attract my soul mate into my life.
My soul mate and I are being drawn together.
My life is filled with passion and romance.
I have found the love of my life.
There is an unbreakable bond between my soul mate and myself.
I welcome love with open arms.
I radiate pure, unconditional love towards my soul mate.
My soul mate is entering my life now.
I open my heart, and trust that true love will follow.
Now you have set a clear intention for your subconscious to attract your soulmate, all you need to do is trust the universe to bring you your soulmate.
You can now allow yourself to drift into sleep taking this feeling of abundant love with you.
This meditation is now complete.

Chapter 4: Meditations For Attracting a Real Twin Flame Relationship (85 mins)

A twin flame is best described as your other half. Someone who has the same spiritual energy and vibrations as you and with whom you share a magical connection. Unlike soulmates, there is only one real twin flame for each person. The magical connection when two twin flames meet creates a lifelong bond that brings two halves together as one. A twin flame relationship is like a mirror that reflects back your real authentic self. In this relationship, you are at your most natural self because you are sharing your life who shares the same frequency as you.

Twin flame relationships differ from other types of relationships because your twin flame is a soul twin. This means the connection between twin flames is the deepest kind and cannot be shared with anyone else because every person has only one twin flame. When twin flames meet there is an instant attraction and bond that you may not really be able to explain because it happens instinctively. If you have always longed for a relationship where your hearts, spirit and energies are in sync, attracting your twin flame or your other half will give you the kind of relationship you want.

In this section, the meditations will help you create a strong vibrational energy to attract your twin flame into your life. The law of attraction enables us to manifest the kind of love we want and all this is possible by tapping into the power of your subconscious to co-create your innermost desires. In this pursuit, meditation is the tool that we use to reprogram our subconscious and set our intentions in order to create the right vibrational energy to get the things we want.

Your twin flame relationship is well within your reach and these meditations will help to draw your other half to you.

Twin Flame Energy Activation – 25 minutes

Twins flames are connected to each other through their chakras and their love energy is identical. To attract your twin flame it is important to first activate your twin flame energy and increase your love vibration so that you can attract your other half.

During this meditation, you may find that as energy centers or chakras are activated you may begin to feel aroused. This sensual feeling is natural because the more you allow yourself to feel the powerful urges stirring inside of you, the stronger the vibratory energy that you pulse out into the universe. Your twin flame will pick up on your energy and send the same energy back to you. So during this session feel free to allow yourself to respond to whatever powerful emotions that are awakened

Let's get started.

Duration: 25 minutes

Start by lying down comfortably on your bed.

Now, find a single point on your ceiling to focus on. Just find something that your eyes can focus on.

Once you have identified your point of focus I want you to now allow your eyes to relax and just keep focusing on this point.

As you focus on this point, you will feel your eyelids start to feel heavier and heavier.

Notice how your breathing is slowing down and you are feeling more and more relaxed as you lie there. Your eyelids are becoming so heavy and you can't keep your eyes open anymore.

Just allow your eyes to close and turn your focus inward by bringing your awareness to your body. You can focus on the rhythm of your breaths as you breathe deeply and slowly.

Now as you allow yourself to relax completely, I want you to start visualizing a beautiful sparkling pyramid that is made up of sparkling iridescent light.

Feel the glow of this beautiful pyramid start to irradiate you in its glow. You are now completely enclosed in the glow of this pyramid and its beautiful light is all around you in a soothing calming glow.

Protected by this soothing glow, visualize yourself standing at the foot of a staircase. This staircase winds up into the sky disappearing into the clouds farther than the eye can see.

You are now going to start walking up this beautiful staircase one step at a time. As you start to walk up the staircase, you feel like you are almost floating and with every step you ascend your body feels lighter and lighter.

As you go higher and higher, your mind is calm and open to receiving energy from the universe and you are sinking deeper and deeper into relaxation.

You may even feel that you're ready to leave this wonderful physical form and just allow your light body to flow gently up the stairs.

Float higher and higher and now you can feel yourself drifting effortlessly through space and time.

As you become lighter and lighter just imagine your physicality becoming so light that you become a light beam, A single sparkling speck of light floating perfectly and beautifully within the immense loving ocean of divinity.

Look about you as you float and notice that you are not alone. You are surrounded by many other radiant rainbow-colored light beings glowing, pulsing, and sparkling.

In this place, you can feel your connection to a divine cosmic law and all about you are unique expressions of gold and silver particles of light that are glowing and sparkling.

Now I would like you to look up and as you do, you see a magnificent sky radiating a soft warm golden glow that caresses your skin lightly.

The air around you is clear and pure and your senses are entranced by the delicate scent of nature and life that is all around you.

Notice how good it feels to be in this astral space surrounded by beauty and light and loving energy.

Here in this place, you are light and free and you can now see very clearly that you are not alone and have never been.

Absolutely nothing can stand between the love and connection you share with your twin flame.

In the radiantly pulsing field of love that you have moved to, the golden glow around you binds you to your other half with unbreakable cosmic energy.

Now look around you and realize that you are not alone. Before you is a magnificent stream of lights that is approaching in a stream of sparkling dancing lights.

The closer this stream of light gets, everything inside you starts to expand and reach out to this familiar being that is approaching you.

You can feel this being inflaming and igniting your passion and you are instantly drawn to them.

As you continue to gaze upon this being of light, you see the light start to shine and flow from this beautiful being deep into your heart.

The light continues to flow connecting your hearts now and forever and as the connection gets deeper and deeper you feel your body begin to ache from every atom of your being and your mind.

Your body is charged with powerful orgasmic energy awakened and you are intensely aroused by the connection you feel to your twin flame.

You feel like a cascade of divine ecstasy is pulsing and moving through you touching and igniting your innermost core.
As you surrender to this passionate connection you may see your twin flame in your mind if it is already someone you know. If it is not someone you have met, they will remain as a being of pure radiant light. At this moment you may choose to project an image of someone you feel a strong physical attraction and soul connection to.
Create an experience that is perfectly in tune with you and what you want to feel with this person. As you look into your twin flame's eyes trace the lines of their jaw, their cheekbones, their neck and their shoulders. Feel their skin come alive beneath your touch.
Trace your fingers lightly and gently along all soft curves and undulations of their body and as you do feel your own skin begin to tingle.
Now place your hand upon your twin flame's heart and feel the heartbeat pulsing and radiating in sync with yours.
In this moment your twin flame places their hand upon your chest and you feel so loved and safe in your connection.
Slowly your twin flame takes you in their arms and kisses you deeply and you can feel the heat and sweetness of their breath passing into yours.
You feel as though your heart has grown wings ready to take flight to rise and soar as you both surrender to passion and two bodies become joined to each other.
Healing energy pours into your heart and soul melding and fusing into each other. Your combined vibrational energy ignites a powerful cosmic force that releases a surge of cleansing and healing energy.
In this moment of pure bliss, I want you to repeat these affirmations quietly in your mind.
I am healed with you.
I am home with you.
I am complete and our field of love may never be broken.
Now, I want you to connect to this moment. Immerse yourself in this feeling of completeness and deep connection. Understanding that you're always connected to your twin flame and that this divine connection is bringing your twin flame to you.
You can now take a deep breath and as you do, allow your mind to carry this moment with you as you slowly bring your awareness back to the present.
Now just close your eyes and dream.
This meditation is now complete.

Harmonize with Your Twin flame and Manifest Your Union -15 minutes

You and your twin flame share the same vibrational energy and frequency. If you want to manifest them in your life, harmonizing with them will give you the power to attract them by aligning your subconscious energy. In love, the perfect union is between people who desire and want to be with each other. If you want your other half to bond and be in sync with your love vibration, it is important to harmonize with them.
This guided meditation will help you manifest a passionate and deep connection with your twin flame.
Let's get started.
Duration: 15 minutes.

I want you to start by getting comfortable. You can choose to sit in a comfortable chair or lie down in bed for this meditation.

Let's shut out all that is going on in your mind, in your emotions and around you by bringing your awareness to your breathing.

Close your eyes and start to take deep slow breaths and as you do focus your attention on the sensations of breathing in and out.

Feel the clean healing energy that enters your body as you inhale and the lightness that follows as you exhale releasing all the tension in your body and mind.

Allow yourself to relax deeper and deeper as you continue taking deep slow breaths.

Release any errant thoughts in your mind and keep focusing on the beautiful rhythm and sensations of breathing in and out.

Allow yourself to relax completely and sink into a feeling of peaceful tranquility and positive energy.

Your natural state of being is in a harmonious union with your true twin flame.

You were created with your twin flame and you have always been together

I want you to feel the love in your heart. The love you have for your twin flame is who you are and nothing can ever extinguish it.

Nothing can ever tarnish this love because your connection with your other half is an indestructible bond forged by the cosmic energy of the universe.

Your twin flame is your forever love and your eternal companion so you are safe and secure knowing that he will always be with you.

You don't need to change yourself to be worthy of your twin flame. Your hearts and minds are perfectly aligned.

You are releasing any thoughts of fear and anxiety about love because you know that you will be forever bonded to your twin flame.

You are letting go of old loves and past hurts because you know that your twin flame is the one who was really meant for you.

You are opening yourself up to perfect love and perfect acceptance that comes from uniting with your other half. You are two beings in one and this connection unites you heart to heart and soul to soul.

Now in this moment, I want you to feel how at ease you are with the truth of love. How peaceful it feels to surrender to the universe knowing that your twin flame is coming into your life right now and you will be united forever.

Anytime thoughts of fear arise, you can always return to this feeling of abundant love and security.

Let this abundant love light the way to your twin flame and commit yourself completely to your twin flame union.

Surrender even deeper into the space of love within you and feel your twin flame's arms wrap around you holding you safe.

They will always return your love to you because you share one love vibration, one heart and one soul.

They are you and you are them, together for all of time.

Take a moment to sit with this connection and allow yourself to fully immerse yourself in it.

When you are ready you can gently open your eyes or allow yourself to drift into sleep.

This meditation is now complete.

Love Affirmations For Twin Flames – 20 minutes

Affirmations help to set your intentions and align your subconscious energy with the things you want to manifest. In this session, you are going to increase your vibrational energy to your twin flame by committing to them and your union. If you want to find, reunite or connect with your twin flame, you can repeat these affirmations daily before you go to bed.

Let's get into it.

Duration: 20 minutes

Find a quiet place where you can sit comfortably or lie down without any distractions.

Now close your eyes and place your hand over your heart.

Begin to take deep mindful breaths and exhaling slowly to calm your mind and release any negative emotions you may be feeling in the moment.

As you breathe in deeply, I want you to focus your awareness on the rise and fall of your chest.

If any errant thoughts pop into your mind simply focus on your breathing. Feel the air enter your body and then feel the tension and negative energy leaving with every exhale.

You are getting calmer and your body and mind are sinking deeper into relaxation.

Now I want you to repeat these affirmations quietly in your mind. As you say them, take time to internalize and connect with each intention.

I open myself to love.

I am surrounded by love every day in every way.

I see love. I feel love. I am love.

I am attuned to the frequency of love and abundance.

I love myself unconditionally.

I am grateful for all that I have.

I have let go of the past.

I release and forgive to open my heart.

I am enough.

I am loved.

I attract positive and healthy relationships.

My heart is always open to love.

I am attracting my twin flame right now.

I am bonded to my other half.

My twin flame and I are in sync.

I am open to giving and receiving love.

I am open to

I am grateful for my twin flame.

My twin flame and I are deeply connected.

I know that my twin flame is out there.

The universe is full of love.

I am ready to connect with my twin flame.

I am attracting my twin flame right now.

I am grateful that my other half is coming into my life.

I draw love and romance into my life with ease.

I spread love to those around me and it returns to me in abundance.

I am magnetic and irresistible to my twin flame.

The more I love myself the more love I receive from others.
I have the power to manifest my twin flame.
My twin flame loves me for who I am.
I am grateful for my twin flame.
My heart radiates with unconditional love for my twin flame.
My twin flame is coming into my life now.
I trust the universe will guide me to my twin flame
I am a magnet of love.
I am loved. I am love.
As you finish repeating these affirmations feel yourself emitting a strong vibrational energy to draw your twin flame to you. Know in your heart and in your mind that you are connected heart to heart.
When you are ready, gently open your eyes.
This session is now complete.

Reuniting With Your Twin Flame -25 minutes

Do you feel like you already met your other half but for one reason or another they are no longer in your life? A twin flame by definition is part of you and is perfectly managed to your energy physically emotionally and spiritually. This means that everyone has only one true twin flame and if you have lost touch with yours for one reason or another, you can attract them back into your life using this meditation.
Let's get started.
Duration: 25 minutes
Find a quiet place and sit in a comfortable chair. You can also choose to lay down for this session.
I now invite you to close your eyes and start breathing mindfully by bringing all your awareness to your breathing.
Take slow deep breaths and exhale slowly releasing any tension or stress you may be feeling.
Let whatever thoughts come to your mind just come and go without attaching to anything like a passing cloud.
Your awareness is on your breathing and the rhythmic rise and fall of your chest as you inhale and exhale.
As you sink deeper and deeper into relaxation, I want you to see yourself now standing on a plateau overlooking a beautiful green and lush landscape.
You can see for miles and miles and as you breathe in, feel that breath being drawn up from the energy of the earth.
Feel how grounding and nurturing each breath is. Feel this vibrant energy that you are breathing in coursing through your body and notice that your senses start to heighten.
You feel how powerful each breath is bringing new life to your body and expanding beyond the boundaries of your skin, connecting you to the earth and your surroundings.
You can now feel that powerful radiant moving into your heart chakra and as you continue to breathe it in, you are opening up your heart.
You can feel your heart expanding and making room for love, connection and joy. With every breath, you take the love is getting richer and stronger filling you up completely.

As you keep breathing in this vibrant love energy, you are getting filled up with a beautiful violet light that is flowing through you and all the way up into the spirit realm connecting with your guides. Your guides can be your guardian angel or your higher self.

See yourself standing before a beautiful majestic path lined and littered with precious gems. Rubies, diamonds, emeralds, and sapphires that shimmer and glow making the path the most beautiful path you've ever seen.

As you keep walking on this path, off in the distance you see a crystal castle. It looks magical and ethereal and just ahead you see a bridge crossing over to the castle.

Standing on the other side of that bridge is your twin flame. He or she stands there waiting for you and as you start to cross the bridge to meet your twin flame you notice their beautiful eyes, the warmth in their smile, the hands that are reaching out to you and the instant attraction you feel for each other.

As you walk closer and closer, you start to feel like there is a powerful force pushing you forward and now you are almost floating towards your twin flame.

This twin flame energy and connection feel familiar to you so you feel safe and you feel like you are coming home where you belong.

When you finally reach your twin flame, they hold out their hand to you and as you put your hand in theirs you can feel the love energy coursing through you getting even stronger and more powerful.

There is a powerful energy flowing from your body into your twin flame and from theirs into yours.

You can feel the energy of the earth beneath your feet rising and connecting you and your twin flame to the earth itself.

As you continue to walk towards the beautiful castle with your twin flame by your side, see yourself now with a golden thread extending from your heart chakra to their heart chakra.

Your steps, breaths and heartbeats are now in sync with each other and you are no longer two beings but one being in two halves.

Now at this moment, I want you to immerse yourself fully in this connection, hold on to the feeling of completeness that you are feeling walking hand in hand with your twin flame. You know that you are exactly where you are meant to be and the person beside you is your other half.

Know that you can come to this beautiful landscape at any time to meet and reconnect with your twin flame no matter what is going on in your life.

Know that your twin flame will always be waiting for you on the other side of that bridge to take you home. All you need to do is walk down the beautiful path and across the bridge that leads you to your other half.

Continue to feel that lightness in your body and in your spirit, knowing that you have established an unbreakable connection with your twin flame.

When you are ready, bring your awareness back to the present by focusing only on your breathing.

You can now open your eyes.

This meditation is now complete.

Chapter 5: Attract Your Ex Back and Reclaim Lost Love (75 mins)

Love can be complicated and sometimes you may end up losing someone that you know is meant for you. Just because a relationship does not work the first time, does not mean that you should give up on being with the person you love entirely. In much the same way that you can use the law of attraction to manifest your soulmate, you can also use this law to reclaim a lost love.

Attracting your ex back takes conscious effort because most of the time after breakups people sink into a negative pool of emotions. This negativity affects your love vibration making it harder to attract positivity back into your life. When you want to reclaim a lost love, the first step is to become conscious of the kind of energy that you are putting out into the universe. If you are constantly depressed, feeling worthless, or unlovable, this energy will take your love interest even further and further away.

As we mentioned earlier, the main principle of the law of attraction is that it gives you back whatever energy you put out. this means negativity will attract more negativity and if you radiate love you will get it back in abundance.

In this section, these meditations will help you reprogram your subconscious to co-create the right love vibrational energy to bring your ex back into your life.

Guided Meditation for Healing a Broken Heart & Releasing Negative Emotions - 20 minutes

For the same reasons you would not put a band-aid on a bullet wound, you cannot build a healthy relationship on a broken heart. Carrying around baggage from breakups and failed relationships blocks your love energy and keeps you from attracting the person you want. Even if all you want is to restart your relationship with your ex, you must first cleanse any residual negative emotions from your subconscious energy to clear the way for a positive love vibration.

This meditation will help you restart your relationship on a clean slate free of old wounds and negativity.

Let's get into it.

Duration: 25 minutes

Start by sitting in a comfortable chair with your feet planted firmly on the ground.

Slowly we are going to shut everything else out of this moment and simply concentrate on breathing.

Breath slowly and deeply, allowing every breath to fill you up completely.

With every exhale start to loosen up allowing both your mind to release any tension or stress.

You are breathing in fresh clean energy and breathing out stress and negative energy.

With every breath, your body feels lighter and your mind is more relaxed. You are sinking into a safe and peaceful space where nothing can hurt you.

Every breath is cleansing you from the inside out, infusing you with positivity and love. As you exhale you can feel all those pent-up emotions start to dissipate into the air.

You are no longer anxious or afraid. You are slowly releasing the pain and the old hurts. You are breathing in positivity and all negativity is being replaced by wholesome and healthy energy.

As you sink deeper and deeper into relaxation, I want you to focus your awareness on your body starting at your feet.

Feel your feet touching the floor beneath you. Feel the earth below you supporting and holding you up.

As you continue to focus on your toes feel a warmth start to spread into your toes, the soles of your feet and your ankles.

You are receiving healing energy from the universe. This energy is a vibrant glow that is covering your feet in a comforting and soothing light.

Now continue to move up your legs and bring your focus to your calves, your knees and your thighs. As your awareness moves up your body, so does the healing energy that is flowing up from the universe into your body.

You can feel it radiate and pulse through you in gentle waves that are warming you from the inside out.

It feels so good that you almost feel like your legs are wrapped in a warm blanket keeping you cozy and warm.

Now you are bringing your awareness to your upper body, your torso, your abdomen, your spine, your chest and your shoulders. As you concentrate on these parts of your body, the soothing energy continues to spread.

You can feel your abdominal muscles relax. The tightness in your chest is gone and your shoulders feel loose and light. The healing energy coursing through you is pulsing in your chest and you can feel it flowing into your heart filling all the empty spaces with love and positive energy.

As you experience this powerful healing energy deep in the center of your chest, you can feel your heart beating and making the radiant energy shine even brighter.

From your chest, your awareness is now on your neck and you can feel the warm energy spreading from your neck into your jaw, your cheeks, your forehead and the back of your skull.

As the healing energy engulfs your entire body, you feel a sense of wholeness and release taking over.

Your body feels light and you can feel yourself start to open up and let the light in to replace all the darkness that was festering inside.

The radiant light is glowing in every part of you and slowly this light starts to radiate from you into the air around you.

Healing energy is coursing through every part of you and covering you all around in a protective glow.

In this moment, you feel safe and protected. You feel in control of your life and your destiny.

Now I want you to visualize a small shoebox right next to you. As you open this shoebox you notice that it is empty.

Now visualize taking a piece of paper and a pen. Take the pen and start to write down the old hurts that you have been holding on to.

It could be the name of the person who hurt you. It could be the way they made you feel. Just write down any negative thought or emotion that has been festering in your heart.

As you write down the name or emotion on the piece of paper, you are going to fold it up and put it in the shoebox.

If you are feeling betrayed, visualize yourself writing that word on the piece of paper and folding it up then put it in the shoebox.

For every negative thought and emotion that you have been holding on to, about yourself, about your relationship or your ex, write it down and put it in the shoebox.

Notice that as you offload all these emotions into the shoebox the healing energy all around you is getting brighter and brighter.

Every negative emotion you release makes room for positivity and healing.

When you have written down all your past hurts, I want you to now visualize yourself picking up that shoebox. This shoebox now contains your past and it has no place in your future.
You have released all those negative emotions from the past and now we are going to set the box on fire and watch it burn.
See yourself lighting the shoebox on fire, and as it starts to burn notice how much lighter and confident you feel.
The anchor that was holding you down is now being detached from you and you are free to be whole and happy again.
As you watch the shoebox turn to ash, you feel an overwhelming sense of relief and healing. You have given yourself a new lease of life and all you can feel in your heart is positivity and openness.
In this moment, I want you to immerse yourself in this feeling of freedom and inner peace. Let yourself open up to the positivity that you have created around you. You are full of love and radiating positive love energy to the universe.
Old hurts no longer have a hold on you. Your heart is filled with positive radiant energy that is going to attract the right relationship and person into your life.
Now take a deep slow breath and as you do start to bring your awareness back to the present.
Concentrate on feeling the breath enter and leave your body as you breathe in slowly and deeply.
When you are ready, you can open your eyes.
This meditation is now complete.

Guided Meditation to Attract Your Ex Back -25 minutes

Relationships can be hard and sometimes you may realize that you lost your soulmate for one reason or another. If you are in this situation where you know in your heart that your ex is the person you are meant to be with, this meditation will help you draw them back into your life.
Let's get started.
Duration; 25 minutes
Find a quiet space and sit in a comfortable chair. Your neck and spine should be aligned in an upright but relaxed posture. Roll your shoulders slightly backward to open up your chest area.
Now I want you to place your hands on your lap with the palms facing upward, ready to receive positivity and love from the universe.
Close your eyes gently and as you do so, start taking slow deep breaths. As you breathe in and out focus all your attention on your breathing.
Every inhale is bringing you a cool vibrant healing energy and with every exhale you are releasing tension, stress and any errant thoughts.
Your whole awareness is focused on the breath entering your body bring in new life and the release of negativity with every exhale.
Nothing else matters but this moment of tranquility and calmness. Your body is getting more relaxed with each inhale and your mind is becoming clearer, open and calm.
With every inhale you are cleansing your spirit, cleansing your heart and cleansing your mind.
With every exhale, you are releasing negative thoughts, unwanted fears and making room for positivity.
As you relax more and more, your body starts to feel lighter and lighter.

Now in this state of relaxation, I want you to visualize a bright golden ray of light start to shine on you. This healing light has a vibrant pulsing love energy that is slowly surrounding you as the golden ray bathes you in its glow.

You can feel this energy start to flow through you and permeate every part of your body. The radiant energy is slowly spreading from your forehead, down to your cheeks, along your jawline, to your neck and the chest below.

Every part of your body that this golden ray of light and energy touches feels a soothing warmth.

As the light continues to spread lower to your abdomen, pelvic region and slowly goes to your thighs and finally to the very tips of your toes, you become fully immersed in this loving healing energy.

You feel safe and protected in this warm glowing energy. As you continue to open yourself up to it, the golden ray is not just in you but also radiating all around you, surrounding you.

You are not just bathed in this purifying energy but you are also radiating it outwards in gentle waves that infuse your surroundings with this vibrant love energy.

With each inhale, the light gets even brighter as it continues to cleanse your heart, your spirit and your mind.

Now in this state of complete relaxation, I want you to see yourself standing before a door. This door leads to your future and behind it is the love that you want to bring back into your life.

As you look at this door, you can see the shiny doorknob that opens the door. I want you to reach out and touch this knob and feel the coolness of it in your palm. You are getting ready to turn this knob knowing that once you do, you will be opening the door to your future.

Now slowly turn the knob and push the door open. In this moment, as you step into the room, you can see your ex standing on the other end of that room facing away from you.

They are bathed in a pool of vibrant light just like the one that is radiating from you and all you need is to connect these two energies to draw him towards you.

I now want you to take a step forward and as you do repeat this affirmation in your mind.

I am getting back together with -say your exes name. I am grateful for having - say your exes name – in my life.

Keep walking towards your ex and when you reach them place your hand on their shoulder. As the two fields of love energies connect, you can see the light all around you pulsing and shining even brighter.

Slowly your ex starts to turn to you and when your eyes connect, you can feel the warmth in his gaze.

Your fields of energy are now completely intertwined and your ex reaches out to take your hand in his.

As you touch you can feel your energy flowing into your ex and their energy flowing into you. You are bound together in this moment and your hearts are beating to the same rhythm surrounded by the same radiant love energy.

I want you to take a moment to immerse yourself in this feeling of reunification and reconnecting with your ex. As you stand there holding hands let yourself feel the powerful energy of love.

Stay in that moment of reunification allowing it to replace all the fears and doubts in your heart.

Now look deeply into your ex's eyes and say, We are getting back together. I belong with you and you belong with me.

See them start to smile as they hear these words from you and then embrace you in a tight hug.

In this moment, you feel accepted and loved. You are safe and secure in your love and you know that your love has been reignited and reconnected even more deeply than before.

Now I want you to take with you this soul connection that you are feeling right now and bring it back with you.

Every time you start to feel doubts or anxiety about your ex, remember this connection and know that the universe is drawing your ex back to you.

Take a moment to internalize this confidence in your love and shared destiny.
When you are ready I want to bring your awareness back to the present by becoming mindful of your breathing.
Focus on taking deep slow breaths and let your breathing lead you back to the present.
You can now open your eyes; this meditation session is now complete.

Meditation for Healing Your Relationship – 20 minutes

Sometimes the more you try to hold on to a relationship the further away it slips from you. If you want to heal a broken relationship, focusing on co-creating the relationship you want will help you avoid having to constantly struggle to hold on. When you reset your love vibration, you allow the universe to fix what was broken and heal what needs to be healed. This guided meditation is intended to help you build a healthier relationship and manifest the kind of connection that you want in your life.
Let us get started.
Duration: 20 minutes
For this meditation, you can choose to lie down on your bed or sit in a comfortable chair.
Now gently close your eyes and lead your mind and body to relaxation with mindful breathing and focusing your awareness on the sensations of breathing in and out.
Inhale slowly and deeply to a count of six, hold your breath for a moment then exhale slowly to a count of six.
Again, deep slow inhale to a count of six, hold your breath and then release slowly to a count of six.
As you practice this mindful breathing clear your mind of any distracting thoughts by simply bringing back your awareness to your breathing.
Let us take another deep and slowly inhale to a count of six, hold your breath for a moment, then exhale slowly.
Now as your body and mind start to relax, allow your breathing to go back to normal. Your awareness is still on your breath and nothing else. Your mind is calm and your body is completely relaxed.
In this moment of complete tranquility, I want you to visualize the person with whom you want to heal your relationship. It could be your husband or boyfriend or any love interest where you feel the relationship is breaking down.
See this person clearly in your mind, take in every detail of their appearance and keep this image in your mind.
As you picture this person in your mind, I want you to pay attention to what you are feeling right now. Are you sad, hurt, angry, or anxious? Whatever you are feeling let the emotion rise to the surface without trying to suppress it.
If you need to cry let the emotion out with no shame or judgment. Just allow it to wash over you.
Become a witness to how this person makes you feel and the thoughts that come to your mind when you think of them.
Now I want you to take a deep breath with these emotions still on your mind and with each exhale you are going to release any negative thoughts or emotions that you feel towards your relationship with that person.
As you exhale, you are letting go of anger. You are releasing past hurts and regrets. You are freeing yourself from anxiety, fear and stress. You are releasing any blockages that are interfering in your relationship.

Continue breathing mindfully and calling to mind all the things you need to release. Remember that to make room in your heart for healing and restoration, you must fast make cleanse and remove the negativity.

Release all those negative emotions one by one and let them out of your system completely. You are no longer anchored in your past because you are going to create the relationship you want. You are going to mend what's broken and breathe new life into your relationship.

Now take this moment to start breathing in new energy into your heart and mind. With every breath you take in, I want you to visualize a stream of bright radiant white light coming into your body.

With every breath you take, your heart is filling up with this positive love energy that is taking up all the room in your heart. This love energy starts to spill over and radiates to other parts of your body.

It is now spreading to your neck and head, filling every pore with positive love energy and creating a glowing field of bright light all around you. Your whole body is now covered with this vibrant energy and you are radiating it from deep inside your heart.

As you sit bathed in this positive radiant glow, I want you to go back to the image of the person that you want to heal your relationship with. See them in the best version of themselves or in the persona you love about them most.

Maybe they are smiling at you, or they could be playing with your children or even just cuddling you as you watch a movie. Whatever positive image comes to your mind right now, keep it in your mind and let this image stir up all the positive emotions that you feel about this person.

Feel your love for this person rise to the surface. Feel your need to care for them. Feel your need to share your life with them. Embrace and acknowledge all the positive emotions you feel about this person.

Now in this moment of positivity, I want you to repeat the following affirmations.

I open my heart completely to you.

I am grateful that you are in my life.

Every day the universe brings us closer and closer.

Our love for each other will never die.

My relationship is secure and supportive.

My relationship is getting stronger.

I enjoy my relationship with you.

I am manifesting a healthy relationship with my partner right now.

I choose to radiate positivity and love in my relationship.

I choose to let go of grudges and past hurts.

I am reconnecting with my partner right now.

I am attracting a happy and healthy relationship.

I give love and receive it back and abundance.

My relationship gets stronger and better every day.

Now, I want you to sit with these intentions in your mind for a moment allowing them to reset your love vibration.

You have created positivity and loving energy for your relationship and started healing your connection with your partner.

Take a deep slow breath in and out, and as you start to bring your awareness back to the present, bring the positive love vibration you have created back with you.

When you are ready, gently open your eyes.

This meditation is now complete.

Love Affirmations To Get Your Ex-Back – 10 minutes

Affirmations are one of the most effective ways to reset your love vibration because they set a clear intention. If you want to get your ex back, these affirmations will align your subconscious energy with your desire.

When saying affirmations, it is always important to be intentional and mindful of what you are saying. Mention the name of the specific person you want to attract back into your life. This will help you create a strong love vibration to attract your ex-back

Let us get started.

Duration: 15 minutes

Lay down comfortably on your bed and close your eyes.

I want you to take time to clear your mind by breathing in slowly through your nose then exhaling through your mouth.

Draw your focus away from any errant thoughts or whatever is going on in your life right now. All of your awareness is on breathing in deeply and slowly exhaling through your mouth.

You can feel your mind start to feel calm and your body is relaxing more and more.

Take another deep breath in and exhale slowly. Now allow your breathing to go back to normal but keep your focus on your breathing.

Concentrate on your breath as it enters your body then leaves. You are now completely calm and relaxed and your mind is clear and open.

Now take a minute to think about the person you want to attract back into your life. Really see them in your mind and say their name quietly.

Keep their image clear in your mind and as you repeat these affirmations, substitute the words my partner with the name of the person you want to attract.

I am in a passionate relationship with my partner.

I truly love and appreciate my partner.

My heart is full of love for my partner.

I am attracting my partner back into my life with ease.

My partner is being drawn back to me.

Getting back together with my love is easy.

I am sending my partner love and they are sending it back to me in abundance.

I am grateful because my partner is coming back into my life.

I am attracting my partner to me with ease.

With every moment I'm moving closer towards my partner.

The universe is manifesting my desire to be with my partner.

There is a deep and profound bond between my partner and me that is being restored.

I am happy and at peace because my desire is coming back to me.

I am full of positivity and love for my partner.

I am grateful that my partner is coming back into my life.

I am attracting my partner back into my life with ease.

I am attracting a healthy and loving relationship with my partner.

I am happy that our deep connection is being restored.

I am releasing old hurts and past love to open my heart to love.

I am loving and my partner loves me for who I am.

I am getting back together with my partner.

My relationship with my partner is getting better and stronger each and every day.
I am surrounded by love and positivity.
My partner is sending me love and I am sending my love to him.
I am manifesting a committed relationship with my partner.
I am a perfect match for my partner.
The love between my partner and me is strong and unshakeable
I am grateful that the universe is filling my life with love.
I am in a passionate relationship with my partner.
My life is blessed with infinite love.
The universe is manifesting my desire to be with my partner.
There's a deep and profound love between me and my partner.
I am completely happy and at peace in my relationship with my partner.
Love comes to me easily.
I am attracting my partner back with ease.
I am in a passionate relationship with my partner.
Getting back together with my partner is easy for me.
My life is blessed with infinite love
I am experiencing the bliss of love
As you finish these affirmations, take a moment to sit with your intentions and commit them to your subconscious mind.
When you are ready, you can allow yourself to drift off into sleep.
This session is complete.

Chapter 6: Meditations for Attracting Love and Being In Love (75 mins)

Love challenges people in different ways. Some have a problem attracting it, others have a problem keeping it and others struggle with both. When you want to attract a soulmate or partner, it is important to also think about how to stay in the relationship and make it flourish. Going from relationship to relationship not only takes a toll on your emotional wellbeing but also every heartbreak diminishes your love vibration.

Co-creating a healthy attitude to being in love and sustaining a relationship with meditation will help you not just find love but also keep it. in this section, the meditations are centered on creating fulfilling and healthy relationships that flourish and last. If you have a problem establishing and maintaining long-term connections practice these meditations consistently to see a change in your love life.

Meditation to Have the Relationship of Your Dreams – 25 minutes

Whatever you envision in your mind you have the power to co-create by using meditation to align your vibrational energy with your desires. If you crave a loving relationship with unconditional acceptance and commitment, practice this meditation as often as you can before going to sleep.

Let's get started.

Duration: 25 minutes

Start by lying down comfortably in your bed. Allow your body to completely relax then gently close your eyes.

Now take a moment to connect with your breath without trying to change it or manipulate it in any way. Simply listen to the natural rhythm of your breathing.

Become aware of the natural flow of your breath as you allow this flow to guide you deeper and deeper into relaxation.

You are letting go of any errant thoughts, any tension in your body and simply sinking into a calm tranquil space full of peace.

I invite you to tune into the natural state of your being. The slow rise and fall of your abdomen as you breathe in and out. Feel the quiet energy that is flowing through you.

There may be aspects of the day that linger in your mind or maybe thoughts about tomorrow. Let them come and go without attaching to anything like a puff of dissipating smoke.

You are focused on your breathing. You are feeling more and more relaxed. As you breathe in your chest is expanding allowing refreshing energy into your being.

As you exhale, the weariness, anxiety and any fears are being released from your body. Your heart center is opening up to receive the endless possibilities of love from the universe.

The more relaxed you feel the more open your heart center or chakra becomes. Letting in loving energy from the universe into your heart.

Love is abundant. Its presence is everywhere and as you sink further into the positive energy all around you begin to understand the truth that love exists all around and within you.

In this moment I want you to quietly repeat these affirmations quietly in your mind,
I am made of love. I am made of love. I am made of love.
Just allow these words to flow into the heart space with each breath. Allow them to open up your heart chakra further dissolving any negative beliefs and thoughts about love.
As the positive love energy flows into your heart allow it to take away any conditioning that has led you to forget why you fell in love, how it felt to be in love, how it felt to love and be loved.
Allow this loving energy flowing into your heart to wash away all the jaded weariness that may have made you indifferent, or cynical about your relationship or love.
With every breath you take, the healing love energy flowing into your heart is reigniting the beauty of love in your heart.
You can feel a warm glow start to ignite in your chest, pulsing to the rhythm of your heartbeat.
Let this love vibration awaken your awareness of the love that runs through each of your cells and as you become more aware of its presence within you, your love vibration is getting stronger and stronger.
In this moment, repeat these affirmations quietly in your mind.
I am made of love. I am made of love. I am made of love.
Now bring your awareness back to your expanding heart chakra. Feel it expand and soften with each breath becoming a radiant light of pulsing love energy that is coursing through you and permeating the very core of your being.
You are sinking deeper and deeper into this field of positive love energy and now I want you to visualize the person you are in a relationship with.
See them vividly in your mind and as you hold this image, I want you to think of a memory between the two of you that makes you happy.
It could be your wedding day, your first date, an experience you shared, or anything else that makes you happy when you think of that person.
Once this moment comes to mind, I want you to notice how it makes you feel. What emotions and thoughts are running through your mind as you think of that moment?
As you reflect on that happy memory, notice how your heart starts to fill with love. This love is making your love vibration even stronger.
Explore in detail the qualities that make this person special. What do you love about this person most? What makes you smile when you think about them? Why did you fall in love with them?
As these answers come to you, take a moment to really hear them deep in your mind and commit them to your subconscious. Hold on to all those positive things that created the love and relationship you have with that person.
Now repeat these affirmations quietly in your mind.
I am so grateful that you are in my life. I am committed to loving you and receiving love from you. I am sending you my love energy right now.
Continue to allow your positive emotions about your relationship to come to the surface.
Call to mind all the things that you may sometimes take for granted. The small details that you stopped noticing when you got comfortable, the little overtures of love you stopped making, the little nagging details that you have let cloud your love for this person.
As you hold these answers in your mind, I want you to slowly direct all the positive energy in your heart chakra to your mind. You will use this positive love energy to cleanse and release these negative notions that are blocking your heart's love vibration.
Slowly feel the love energy rise from your chest, spreading slowly to your neck and flowing into your head. It is lighting up every part it touches with a radiant bright glow that lights up and removes all darkness and negativity.

Now the only vision left in your mind is of the positive things you love about your partner and your relationship. You are immersing yourself in the positivity of love and letting go of any love blocks in your subconscious.
In this positive space, repeat the following affirmations.
I am so grateful that you are in my life. I am committed to loving you and receiving love from you. I am sending you love energy right now.
Take a moment to connect with this intention and feel it deeply in your heart and mind.
You are resetting your love vibration to manifest the loving relationship you have always wanted.
Melt into this present moment with complete trust and faith that your soul is manifesting the deepest and most fulfilling love for you.
The love of your dreams is manifesting right now and you no longer need to struggle with your relationship.
Before drifting off into sleep allow your mind to keep holding the positive love energy that you have created.
You can now bring your awareness back to the present by tuning in to your breathing and allowing it to carry you into a deep restful slumber.
This meditation session is now complete.

Manifest Your Crush – 15 minutes

Are you attracted or drawn to someone who does not even know you exist? You can use the law of attraction to create a connection between you and the person you want to bring into your life. When you have a crush on someone, sending them heart energy will actually cause them to be drawn and attracted to you.
This meditation will help you manifest your crush whether they are currently in your life or not. You can practice it at night before going to bed or first thing in the morning.
Let's get started.
Duration: 15 minutes
Once you are sited or lying down comfortably, close your eyes.
Now take some deep breaths in through your nose and allow the air to flow down into your chest or your heart center.
Exhale slowly allowing your body to slowly relax and ease into a peaceful and calm state.
Continue to breathe deeply and mindfully keeping your focus on this natural rhythm of breathing in and out.
All your attention is focused inward and you are releasing any errant thoughts that pop into your mind.
Bring your attention down to your heart center and as you focus on your heart center take your hand and place it above your heart.
With your heart above your hand, I want you to visualize your crush in your mind right now. See this person in vivid detail and every aspect of their being. See their face, their body, the color of their eyes, their hair, their smile and every other part of them that comes to your mind.
Hold this image of your crush in your mind and allow yourself to feel all the emotions that come to the surface every time you are near them or around them.
As these emotions come to the surface, you are going to go a step further and now visualize your crush holding you, with his arms around you holding you close to his chest.

As you stay in this embrace you can feel warmth spreading from him to you and you can also feel yourself radiating love energy that is flowing from you into him.
Notice how grateful and at peace you feel with your crush next to you, holding you and sending you their love energy.
It feels so good to be in your crush's presence and you can feel yourself relaxing into the warmth and safety of their arms.
There's a very beautiful exchange of love happening between the two of you right now and you can feel your crush radiating the same joy and love that you are feeling.
You can feel that there's nowhere else your crush would rather be. They are happy and content to be holding you in their arms.
In this embrace I want you to feel the connection between you and your crush. Immerse yourself in the feeling of loving them and having them return that love in abundance.
And now you can hear your crush say to you,
I claim you and I love you. I'm not going anywhere.
Let these words penetrate deep in your mind and give you confidence in your connection with your crush.
You are manifesting them into your life and the connection between you is real and strong.
You are sending them strong love energy and they are letting their love flow into you, connecting with your heart chakra to create a powerful love vibration.
In this moment take a deep breath and repeat these affirmations. You can replace the words my crush with the actual name of the person you want to attract.
I am attracting my crush into my life right now.
I can feel the strong love energy from my crush.
My crush is deeply connected to me.
I release my love energy to my crush and trust the universe to bring him into my life.
I am attracting my crush with ease.
Love comes easily to me.
I am surrounded by love and abundance.
My crush is being drawn to me right now.
Now take a moment to let these affirmations sink deep into your subconscious. Your heart and soul have reached out to the person you are attracted to and the universe will draw them into your life.
Now you can bring your awareness back to the present, holding on to the confidence that your crush is being manifested into your life.
Focus your awareness on breathing in slowly and exhaling. With every breath, you are becoming more aware of your surroundings but the feeling of love and the deep connection with your crush remains with you.
You can now gently open your eyes.
This meditation is now complete.

Guided Meditation to Harmonize Your Relationship – 25 minutes

Conflicts and misunderstandings are a natural part of relationships. However, if you want to build a harmonious relationship, the law of attraction can help you clear blockages and misunderstandings by attracting harmony between you and your partner, If your relationship gets tumultuous at times, this meditation will help you attract a loving and harmonious energy to your relationship.

Let's get started.

Duration: 20 minutes

Find a comfortable and quiet space and sit comfortably.

Gently close your eyes and align your spine with your neck in an upright posture that opens up your chest area.

Now place your hands on your lap with the palm facing upwards opening yourself up to receive positive energy from the universe.

Now start taking deep mindful breaths allowing the natural rhythm of your breathing to clear your mind.

Feel your body start to relax as you take deep rhythmic breaths followed by slow relaxing exhales.

Let any errant thoughts come and go without attaching to them. Your awareness is on your breath and your breath is bringing you peace and tranquility.

With every deep breath, your body is sinking deeper into relaxation and you can feel the tension leaving your body every time you exhale.

Your body is sinking deeper and deeper into relaxation and you feel your mind and heart slowly releasing negative energy.

Now bring your awareness to the heart chakra in the center of your chest. Now as you inhale you will feel the breath transform into healing energy that is flowing into your heart chakra in gentle refreshing waves.

You can feel this positive energy start to purify your heart chakra clearing out resentment, anger, bitterness, grudges and pain.

Every time you breathe in, the positive healing energy flowing into your heart chakra gets stronger and infuses you with a cleansing warmth that is now radiating in your chest.

When you exhale you can feel the healing energy in your heart chakra start to spread throughout your body.

Inhale deeply through your nose into your heart chakra, hold your breath for a moment and feel it become a powerful healing energy flowing into your heart.

As you exhale you can feel this energy spreading throughout your body easing stress and tension.

In this moment of calmness and clarity, I want you to repeat these affirmations,

I radiate love and goodwill to others.

I open my heart to healing positive energy.

I am attracting harmony and peace in my relationship.

My partner and I are deeply connected.

I am releasing all resentment and opening my heart to love and joy.

I am sending my partner heart energy.

My relationship is happy and harmonious.

My partner and I are living in peace and love.

I am attracting harmony and peace in my relationship.

I open my heart to healing positive energy.

I am grateful for my partner.

I am thankful for my relationship.
My relationship is founded on true love.
The universe is sending me love and harmony.
Now, I want you to visualize your partner in your mind. See them sitting next to you right now. They are surrounded by a vivid bright light that is pulsating all around them.
Now I want you to take your hand and reach out to your partner. Take their hand in yours and notice that your two energies are starting to merge and interconnect.
Your partner's energy is now intertwined with yours and the positive healing energy is flowing from your heart chakra into theirs. Your partner's energy is also flowing from their heart chakra into you. There is a smooth flow of healing positive energy flowing between the two of you.
As you visualize this smooth flow of energy connecting the two of you, I want you to feel the rhythm of your heart and breath start to sync with that of your partner.
Your breathing is mirroring your partner's natural rhythm and you are radiating the same radiant energy from your heart chakras.
As you sit holding hands, I want you to feel the connection between you and your partner getting deeper and deeper. You are establishing a shared love energy vibration that will help to bring peace and harmony into your relationship.
This shared energy is making you two halves of the same being that complete and complement one another.
You can feel your partner's love energy flowing through your body just as your energy is flowing through your partner,
This shared energy will connect you two deeply and intricately and from now on in moments of conflict, you will come back to this harmonious space where you are sharing the same love vibration.
Take a moment to immerse yourself in this positive shared love vibration.
When you are ready to bring your awareness back to the present, focus on your breathing and tune into the sensations in your body.
Take deep mindful breaths until you become aware of your surroundings. You can now open your eyes.
This meditation is now complete.

Affirmations to Attract Emotional Intimacy and Reconnect with Your Partner -10 minutes

You may sometimes feel like the emotional intimacy in your relationship is fading or waning. If you would like to rebuild the intimacy in your relationship, you can reset your love vibration and increase it to attract the level of intimacy you want in your relationship.
With time intimacy can diminish naturally in relationships but with these affirmations, you can keep attracting intimacy back into your relationship.
Let's get started.
Duration: 10 minutes
Start by sitting comfortably or lying down in your bed.
I invite you to close your eyes and shut everything else apart from the gentle rhythm of your breathing.
Feel the air enter leave your body in a soothing rhythm that guides you to peace and tranquility.

As you continue focusing on your breath, you can feel your mind start to relax and any tension in your body is being released.
As you sink deeper and deeper into relaxation, I want you to take your hand and lay it on the center of your chest.
Now I want you to repeat these affirmations slowly and quietly in your mind, connecting deeply with each intention as you say it. You can use your partner's name where appropriate.
I respect my partner.
I can be my true self around my partner.
I communicate my wants and needs clearly to my partner.
I am attentive to my partner's needs and desires.
I go out of my way to support my partner.
I am tuned into the wants and needs of my partner.
I deserve to have a healthy relationship.
I respectfully communicate my feelings.
I attract healthy relationships easily.
My partner respects and cherishes me.
My partner's feelings are important to me.
I respect and cherish my partner.
I am positive and loving.
I support my partner unconditionally.
I am in a lasting and loving relationship.
I always honor my relationship I always.
My connection with my partner grows deeper and stronger every day.
My partner respects and cherishes me.
My partner and I are happy together.
My relationship with my partner is joyous.
We are committed and devoted to each other.
I feel safe and secure in my relationship.
I am confident in my relationship.
I share a deep emotional bond with my partner.
I am grateful for my relationship and my partner.
Our relationship is growing stronger and more loving every day.
The universe is sending us positive love energy and connecting us deeply.
I am attracting a deeper emotional connection in my relationship.
Now you can slowly bring these intentions with you as you bring yourself back to the present.
Breath in deeply and start to bring your awareness back to your body. When you are ready you can open your eyes.
This session is now complete.

Chapter 7: Meditations For Emotional Balance and Gratitude (65 mins)

A healthy relationship full of love is one of the best gifts the universe can bring into your life. People spend their whole lives looking for that one deep connection that will make them feel like they are part of something. We all want to share our lives with someone or people who we love and people who love us in return. Having someone to build a life with and share experiences with makes life more meaningful and fulfilling. This means any effort that you put towards attracting love to your life is always well worth the effort.

Love may seem elusive and out of reach but when you start to align your subconscious energy with your heart's desires you will attract your soulmate or twin flame into your life. In this quest for love, people often overlook the most relationship of all: their relationship with themselves.

Even the most beautiful and deep connection cannot survive if your relationship with yourself is not right. That is why it is important to work on creating the person you need to be in order to attract the right person for you. Like energies attract each other so if you are broken on the inside you will keep attracting broken people into your life.

In this section, we shall focus on the inner energies that influence how we feel about ourselves. These are the energies that keep fueling your negative beliefs about love and blocking your pathway to attracting your soulmate. By co-creating a balanced internal energy, you will make it possible to radiate the kind of positive energy you need to manifest love not just for others but also for yourself.

Guided meditation For Emotional Balance - 25 minutes

Emotions are at the core of the human experience and this means they control how we experience life. If you are constantly in emotional turmoil, you will find it hard to attract love because your subconscious energy will always be skewed towards the negative,

In this meditation, you will learn to manage and control your internal energy in order to reset your subconscious mind to a positive frequency. You can practice this meditation anytime you start to experience negative emotions such as jealousy, anger pessimism and self-doubt.

Let's get started.

Duration 25 minutes

Start by sitting on a comfortable chair with your back straight.

Now close your eyes and place your hands on your knees. Focus on bringing your awareness to your breathing by paying attention to how you feel when you inhale slowly and deeply and then exhale slowly.

Continue to take slow deliberate breaths allowing your mind to only concentrate on this simple act of breathing. In this moment you can feel your mind start to calm down and your body is gradually starting to loosen up and relax.

Feel every breath as it passes into your nostrils and fills your chest with clean wholesome energy and feel every exhale take with it all the stress and tension in your body.

Feel your body sink deeper and deeper into relaxation and embrace the feeling of tranquility that is settling over you.

You are at peace. Your mind is at ease and your body feels as light as air.

Now, I want you to bring your attention to the center of your chest which is your heart chakra. As you breathe in, feel your heart chakra start to slowly expand letting the air in and opening up.

In this moment, you feel the energy in your chakra pulsating in gentle waves that are soothing and calming. This simple act of breathing in is bringing you healing energy from the universe into your heart chakra.

Now, take your hand and place it above the center of your chest where your heart chakra is expanding and radiating calm energy.

Use the hand above your chest to slowly massage that area of your chest and as you do the gentle soothing motions, say out loud, I am attracting emotional balance into my heart.

Continue to rub your chest slowly and gently and as you do so feel the energy that is pulsating in your heart chakra start to spread to other parts of your body. This soothing energy is a vivid green color signifying the vitality that is spreading throughout your body.

You can feel the energy as it spreads with a soothing warmness down to your abdomen, flows into your legs and finally your toes. This vibrant energy is now anchoring you to the earth beneath your feet and you feel supported by the universe.

The healing energy is also spreading upwards into your neck, flowing into your head and you can feel it cleansing your mind of dark thoughts and negativity.

From head to toe, every pore of your being is infused with this vibrant energy. Now place your hand back on your knee and continue to feel the healing energy course through your body.

With every breath, you take this healing energy gets brighter and starts to radiate outwards surrounding you in an aura of glowing green light. You are not just filled with healing energy but you are now radiating this positive radiance outwards into the world around you.

Anyone you come into contact with from now on will feel the positivity radiating from deep inside your heart chakra. Every thought and every emotion will be infused with the positivity and radiance of this energy.

You will only attract people with a similar positive energy that will bind you together in a healthy and balanced relationship.

This aura of positive energy will act as a shield that will filter out negative emotions and only allow positivity in. You will no longer be affected by other people's opinions because you have the power to create your own energy from deep inside your heart chakra.

You are taking control of your emotions and of your life in general. You will no longer be affected by external negative energy because you have a field of positive energy all around you at all times.

Your connection to the universe means that you will always have a never ending supply of this positive healing energy. All you need to do whenever you feel anxious or distressed is to come back to this moment of peace and tranquility.

Now, I want you to take a deep breath and as you breathe out, start to bring your awareness to your surroundings. Feel the ground beneath your feet and as you continue to breathe slowly and deeply, gradually bring your awareness to the present.

When you are ready you can open your eyes.

This meditation session is now complete.

Guided Meditation for Detachment From Over-Thinking and Anxiety – 20 minutes

The law of attraction relies on the infinite energy of the universe to help you manifest the things that you want. This means when you co-create the right subconscious energy to attract the person you want, you do not need to struggle or overthink what may or may not happen. Anxiety redirects your subconscious energy from focusing on the things you want to the things you are afraid may happen.

If you are prone to worrying yourself with thoughts like, *what if he doesn't like me, what if we break up, what if he meets someone else* and similar thoughts of fear and anxiety, you will never be able to manifest the things you want. In fact, focusing on your fears attracts them and causes the universe to manifest the things that you are afraid of most. In this meditation, the goal is to detach yourself from worry and focus on aligning your energy with your desires.

You can practice this meditation every time you find yourself overthinking and worrying about love or anything else that disrupts your inner peace.

Let us get into it.

Duration: 20 minutes

Start by sitting or lying down comfortably in a quiet space that is free of any distractions.

I now invite you to close your eyes and allow yourself to shut out all thoughts and external noise by simply bringing your awareness to your breathing.

Feel the rise and the fall of your chest as you breath in and out allowing your breaths to guide you into a calm and relaxed state.

Every breath is easing the tension in your body allowing you to relax and sink into a state of tranquility.

Become aware of your ribs expanding with each breath and notice how they gently contracting as you exhale.

Now bring your awareness to the rest of your body feeling the warmth on your skin, the gentle tension in your leg muscles, the arch of your spine and the sensations that you are feeling right now.

If any thought pops into your mind simply let it come and go without exploring it or attaching to it.

Become aware of your resting body's subtle movements. Notice any parts of your body that may feel more relaxed than others. If you find an area of tension, slowly bring your awareness to it, relaxing it and feeling the tension ebb away.

In this moment, you are completely relaxed and at ease with yourself. There is no need to rush no need to be anywhere else at all.

This time now is the time for you to learn to simply observe and accept that you can rest and remain here fully in the present moment.

Understand that in this moment you are learning to live in the present without worrying about what has happened or what will happen. You are anchored in the here and now and you can allow yourself to just breathe.

As you continue to immerse yourself in the present, start to breathe in a little slow so that you are taking long slow breaths and then exhaling slowly.

Do this by allowing your very next breath in to become just a little slow and then allowing your next breath to become just a little longer gradually slowing your cycles of breathing without straining yourself.

You can feel that calm and relaxed aura of simply being present without feeling the need to control or dictate anything.

You are letting your body and your mind follow their natural rhythms and it feels good to release your natural instincts and simply let yourself flow with the natural rhythms of your body.

Now I want you to start observing the thoughts that are popping into your mind at this moment. Whatever it is that your mind may wish to create, become aware of the temporary nature of thoughts and realize that you can choose to observe them as they come and go without attaching to them.

You have the power to choose which thoughts you allow to dominate your consciousness and which ones to ignore. Just as your body follows its natural rhythms, you can allow your mind to process thoughts as creations of the mind that are not bound or attached to you. You can choose to release them and allow your mind to create others.

Understand that there is no need to try to control thoughts or change them because you can detach from them and release them freeing yourself from them.

Choose to witness thoughts come and then go like a shooting star that flashes across a clear night sky and then disappears into nothingness.

Understand that each thought carries a field of energy and that this energy seeps into your subconscious. The more negative thoughts you attach to, the harder it is to radiate a positive subconscious energy.

Some thoughts have a particularly strong energy and they like to call attention to themselves but this energy cannot taint your subconscious if you choose to detach from the thought.

Now I want you to think of the worries that plague your mind constantly. The things that keep you up at night and steal your joy. Maybe you worry about finding love, maybe you are anxious about your relationship, or anything else that you constantly fret about.

Allow those thoughts to rise to the surface, and as each one pops into your head I want you to simply shift your focus to the natural rhythm of your breath. Notice how easily the thought disappears when you do not attach to it.

One by one as the worries and fears come to you, detach yourself from them by bringing your awareness to your breathing and focusing on only the sensations of breathing and the natural rhythms of your body,

You will notice that the thoughts only have power over your subconscious energy if you allow yourself to attach to them and dwell on them. If you simply release them as they come, you remain in full control of your internal energy and emotions.

Whenever you find yourself starting to overthink or worry, you will simply come back to this moment and release the thoughts that come into your mind. When you start to feel overwhelmed simply start to breathe mindfully concentrating fully on the rhythm and sensations of your breath.

You will no longer be a prisoner to negative thoughts or obsess over what may or may not happen. Your focus will simply be on living in the moment and creating the positive energy you need to manifest your heart's deepest desires.

Now, you can slowly start to bring yourself back to the present knowing that you have the power to control your thoughts and the energy they give you.

Focus on taking deep slow breaths and observing how your body feels. Bring your awareness back to the present and when you feel ready you can open your eyes.

This guided meditation is now complete.

Trust Your Journey – 20 minutes

The law of attraction is one of the most powerful forces of the universe. Everything is energy and all your desires can either be fueled by positive energy or obstructed by negative vibrations. A big part of manifesting and attracting the things you desire is trusting the universe to bring you the things you want. This is why meditations to attract the things you want, focus only on shifting your subconscious energy and not trying to control the outcome.

If the law of attraction is to work for you, it is important that you trust your journey and let the universe manifest the energy that you have created. If you keep trying to control the outcome, you will block the natural flow of abundance from the universe. In this meditation, the goal is to develop confidence and the belief that the universe is working to bring you all the desires of your heart. If you focus on realigning your internal energy, you can leave the outcome to the universe and trust that in good time the things you want to attract will come to you.

Let's get started.

Duration: 20 minutes

I invite you to make yourself comfortable and find a posture of effortless ease where you can be relaxed. For this meditation, you may choose to lie down or sit in a comfortable chair.

Now I invite you to close your eyes and start to bring your attention inward as you settle into relaxation and tranquility.

Now let us sink deeper into a feeling of relaxation. I want you to take a deep breath and as you inhale, hold for a moment then exhale slowly making sure that your exhale is longer than the inhale.

One way to do this is to inhale to a count of four, hold your breath for a moment then exhale to a count of six.

Continue with this rhythmic breathing allowing it to soothe you into complete relaxation and free you of any tensions and stress.

As you relax completely allow your breath to return to normal and then scan your body noticing how each part feels. Take note of any part that feels tense and as you bring your awareness to the tense muscle feel the tension ease and relaxation set in.

Now bring your attention back to your breath and feel the air flowing softly through your nose deep into your lungs.

With every inhale you can feel a vibrant energy flowing into your body. The universe is giving you life and all you have to do is to breathe it in and allow it to fill your lungs.

As you continue to feel the universe breathing its life into you, I want you to think of something you may be yearning for right now. Allow yourself to think about how this thing is always on your mind and you keep trying to make it happen. However the harder you try to bring it to you the further away it slips.

With the image of whatever you are yearning for still in your mind, I want you to repeat these affirmations,

Everything I want is already available in the universe in abundance.

The infinite power of the universe is strong enough to manifest all my hearts desires.

I trust the universe to bring me the person or thing I desire the most.

I yield to the infinite wisdom of the universe and allow myself to surrender to its power.

I trust my journey and believe that it is leading me to all my heart's desires.

I am confident that my heart's desires will come true.

The universe is manifesting the thing I desire the most.

Each and every day the healing energy of the universe brings me life and positivity.

I am open to all the possibilities available to me through the power of the universe.
My heart's desire will manifest at the right time.
I am surrendering to the infinite power of the universe and trusting it to fulfill my heart's desire.
I am not afraid of what the future holds because I trust my journey.
I no longer need to control everything because the universe will always give me what I desire.
I am grateful that the universe is manifesting everything I desire.
I attract positive energy from the universe easily.
As you finish these affirmations, take a moment to internalize these intentions and commit them to your mind.
When you are ready take a deep breath and as you exhale start to bring your awareness back to the present. Once you feel yourself becoming aware of your surroundings, you can now open your eyes.
This meditation is now complete.

Total Meditation Time – 8 hours 45 mins

Conclusion

Finding love does not have to be difficult or nerve-wracking. The infinite positive energy of the universe is available to us all to help us manifest all our heart's desires. When you surrender to the power of the universe and use the law of attraction to manifest your love, you will start to witness significant changes in your love life. The law of attraction works perfectly every time and anything that you truly want to manifest in your life will be drawn to you.

There is no limit to what you can do by harnessing the law of attraction and using it to manifest love and healthy relationships. Using this infinite power you can connect with your soulmate, get your ex back and even reignite the passion in your relationship. The only thing you need to enact is harnessing your subconscious energy to align it with the things you want to manifest. Positive thoughts alone are not enough to attract the love you want because your subconscious mind is a much more powerful reservoir of your love vibration and energy. That is why we use meditation since it is the most effective way to access your higher self or your subconscious mind and reset your love vibration.

In these meditation sessions, we have equipped you with all the techniques you need to turn your love life around and start enjoying the love you always wanted. The beauty of meditations is that they are simple to practice even for beginners and you can practice them as many times as you need to get the result you want.

The relationship you have always wanted is now within your reach. The crush you have been yearning for can now become more than a dream and manifest into reality. If you have always wanted to find your soulmate or your other half, you now know how to do it. All you need to do is trust the infinite power of the universe and the law of attraction to bring you all your heart's deepest desires.

We hope this book helps you to manifest the love life you have always wanted using the principle of the law of attraction. Thank you for listening.

CPSIA information can be obtained
at www.ICGtesting.com
Printed in the USA
LVHW060106200422
716703LV00005B/242

9 781801 347587